Yes We Can?

The first edition of this book offered one of the first social science analyses of Barack Obama's historic electoral campaigns and early presidency and earned wide use in undergraduate race and ethnicity courses throughout the United States. In this second edition the authors extend that analysis to Obama's service in the presidency and to his second campaign to hold that presidency. Elaborating on the concept of the white racial frame, Harvey Wingfield and Feagin assess in detail the ways white racial framing was deployed by the principal characters in the electoral campaigns and during Obama's presidency. With much relevant data, this book counters many common-sense assumptions about U.S. racial matters, politics, and institutions, particularly the notion that Obama's presidency ushered in a major post-racial era. Readers will find this fully revised and updated book distinctively valuable because it relies on sound social science analysis to assess numerous events and aspects of the historic 2012 presidency campaign.

Adia Harvey Wingfield is an associate professor of sociology at Georgia State University. Her research focuses on the ways intersections of race and gender shape various groups' experiences in different occupations. Her recent work addresses the experiences of black male nurses, minority faculty at independent schools, and black female entrepreneurs.

Joe R. Feagin is Ella C. McFadden Professor at Texas A&M University. Feagin has done research on racism and sexism issues for 48 years and has served as the Scholar-in-Residence at the U.S. Commission on Civil Rights. He has written many scholarly books and articles in his major research areas, and one book (*Ghetto Revolts*) has been nominated for a Pulitzer Prize. He was the 1999–2000 president of the American Sociological Association.

Yes We Can?

White Racial Framing and the Obama Presidency

Second Edition

**Adia Harvey Wingfield
and Joe R. Feagin**

Routledge
Taylor & Francis Group

NEW YORK AND LONDON

Second edition published 2013
by Routledge
711 Third Avenue, New York, NY 10017

Simultaneously published in the UK
by Routledge
2 Park Square, Milton Park, Abingdon, Oxon OX14 4RN

Routledge is an imprint of the Taylor & Francis Group, an informa business

First edition published by Routledge 2010

Library of Congress Cataloging in Publication Data
Wingfield, Adia Harvey, 1977–
Yes we can?: white racial framing and the Obama presidency/Adia
    Harvey Wingfield and Joe R. Feagin.—2nd ed.
    p. cm.
Includes bibliographical references and index.
    1. Presidents—United States—Election—2008. 2. Presidents—United
States—Election—2012. 3. United States—Politics and government—
2009. 4. Political campaigns—United States—Sociological aspects.
5. Elections—United States—Sociological aspects. 6. Obama, Barack.
7. Obama, Barack—Public opinion. 8. United States—Race
relations—Political aspects. 9. Race discrimination—Political aspects—
United States. 10. Post-racialism—United States. 11. Whites—United
States—Attitudes. 12. Public opinion—United States. I. Feagin, Joe
R. II. Title.
E906.W56 2012
324.973—dc23
2012022065

ISBN: 978-0-415-64536-2 (hbk)
ISBN: 978-0-415-64538-6 (pbk)
ISBN: 978-0-203-07873-0 (ebk)

Typeset in Adobe Caslon and Copperplate Gothic
by Florence Production, Stoodleigh, Devon, UK

Printed and bound in the United States of America
by Edwards Brothers, Inc.

CONTENTS

PREFACE

On a cold January inauguration day in 2009, history was made and witnessed by millions of television viewers across the globe. In Washington, D.C., a record-breaking crowd of over one million people of all ages, racial groups, and nationalities personally gathered on the national mall to be present for the inauguration of President Barack Obama. This dramatic scene was unlike any other in this country's history, in large part because it marked the onset of a presidential administration led by the first African American president. Indeed, many in the audience were driven by the desire to be a part of this unique moment, and braved cold temperatures, large crowds, and long waiting periods in order to say that they were there.

In the wake of Obama's dramatic 2008 election, many have argued that his presidency marks the end of the tumultuous racial history of the United States, and indicates that white racism has now been defeated and rendered inconsequential. Ironically, however, this argument seems to conveniently forget all of the ways in which both the 2008 and the 2012 election cycles were more overtly racialized than any presidential elections in more than a century. How do we reconcile the image of a "post-racial" America with the recent spectacle of whites who have depicted candidate and President Obama through crass racist imagery that evokes historical representations of blacks' subhuman characteristics and have even likened him to a monkey? Or with white Americans who, after the 2008 election, committed numerous hate crimes against Americans of color across the country? Major issues such as these warrant a much more in-depth analysis of the ways in which racial issues have been part and parcel of the successful 2008 presidential campaign and his presidency.

In this book, we attempt to address these racial questions in detail. As social scientists who study racial discrimination and inequality, we see a unique opportunity here to expound and develop further existing conceptual frameworks so that they speak more clearly to the still-difficult reality of racial relations in a country where racial stratification and discrimination remain severe and pervasive. Yet, at the same time, this is a country that has managed to achieve a major political milestone in electing a black man as president who, had he been born a generation or two earlier, would likely have faced the threat of injury or death simply for attempting to register to vote in southern or border states. We also see the chance here to offer a sound social science analysis of the white racial framing that was used extensively throughout the 2008 and 2012 primaries and general elections—and that has been routinely used since the election. Having witnessed media analysts, pundits, politicians, scholars, and everyday citizens offer their interpretations of these distinctive and unprecedented political events, we feel that it is very important, timely, and necessary to continue to provide an assessment grounded in social science thinking and analysis with a critical bent. Thus, in this book we attempt to use relevant social science theory and data about racial matters to examine closely and systematically the critical social issues of this historic presidential campaign.

In Chapter 1, we discuss several major approaches that social scientists have used to understand racial discrimination and inequality, and lay out with a few examples the central conceptual framework guiding this book —a systemic racism approach. We elaborate on a key feature of systemic racism, the concept of the white racial frame, to incorporate in our analysis the idea that this frame has at least two major versions—a hard racial framing and a soft racial framing. The hard version of the old white racial frame is relatively blatant and open in its use of racial stereotyping, imagery, emotions, and interpretations, while the soft version of the white racial frame does not show its blatant racism in public but prefers to accent a color-blind imagery and a set of emotion-laden assertions playing down the reality of racism. We suggest here that both these versions of the white racial frame were used repeatedly over the course of both the 2008 and the 2012 primary seasons and the following presidential elections, as well as during the years Obama has made his many decisions as president.

Over the next few chapters, we first show this to be the case with many significant examples from the unprecedented 2007–2008 presidential campaign. We consider major issues that arose throughout this long campaign season as case studies that illustrate the complex and troubling use of white racial framing, as well as other significant aspects of systemic racism. Thus, in Chapter 2, we examine early debates that ranged over whether Obama was "too black" for white voters, or "not black enough" for African Americans, and we critically assess these debates in the context of hard and soft racial framing. In Chapter 3, we address in detail the ways that sexist framing and actions interacted and intersected with racial framing and actions, particularly during the Democratic primary season in the contest between Senator Obama and Senator Hillary Clinton.

Then, in Chapter 4, we explore the ways that Obama's white political opponents used the hard version of the white racial frame to depict and attack him; and we also assess Obama's distinctive efforts to counter these attacks by constructing an image of himself as a "cool" politician and using his own version of a soft (color-blind) racial framing to do so. In Chapter 5, we examine the major national controversy over Senator Obama's relationship with his longtime pastor, Dr. Jeremiah Wright, and show that it was understood by most white Americans through a hard racial framing—and that the available black counterframe was mostly ignored or overlooked. In Chapter 6, we explore further the ways in which the hard version of the white racial frame was regularly used to predict, contextualize, and interpret the voting patterns of voters of color, especially nonblack voters of color. And in Chapter 7 we examine in detail the remarkable outcome of the dramatic 2008 election, including who voted for whom and why. After that discussion, in Chapter 8, we explore many of the distinctive reactions to that 2008 election in the

United States and across the globe—reactions positive and negative. Using these data, we examine the implications of these national and international reactions for assessing the reality of persisting systemic racism for the United States.

This second edition adds two chapters that focus specifically on the aftermath of Obama's 2008 election. In Chapter 9, we examine the numerous ways that Obama's presidency has been racialized and explore examples of hard racial framing and soft racial framing used both by President Obama and his many opponents during his time in office. We also examine how the Republican Party has substantially become the "white party" of the United States. In Chapter 10, we assess the long 2012 presidential campaign and the subsequent November election. We assess the electoral strengths and strategies of both major political parties. In conclusion, we discuss the ongoing ways that white racial framing and systemic racism continue to be aggressively present and corrosive for much heralded U.S. values of "liberty and justice for all."

ACKNOWLEDGMENTS

In their final form, books bear only the authors' names, but they are typically a culmination of various types of efforts from a wide array of people. Adia would like to acknowledge the support of many people who made this work possible. I want to dedicate the second edition this book to Amina Harvey, who is really the best sister anyone could hope to have—funny, smart, beautiful, stylish, classy, and so cool that I don't even mind being the nerdy big sister! You are and always will be one of my favorite people in the whole world. I also thank my husband, John Harvey Wingfield, as well as my parents, William and Brenda Harvey, for ongoing emotional support, encouragement, and helping me to keep everything in perspective. Thanks also to Brandon Wingfield for being a good kid—excuse me, young adult. Finally, thanks (and welcome!) to my baby girl Johari for coming into and enriching our lives.

Joe would like to thank the many sociology undergraduates and Ph.D. students and colleagues he has had in recent years, who contributed to his general development of the white racial frame concept and to his thinking about the role of systemic racism in U.S. politics. I would also like to thank my wife, Clairece Feagin, and my students and colleagues Ruth Thompson-Miller, Louwanda Evans, Candace Hill, Glenn Bracey, Jeff Long, Jenni Mueller, Shari Valentine, John Foster, Rachel Feinstein, Bernice M. Barnett, and Donny Barnett for many fruitful discussions on the Obama elections and related racial issues as this book was being developed and revised.

Both Joe and Adia would also like to thank their reviewers for the two editions:

Jake Wilson, California State University Long Beach
Sean Noonan, Harper College
Alan Rudy, Central Michigan University
Lori Martin, CUNY John Jay
Stacye A. Blount, Fayeteville State University
Kathleen Fitzgerald, Loyola University of New Orleans
Jamie Daisy Purdy, Northern Arizona State University
Frances Moulder, University of Connecticut
Bill E. Lawson, University of Memphis
Tim McMillan, University of North Carolina at Chapel Hill
Traci Burch, Northwestern University

1

WHITE RACIAL FRAMING AND BARACK OBAMA'S FIRST CAMPAIGN

In an interview soon after the November 2008 election of Senator Barack Obama, the conservative Republican Secretary of State Condoleezza Rice commented thus about the election:

> I was just enormously proud of Americans for I think setting race aside. I think what you really saw here was that race is no longer the factor in American identity and American life, and that's a huge step forward . . . But it is very clear that the message of America as a place that has overcome its wounds, America as a place where race didn't matter in preventing the election of the first African American President.[1]

After the remarkable 2008 election, Secretary Rice's viewpoint was often stated by hundreds of other commentators across the country.

The election campaign and resulting election of Senator Barack Obama as the first African American president in U.S. history were indeed striking in their impact on U.S. society. However, this rosy view of "the end of racism" or a "post-racial America" is very much out of touch with the everyday realities of continuing racial hostility and discrimination in this society. In 2008, a substantial majority of whites did not vote for Senator Obama. In addition, then as now, many research studies have shown widespread racial discrimination in areas such as housing and employment. This post-racial notion is just a whitewashed fantasy.

Indeed, one of the most disturbing aspects of the 2008 campaign and Obama's presidency has been the great hostility and negative reaction of many white Americans to Obama and his family. For example, just a few weeks before the November 2008 election, a major Florida newspaper reported that an inflammatory email message from a Republican volunteer had been forwarded by the influential chair of the Hillsborough County Republican Party, who suggested that his team pass it along to help "us to win this election." The political message was all in screaming capitals:[2]

> THE THREAT: HERE IN TEMPLE TERRACE, FL OUR REPUBLICAN HQ IS ONE BLOCK AWAY FROM OUR LIBRARY, WHICH IS AN EARLY VOTING SITE. I SEE CARLOADS OF BLACK OBAMA SUPPORTERS COMING FROM THE INNER CITY TO CAST THEIR VOTES FOR OBAMA.

The email was sent around in these capital letters, thereby indicating a high level of emotion, probably including some fear. The message signals an image of African Americans that is quite stereotyped and negative— one of scary black folks "coming from the inner city" and voting "in carloads" in this whiter Florida area. The pointed email continues:

> THIS IS THEIR CHANCE TO GET A BLACK PRESI- DENT AND THEY SEEM TO CARE LITTLE THAT HE IS AT MINIMUM, SOCIALIST, AND PROBABLY MARXIST IN HIS CORE BELIEFS. AFTER ALL, HE IS BLACK—NO EXPERIENCE OR ACCOMPLISHMENTS —BUT HE IS BLACK.

Notice again the level of racialized emotion. In this turbulent 2008 campaign, some conservative Republicans saw their efforts as still fight- ing a cold war against "Marxism," a theme that was part of the national

Republican political effort. These political themes seem to have been cover for viewing Senator Obama in older antiblack terms, as the harping on his blackness suggests. The email continues in capitals:

YOU AND I UNDERSTAND THE DANGERS THE POTENTIAL OBAMA PRESIDENCY PRESENTS TO OUR WAY OF LIFE ... THERE IS ONLY ONE WAY TO STOP OBAMA: VOTE!!!—(AND GET EVERYONE YOU KNOW TO VOTE)

So, once again the writer accents an emotional we/them language of "dangers" and threats from Senator Obama and his black supporters. Punctuated by several exclamation points, the widely circulated email continues in the "get out the vote" vein, with an accent on getting out the (presumably white) vote immediately.

Together with the numerous negative comments from white readers placed after the news report on this story at a Tampa Bay, Florida website, this email message points up the naïveté in the "end of racism" comments of conservative analysts such as former Secretary Condoleezza Rice. In the pathbreaking 2008 election most whites did not vote for Senator Obama as the first black president, even in the midst of the greatest economic crisis the country has faced in 60 years. According to exit polls, only about 43 percent voted for this African American candidate, including less than a majority of whites in 32 of the 50 U.S. states. (See Chapter 10 for how he did with white voters in the 2012 election.) In this book, we examine, among numerous other issues, the powerful character and significance of the negative and racist responses by many whites to the Obama political candidacy and presidency as a way of examining the continuing importance of systemic racism in this country.

The racial hierarchy at the heart of systemic racism has from the beginning been a central, provocative, and driving force in North American society. From the onset of this society, the oppressive treatment of Americans of color has coexisted uneasily with the professed ideals of equality, freedom, and liberty and justice for all. In the mid-1800s, the astute French visitor and famous political commentator,

Alexis de Tocqueville, cited this as a major contradiction in U.S. society, and numerous others since then have urged this country to resolve this issue of racial oppression and to live up to its rhetorical ideals and promises of liberty and justice. Yet, after 400 years of this North American democratic experiment, racial inequality still prevails and is characterized by marked racial disparities in virtually all major institutions. Today, for example, black Americans still experience generally higher rates of illness, poverty, unemployment, and incarceration than white Americans.[3]

Social scientists have employed several perspectives to explain these racial disparities and the continuing reality of a racial hierarchy in this society. In this book, we argue that systemic racism and its attendant concept of the white racial frame offer the best analytical framework from which to understand the extensive, ongoing racial dynamics of the exciting and unprecedented 2008 presidential campaign of Senator Barack Obama.

Contemporary Theories of Race and Racism

Over recent decades, several social science theories have been advanced to explain persistent, ongoing racial inequalities in U.S. society. Many social science theories have assumed that U.S. racial relations regularly follow what sociologist Robert Park once described as an adaptive cycle of contact, competition, accommodation, and assimilation. Since the 1920s, Park and his later followers have generally focused on immigrants and "ethnic groups" and have argued that this cycle of assimilation can be applied to the experiences of all such groups in society. Social scientists working today in this tradition of Robert Park—and in the more recent tradition established by assimilation theorists such as Milton Gordon— have rarely challenged the underlying assumption that an ethnically driven model can be easily applied to U.S. racial groups.

While these important mainstream theories have provided some useful conceptual tools for understanding patterns of adaptation and discrimination in this society, their theoretical discussions have significant limitations and carry hidden assumptions that frequently trap social scientists and other analysts into a limited understanding of this society's extensive patterns of racial oppression. Included among these are the traditional concepts of race, prejudice, bigotry, stigma, stereotype, ethnicity, assimilation, integration, and discrimination. These terms have been widely used, but they do not provide the essential array of conceptual models necessary to make sense out of a highly racialized society such as the United States.

Even a quick look at today's social science journal articles and textbooks reveals the frequency and limitations of these conventional concepts. Interpretive approaches using them often start from a liberal social science perspective that views racial "problems" as not foundational to this society, but as more or less temporary "cancers" tacked onto an otherwise healthy democratic society. In addition, the conventional prejudice-causes-discrimination model of the mainstream tradition is oriented to individual or small-group processes and does not examine well the deep structural foundation in which acts of discrimination are always embedded.[4]

With the development of the racial formation perspective in the 1980s, however, social scientists such as Michael Omi and Howard Winant helped to shift the focus from the older assimilation/ethnicity approach to an approach accenting racial institutions and formations.[5] The racial formation theory argues that racial thinking is not only a central organizing principle of U.S. society, but that racial thinking is embedded in social actions at the macro and micro levels. This approach specifically emphasizes the ways in which racial thinking is imbedded in the legal and political system, which they argue plays a significant role in shaping racial interactions at the micro level. Racial formation theory refocused sociological attention on the ways "race" exists as a societal concept distinct from ethnicity, and one that shapes social interaction in a myriad of ways. While influential, the racial formation theory has been accurately criticized for overemphasizing the role of the legal and political system (the state) in shaping racial inequality, and for overlooking the major racial inequalities and realities in other institutional systems. The approach of Omi and Winant accents an array of competing and changing "racial formations" over time in this society and neglects to assess in detail the antiblack racial formation that has long been the most central and integral part of the U.S racial structure. Furthermore, their approach also fails to name clearly and examine well the principal creators and controllers of the foundational and systemic racism of the United States—those whites in the political–economic elite and other whites with substantial societal power.[6]

Several critical social scientists have worked to move analysis of U.S. society in the direction of an even more critical approach. For example, social scientist Eduardo Bonilla-Silva has attempted to correct some weaknesses in racial formation theory with an introduction of the concept of racialized social systems.[7] Bonilla-Silva argues that in U.S. society, racial groups are hierarchically ordered and that this unequal ranking produces inequality in major institutions. This inequality is legitimized through ideological practices that change in accordance with shifting racial practices. According to this framework, the eras of slavery and legal segregation marked earlier racialized social systems where racist practices and ideologies were more overt and obvious. The current racialized social system, however, is one in which practices of inequality are more covert and hidden and are thus justified by a "color-blind" ideology in which most whites disavow awareness of racial difference in order to continue practices that perpetuate substantial racial inequalities. This theoretical perspective is an important step forward in understanding the ways in which continuing white racism shapes social institutions and interactions, and it offers key insights into how a racial ideology sanctions racial practices. We will see how this color-blind ideology operates throughout the election campaigns of 2007–2008 and 2011–2012.

Still, in our view this important "color-blind racism" analysis, which was first developed in the 1990s by Leslie Carr, does not go far enough in assessing just how foundational and systemic that racism—especially antiblack racism—remains for this particular society. Additionally, this perspective fails to explain how and why whites still engage in a great many overt and explicit racial practices that still perpetuate extensive racial discrimination across the society. It also does not go far enough in positioning the country's racist ideology as part of a larger societal worldview, one that we term the "white racial frame."[8]

Systemic Racism: A Brief History

The systemic racism framework fills in this gap by arguing that in the U.S. case, enduring racist practices, perspectives, and institutions are quite fundamental and foundational in this society—and that in several important ways, they have changed less than these other theoretical approaches suggest. Specifically, the systemic racism perspective developed by Joe R. Feagin and his colleagues suggests that white racism is not an incidental part of this society, but is endemic and foundational. It is much more than an undesirable component of an otherwise healthy societal whole. Building on the visionary research and activism of black intellectuals such as W. E. B. Du Bois, Ida B. Wells-Barnett, Kwame Ture, and Oliver Cromwell Cox, contemporary systemic racism theorists argue that white-on-black oppression and inequality were built into the foundation of this society in the 17th century and have been manifested for centuries in its major institutions—including the legal and political system, the mass media, the educational institutions, the labor market, and other economic institutions. Du Bois was one of the first social scientists to draw attention to the ways in which deep societal structures impacted group outcomes and to emphasize the ways in which these outcomes were often racialized in the United States.[9]

The contemporary systemic racism perspective develops these important ideas further in considering the many substantial ways in which contemporary racism is still a core part of, and reproduced through, the various institutional systems of U.S. society. As we will demonstrate in later chapters, systemic racism is complex and is both class-shaped and quite gendered, thereby frequently creating differential racial outcomes for men and women of color.[10]

One major contribution of the systemic racism perspective is that it puts racial oppression and inequality in their full historical context, and emphasizes the ways in which white-on-black oppression and inequality have been foundational, and thus critical, to the continued functioning of North American social institutions and systems. For example, in his books Feagin traces the ways in which racial oppression, hierarchy, and inequality have been at the core of this society since its inception.[11] Rather than mirroring mainstream analysts' tendencies to suggest that racism is a minor, steadily declining part of society, by examining North America's long racial history the systemic racism analysts have shown that the nature, character, and indicators of racism have in numerous ways remained remarkably consistent and persistent over time.

In the early stages of North American society, the legally sanctioned system of slavery and the widespread genocide directed against Native Americans marked conspicuously overt aspects of the ways that racial oppression was endemic to societal institutions and structure. Domestic policies that emphasized whites' power, citizenship, and rights led to Native Americans' mass displacement, and a stereotyped framing of Native Americans as dangerous and heathen savages justified their wholesale slaughter or major physical displacement by whites.[12] Furthermore, the system of slavery abolished all of African Americans' human rights as individuals and rendered them subject to property ownership from whites who could afford to buy them. Even African Americans who were not enslaved had, by decree of the Supreme Court, "no rights a white man was bound to respect."[13] With laws, social customs, and governmental and economic systems based on principles of slavery and genocide, racial oppression and inequality were embedded early and deeply into the basic foundation of this society. This racial oppression and inequality were sanctioned and defended by major founders such as George Washington, Thomas Jefferson, and James Madison, who argued among other racist arguments that the innate inferiority of black Americans mandated their subordination and, if freed, a necessary separation of "races."[14]

The extremely oppressive North American system of slavery was legalized and legitimated by the European colonists and their descendants. It principally targeted black Americans and lasted nearly two and a half centuries, more than half this country's history. It persisted from 1619, when the first Africans were purchased by European colonists off a Dutch-flagged ship in Jamestown, Virginia, until 1865 with the passage of the 13th amendment, which finally prohibited slavery. Of course, virtually no African Americans, whether enslaved (most of them) or free, participated significantly in the politics of this country during the two centuries of slavery. With rare exceptions, they were not able even to vote, much less to hold political office. The bloody centuries of slavery were followed by Reconstruction, a brief period in which African Americans made unprecedented advancements towards racial equality, including some significant political participation.

Reconstruction lasted from about 1866 to 1877, during which time freed black Americans were able to vote and campaign for the first time and black politicians served in elected office. Significantly, the first black person ever to serve as U.S. senator was Hiram Revels, who was elected to represent the state of Mississippi and served from 1870 to 1871. Blanche Bruce, also of Mississippi, became the first black person to serve a full term in this congressional body, from 1875 to 1881. Both men represented the Republican Party, which in those days was considered the "party of Lincoln" and thus the political party that represented the interests of black Americans. Indeed, both Revels and Bruce were advocates for racial equality, and Bruce's wife Josephine was a contemporary of Ida B. Wells-Barnett, the well-known journalist and crusader for equal rights for black men and women. In this era, there were also numerous black employees who worked in newly integrated workplaces, and many public accommodations and other societal spaces were racially integrated for the first time. Yet, massive political pressures and violent resistance in Klan-type groups by southern whites meant that this condition of significant racial progress in the economy and politics was short-lived. The violent white backlash quickly reversed the modest trend to racial desegregation and resulted in the Jim Crow era of extensive and legal racial segregation.

This totalitarian-like era lasted from the 1870s to the late 1960s. This time period reinforced racial oppression and inequality, further entrenching it as a basic and systemic aspect of U.S. life and society. Under Jim Crow, racial inequality remained codified into law, the educational and economic systems, and public accommodations and other public social spaces. Blacks were legally prohibited from testifying against whites, serving on juries, and voting. They could not campaign for or serve in political offices in most areas, the only exception being small all-black towns. They were paid much less than whites and openly denied access to better educational facilities and most decent-paying jobs. In public social arenas in southern and border states, blacks were often expected to step off sidewalks when whites approached, avoid direct eye contact, and most infamously, use segregated public fountains and other facilities. As in the era of slavery, Jim Crow established white-on-black oppression in all major societal sectors and reinforced its importance and centrality in the society as a whole. Moreover, in northern areas of the country, blacks generally experienced significant de facto racial segregation, which resulted in their concentration in crowded, underserved areas of the cities. Du Bois' classic social science work, *The Philadelphia Negro*, explored with field research the ways in which racial oppression and segregation functioned outside the south to create yet more oppression and disadvantages for African Americans.[15] There was thus little opportunity for them to run for political offices, and much pressure not to vote, in the north as well.

Systemic Racism Today

In our time, there is a curious tendency among a majority of whites to downplay this extensive racist history and argue that, since the 1960s civil rights movement, racism has ceased to function as a major factor shaping this society. Considering that most of this country's history has been grounded in the extreme racial oppression of slavery and Jim Crow—which openly and deeply shaped the legal, political, economic, educational, and other institutional systems of this country—we find this claim disingenuous and ill-informed. Coupled with slavery and the period of legal segregation, which persisted until the civil rights laws of the 1964–1968 era, the period of legally sanctioned racial oppression and inequality lasted for nearly 350 years. In contrast, the period of time that overt racial discrimination has been officially and legally prohibited is a mere 44 or so years. These numbers display in stark terms the length of time that racial oppression has been an accepted, taken-for-granted part of this society's foundational social structure.

In present times, attempts to rectify ongoing racial discrimination and inequality in employment, housing, education, politics, and other areas are often met with whites' oxymoronic claims of "reverse discrimination" and arguments that ending official discrimination was sufficient and that efforts to create a level playing field create an unfair burden now for whites.[16] These arguments ignore the effects of historical racism and inequality, and the fact that centuries of such institutionalized oppression still shape racial discrimination and disparities that persist to this day. As such, these arguments help to permit racial inequality to continue, as is evidenced in whites' outpacing African Americans and some other groups of color on most major measures of economic success and stability, health and well-being, and educational attainment. We also see significant racial disparities in important political bodies such as the U.S. Senate.[17] In other words, it is difficult to claim that racial discrimination and inequality have ceased to be a central societal reality when whites as a group have more wealth, better health, and higher incomes than blacks, and justify this reality by citing old racially framed perceptions that black Americans are lazy, unintelligent, or generally inferior.[18]

Today, whites continue to actively support and maintain racial inequality in various societal settings. As social science research on wealth and inequality routinely shows, white choices about residential mobility and access to transformative assets reproduce racial wealth gaps.[19] Because whites are more likely to have access to inherited wealth in the form of gifts, loans, and cash assets from parents and other relatives, they can use this economic cushion to relocate to neighborhoods that would otherwise be unattainable. Significantly, racial composition plays a key role in decision making, with whites often intentionally or tacitly seeking out neighborhoods that are mostly white. The perception that whiter neighborhoods are "better" neighborhoods perpetuates residential segregation and further devalues areas that are comprised mostly of citizens of color. By acting on these ideas, whites help, albeit sometimes unwittingly, to maintain and benefit from continuing racial inequality.

Moreover, one major study of the white male elite has shown that white men with high levels of influence in the U.S. political, legal, educational, economic, and social spheres regularly rationalize continuing white-on-black oppression by arguing that African Americans are less intelligent, hard-working, and honest than whites.[20] These white men admit to feeling more comfortable with whites than with people of color. This feeling of comfort guides their decisions in many arenas—hiring, employment, choice of partners, and political choices—and thereby reinforces much white advantage. In one example, a white employer describes how feeling more comfortable with a prospective white worker eventually led to this employee's hire over a black applicant:

> I had a [black] candidate for a job in my organization, and I
> just didn't know if he was going to work out . . . and I knew if
> I picked the white candidate I could transfer him, I could demote

him, I could fire him if he couldn't do the job, [but] if I chose the black candidate he was mine forever . . . I wouldn't be able to fire him with all the pressure of affirmative action—he would just be mine forever. I took the white candidate. I agonized over that one not only when I made it, but later. And I would do it again . . . because all I know about that person [the black candidate] is where he graduated from, and that could have been a standard much lower than that school normally has.[21]

In this case, this white employer ultimately chooses the candidate with whom he feels most comfortable. Operating out of a traditional white framing of black Americans, he justifies this by preemptively deciding that the black applicant will not perform satisfactorily and that his educational experience was likely substandard—despite the speaker's implication that the college from which the black applicant graduated typically holds students to high standards. Here, the greater level of comfort and familiarity with whites in general results in a concrete lack of opportunity for an apparently qualified African American worker. We use this example to accent a much larger racial problem and reality in this society. This white-comfort process is not unique to the employment process, for, as we will see in later chapters, white comfort with white or black political candidates significantly shaped the 2007–2008 and 2011–2012 presidential campaigns. Like employers in workplace settings, white politicians and voters periodically make premature or preemptive judgments about whether a candidate of color will perform satisfactorily or whether he or she has the "right" education or experience.

Much social science research today shows that racial oppression and inequality are, in fact, pervasive and core aspects of the U.S. social structure. The research also indicates that whites, as a group, are complicit in maintaining systems of racial discrimination and inequality as well as their personal privileges and advantages over people of color. Rather than being passive, innocent bystanders who are uninvolved in— or active dissenters who work to dismantle—the racist structures that offer them undue or unjust advantages, a majority of whites actively work to protect these unearned racial opportunities. More importantly, they do so in collusion with the major economic, social, political, and legal systems originally constructed by whites with the intention, though not the sole purpose, of supporting white privileges and advantages over Americans of color.[22]

What enables whites to maintain a high level of complicity with racist patterns and institutions that further racial oppression and inequalities? How do they justify their active or passive participation in these racialized systems? We argue that the extreme and systemic nature of U.S. racial oppression and inequality necessitates a broad perspective and emotion-laden frame that justifies the routine exploitation and numerous disadvantages facing African Americans and other Americans of color. In order for systemic racism to succeed, we argue, it has relied on the existence of a legitimating and shaping white racial frame.

The Dominant White Racial Frame

As Feagin has explained this concept, the dominant white racial frame consists of the array of whites' sincere fictions, stereotypes, images, emotions, narratives, interpretations, and discriminatory inclinations that legitimizes systemic racism and inclines or allows whites to participate in the routine exploitation of people of color. In general, this white racial frame portrays whites as inherently more moral, intelligent, kind, and hard-working than most people of color. It rationalizes the dominant racial hierarchy. This centuries-old hierarchy is a societal ladder that positions whites firmly at the top and slots subordinated racial groups into hierarchical ranks, with many Asian Americans and certain light-skinned Latino/as viewed as preferable to African Americans, but still not equal to whites.[23]

Emotion-laden stereotypes and sincere fictions about Americans of color abound in the white racial frame. Asian Americans are generally seen as passive and nonthreatening, or as "model minorities" (a white-created term), but are still considered racialized "others" who threaten white Americans' racial hegemony. Blacks are depicted in the dominant white frame as prone to criminal behavior, dangerous, dirty, lazy, and less intelligent than whites. In numerous ways, Latino/as are envisioned similarly in the white frame. They are imagined to be dirty and to have criminal proclivities. Unlike African Americans, however, Latino/as, especially immigrants, are often cast as hard-working, although best suited for low-wage, manual labor. These stereotypes serve to justify and legitimize individual actions, policy decisions, and institutional processes that reproduce systemic racism in the larger society. These usually emotion-laden stereotypes and images work in complex yet interconnected ways out of the dominant white racial frame and ultimately uphold systemic racism.[24]

This old white racial frame is gendered, so that the stereotypes and images of people of color diverge along *gender* lines. The dominant frame, for example, constructs black and Latino men in particular as physically threatening with criminal proclivities. Black men are specifically construed as potential rapists who often prey on white women. Asian-American men are alternately represented as asexual, quiet types, or as foreign gang members, while Asian-American women are highly sexualized or docile and submissive. Black women are depicted as sexually promiscuous, a stereotype that creates prevailing images of black women as deficient mothers who have many children out of wedlock. Importantly, these stereotypes vary by class, with working-class black men and women subjected to controlling images that justify their low economic status and differ somewhat from the gendered images applied to their middle- and upper-income counterparts. While black working-class women may encounter commonplace images of the "bitch" and the bad black mother, their middle- and upper-income counterparts are more likely to face images of the modern "mammy" or the black "lady."[25]

A critical part of the white racial frame, these stereotyped ideas and images are usually emotion-laden and regularly shape whites' individual and institutional behaviors to maintain and reify white-on-black inequality. This occurs as these racialized images dominate individual minds to shape interpersonal interactions in everyday life. These racial images, almost always negative, regularly give rise to discriminatory responses loaded with much emotion. For instance, when white women see black men and reflexively clutch their purses, lock their car doors, or cross to the other side of the street, these responses clearly suggest they are using white racial framing of black male criminality and white female vulnerability to make sense of their surroundings. Furthermore, when white employers are reluctant to hire working-class black women because they expect these women will be unreliable single mothers, these employers also utilize a white framing of black female sexuality to inform their hiring decisions.[26]

The white racial frame legitimates and shapes societal institutions as well as individual actions, and it is in turn shaped by those institutions. For example, sociologist Wendy Moore describes how the legal system systematically advantages whites through policies, rulings, and interpretations that deny full participation, citizenship, and opportunity to Americans of color.[27] Similarly, a white racial framing shapes much of the operation of the mainstream mass media, as is evidenced in frequent depictions of black people as less honest, forthright, and moral than whites.[28] Though she does not use our terminology of the frame, Ann Arnett Ferguson's ethnographic study of a public school shows how institutional policy is grounded in a white racial framing that often views black boys as criminals and deviants.[29] With most individuals and major institutions guided by the dominant frame, an array of behaviors, stereotypes, emotions, images, and actions that maintain ongoing inequality are thereby legitimized.

All whites benefit from the white racial frame, even though many are adversely affected by class and gender inequalities. Thus, working-class whites gain from a white racial framing that makes employers reluctant to hire blacks for certain skilled blue collar jobs.[30] Even though these whites are disadvantaged by their class position, especially in environments of economic restructuring and decline in job opportunities, the white frame offers them advantages over other racial groups. Similarly, white women of all class levels encounter widespread, institutionalized sexism that limits their occupational options and earnings. Yet they too benefit from white racial framing that favors them in hiring decisions over women and men of color.[31]

Whites benefit from the white racial frame because it offers them undue or unjust advantages in the workplace, political sphere, education, media, health care, and other societal areas. Perhaps more importantly, the white racial frame offers important psychological, social, and emotional justifications that enable whites to participate, both actively and passively, in a systemically racist society. It legitimates both active discrimination and passive bystanding when others discriminate. For example, the aforementioned research on elite white men shows that utilizing a white racial framing of black people as likely criminals allows whites to justify racial discrimination overtly. When asked what they would do, hypothetically, if they witnessed a white jewelry store clerk ignore two black patrons in order to serve white men first, these elite men often relied on the white frame's image of black criminality to justify both the store clerk's behavior and their own unwillingness to intervene. In a telling example, one respondent stated:

> Maybe [the clerk] is worried about them shoplifting. I guess if five guys carrying guns walked into the store, and I was working in the store, I might be a little inclined to stay away from them too . . . Also there is another reason, another angle that could be. And that is . . . maybe because most black people don't make much money, maybe . . . [the clerk] doesn't figure there's any money in the sale . . . he's trying to do his job.[32]

In his mind, this elite white respondent immediately equates the mere presence of black customers in the jewelry store with possible criminality. Note that this example also underscores the ways the dominant racial frame is gendered, as this white respondent assumed that the black patrons were men even though that was not mentioned in the hypothetical question. Further, though the hypothetical example specifies that there are only two black customers in the store, this man multiplies the number of black patrons and introduces weapons, criminal proclivities, and poverty into this scenario. These embellishments enable the respondent to explain and justify the white clerk's discriminatory behavior. By relying on the dominant racial frame, these elite male respondents often indicated that they were more or less comfortable in colluding in the societal processes of racialization and racial discrimination.

Although whites benefit from the dominant racial frame, they are not the only group that is susceptible to its messages. Because this frame is so pervasive in and foundational to the societal structure, Americans of color often internalize some of its racial stereotypes, controlling images, and sincere fictions as well. Research on black women salon owners, thus, suggests that even as they challenge aspects of the racial frame in their daily lives, they simultaneously internalize certain of its stereotyped messages that some black women (usually working class) are loud, crass, and "ghetto."[33]

Other research shows that Asian Americans may also buy into the white racial frame's images about black Americans and Latino/as.[34] This process can become largely invisible, inasmuch as major societal institutions, especially the media and educational system, socialize all citizens to buy into the white racial frame and accept many of its notions and premises. For many whites, this racial framing becomes "normal" and basic. Unlike whites, however, people of color as groups usually benefit only modestly, or not at all, from using elements of this white frame to shape their interactions and behaviors in society. Only a few favored individuals of color, such as Justice Clarence Thomas on the U.S. Supreme Court, have benefited a lot from greatly buying into the white racial frame. Since the dominant frame justifies racial oppression and inequality that heavily favor white Americans, use of its elements generally does not offer people of color, even those who appear to garner some privileges, full access to the power and opportunities generally available to whites. Certainly, much popular opinion, especially among whites, on racial matters ignores systemic racism and reduces racism to personal beliefs and attitudes, hence the contention that "anyone can be racist." However, it is important to recognize that while people of color may employ hard or soft racial framing to facilitate their individual upward mobility, personal gain, or professional opportunity, doing so regularly reinforces the structural and institutional barriers that disadvantage people of color as a whole.

Moreover, to varying degrees, groups of color in the United States periodically deploy counterframes that challenge basic elements of the white racial frame. In response to the dominant frame that posits white women as the epitome of beauty, for example, black women develop and rely on a counterframe that defines beauty by physical features commonly found among black women and that emphasizes intangible criteria such as emotional strength and character.[35] Similarly, many black Americans employ a counterframe that encourages critical analysis of racist stereotypes and racial inequality in society. This black counterframe helps to challenge the white racial frame that suggests that inequality stems solely from blacks' personal, moral, and individual shortcomings.

Hard and Soft Racial Framing

A broad white racial frame has persisted now for several centuries. Many important aspects that are in the white frame today have persisted from the very distant past, while other significant components have been added in recent decades. As we have suggested, this dominant racial frame has many elements, and people ordinarily select from these diverse elements and use them in different and variable ways. Some whites still openly emphasize that certain racial groups are biologically inferior. Yet others may or may not believe this, but they do not articulate it openly and make use of a more subtle or covert racial discourse in viewing and openly discussing Americans of color. There are numerous variations in between. Different people and different groups, both white and not white, select from this old and broad frame and employ elements that facilitate their racialized framing and consequent everyday actions.

We thus view the concept of the white racial frame as providing a more comprehensive conceptualization of how racialized issues and situations are presented, experienced, and interpreted than other theoretical approaches. While the concepts of color-blind ideology, new racism, or subtle racism are innovative and useful, they tend to accent just certain cognitive and discursive aspects of contemporary racism. The white racial frame concept is broader and not only encompasses the diversity of pro-white and anti-other cognitive, ideological, and rhetorical explanations of contemporary racism, but also highlights the imagery, sounds (language), and emotional aspects of racialized behavior and action. Furthermore, the white racial frame concept provides a lens for better understanding how verbal-cognitive material such as stereotyping translates into everyday interracial interactions and recurring racial discrimination. In Feagin's previous work and in our conceptual work here, the white racial frame concept is also theoretically extended to describe and interpret the *counterframes* that African Americans and other people of color regularly use to challenge the old white racial frame.

In its everyday use, thus, one can roughly distinguish two differing versions of the dominant white racial frame—what we term (1) hard racial framing and (2) soft racial framing.

Hard Racial Framing

Much overtly racist commentary in public. "Races" are inherently and biologically unequal, as well as culturally unequal. Whites are superior. Black people are "N-words" who should know and keep their "place" in society, and should be openly treated in unequal ways. Other people of color are very negatively evaluated. Assertively, white people are biologically and culturally superior and justifiably dominant.

Soft Racial Framing

Little overtly racist commentary in public. "Race" and racism are receding and are no longer very important in this increasingly "color-blind" society. People of color are more subtly or covertly stereotyped, but are still responsible for their own problems. Those people of color who behave according to white norms and accept much white racial framing are much more acceptable in society. Whites are viewed as more culturally superior than biologically superior, and whiteness is centrally but somewhat less aggressively asserted, at least in public.

In all its expressions, this white racial framing views whites as the dominant and superior group, and other racial groups as justifiably on lower rungs of the racial ladder. This framing is essential to the legitimization and maintenance of the U.S. system of racial oppression. The framing generates and shapes actions, which in turn reinforce the framing. Whites rely on this dominant frame to implement and normalize ongoing racial discrimination and inequality, as well as to justify the ways in which they participate in and benefit from this discrimination and inequality. However, there are important differences in the ways this occurs.

For some whites, harsh and blatantly racist elements from the white racial frame are still used in overt and public ways to argue openly for the subordination or inferiority of African Americans and other Americans of color. For example, this is evident in examples of whites who candidly and publicly state that they find African Americans dirty, lazy, ape-like, or otherwise repugnant.[36] Consider the text below from a handwritten letter on a New Jersey public school's stationery that was penned by a white person, apparently male. The letter was in response to a newspaper article discussing research on discrimination in which the second author was briefly quoted:

> So we should give privileges to placate filthy dirty subhuman coons, your nuts [sic]. Never! Never! I'm telling you . . . Whites such as myself are just itching to take to the streets and exterminate every dirty nigger ape as well as every white nigger loving commie dog (such as your self). Simpson is the catalyst that will finally awaken the latent, dormant nigger hatred extant in this county. There will be no compromise, no quarter given . . . First we elect Buchanan types, next suspend habeus corpis [sic]. Third disenfranchise and resegregate niggers. Then either deportation or extermination . . . The only good nigger is a dead nigger. WHITE RAGE.[37]

We have shortened his letter, but even this excerpt shows how extremely strong and emotionally held the dominant white racial frame is for some whites, even inclining people such as this likely well-educated letter writer to forecast white violence as coming against black Americans and whites who might be their allies. This is what we mean by a "hard" racial framing. Such harsh, blatant, and venomous use of elements of the old white frame is still commonplace in this society, as is conspicuously evident at numerous internet websites and in the many and various hate crimes that have taken place during and after the Obama presidential campaigns, as shown later (see Chapter 7).

Note too that this white letter writer's hero seems to be former MSNBC commentator and former presidential candidate, Pat Buchanan. Buchanan periodically uses a relatively hard version of the white racial frame publicly to explain U.S. racial matters. He has spoken positively of Adolf Hitler's achievements and argued that African Americans are unassimilable and often criminal.[38] In numerous contexts, he has accented what he views as the justifiable societal dominance of white

European Americans. He makes this clear in a comment about immigration: "If we had to take a million immigrants in, say, Zulus next year or Englishmen, and put them in Virginia, what group would be easier to assimilate and would cause less problems for the people of Virginia? There is nothing wrong with us sitting down and arguing that issue that we are a European country, English-speaking country."[39] Here he ignores the history of Virginia, which early on was nearly half African American in its population, and the fact that many whites today have ancestries that do not go back nearly as far as those of many African Americans in Virginia. Buchanan also ignores the history of oppressive white colonization that helps account for the white population in Virginia today, and the fact that this colonization involved the genocide targeting Native Americans who previously lived in this region. While Buchanan's framing of U.S. society is not overtly violent like that of the letter writer, his emotion-laden words do signal a hard white framing of society.

In contrast, many other whites do not operate publicly out of such a hard, blatantly racist framing but operate instead out of a "softer" racist framing of whites and other Americans of color, though one that still draws important elements from the contemporary white racial frame. Take this example of an elite corporate executive in the aforementioned white elites' study, who compares black Americans to whites and Asians in assessing black community problems:

> It has to do with family values . . . If you ask me what I [think] about an argument or a thesis that the family structure is stronger in Asian families or white families than it is in black families, there, I think that there's probably some legitimate issues . . . The problem with black kids today has a lot to do with family structure. I don't know if family structure was influenced by racism, or at least recent racism . . . I just don't see it.[40]

This white executive relies on racial stereotypes about black family structure and a willful ignorance about the intergenerational effects of racial oppression to form his racialized conclusions, which are not violent or as venomous as the previous commentators but are consistent with the sincere fictions and "common-sense" assumptions about African

Americans that predominate in the age-old racial framing. Though all these types of racialized statements and framing reinforce patterns of white-on-black oppression and inequality, there are important differences in the ways they are used and deployed in everyday life.

The hard version of the white racial frame shapes resultant behaviors on racial matters. Individuals who openly subscribe to the old white supremacist ideology that racial groups are biologically different and that people of color are fundamentally inferior may, at the extreme, engage in open racial harassment and violent discrimination against them, as the letter writer above suggests he and others will do. In less extreme cases, those operating out of this harsh version of the dominant frame may seek to establish and maintain great physical, emotional, and social distance from people of color. These white individuals often openly state that they do not enjoy living in areas with people of color, especially African Americans, or that they are heavily invested in their racial identity as whites, so much so that the very thought of their children being in interracial relationships makes them physically ill.[41] Overall, those who regularly and openly operate out of the hard version of the white racial frame are guided by their conviction that "race" is a legitimate and reliable biologized and cultural marker of difference and that black Americans or certain other people of color do and should occupy a deservedly lower spot on the U.S. racial hierarchy.

The soft version of the old racial frame differs from the hard version in its often toned-down assessments of racial matters. The soft version of the frame suggests that white racism is now dead or rapidly dying, and that "race" is receding as an important marker of social differences in a "color-blind" or "post-racial" United States. In this perspective, individual effort is the only thing that is critical to personal advancement and opportunity for Americans of color. Those who employ this softer racist framing are likely to suggest, at least in public, that they do not see, or are uncomfortable discussing, an array of contemporary and historical racial issues. Instead, in public and racially mixed settings they tend to profess a rosy vision of U.S. society in which they make no mention of structural racial inequalities and commonly articulate the view that individuals of whatever backgrounds should be viewed as more or less alike. They are likely to espouse the "post-racial" view that "race doesn't matter anymore."

For example, during the 2008 presidential campaign, the prominent white media commentator, Chris Matthews, described his discomfort in acknowledging white voters as a *racial group*. In a revealing statement, Matthews confessed:

> We've known that ethnic and racial issues always get in the way of arguing over issues—real issues. But this conversation as it's turned—I even hate saying things like "white working class voters." I was taught growing up, don't even say words like "blue collar," don't even get into that kind of elitist talk. We're not sociologists, we're Americans.[42]

Matthews' statement can be viewed as an example of the soft racial frame, wherein he was uneasy in publicly recognizing or talking about racial distinctions and how they may have impacted contemporary voting patterns. Note also Matthews' assertion that talking about racial matters gets in the way of discussing the "real" issues, and his implicit marginalization of racism and racial issues as serious problems. For him, even having to acknowledge racial and class differences creates a marked sense of personal discomfort, a common reaction for whites who harbor much old racist thinking in their minds but are unwilling to face that framing.

This soft version of the dominant racial frame also drives behavior. Unlike the hard racial frame, individuals who subscribe to this soft color-blind framing are less likely to openly describe people of color as unequal and publicly attack them as deficient. Because their ideological bent contends that racial differences are no longer a central issue, they may sometimes even take exception to whites who express openly blatantly racist statements. However, the perspective of this soft frame means that individuals rarely examine, much less acknowledge, the existence of individual actions and structural processes that create and maintain societal patterns of racial discrimination and inequality. The soft frame allows whites to ignore the ways that racial characteristics shape most social, economic, and occupational aspects of their lives. Thus, an individual who uses this soft racial framing may argue that "race" does not matter to them because they have a black friend or acquaintance, without considering that racial characteristics do shape their choice of most friendships, social activities, and romantic partners, so much so that interactions (especially equal status interactions) with African Americans and other people of color are rather infrequent. The emotional and cognitive logic of this soft framing is that individual choice and responsibility trump structural processes. Importantly, this type of framing still allows whites to maintain a distance from Americans of color without acknowledging the racial implications of their actions.

Those publicly operating out of the soft racial frame may view certain Americans of color as virtuous. Some African Americans are thus seen as "exceptions to their race." Researchers Sut Jhally and Justin Lewis describe this process in their study of the impact of the very popular 1980s television program *The Cosby Show*, now often seen in reruns.[43] They found that some white audiences' genuine affection for Bill Cosby functioned as a discursive process wherein they downplayed their negative feelings about blacks in general by emphasizing their positive feelings for one (fictional) black person. In this interpretative process, white viewers are thus able to point to individual blacks who are acceptable and safe "exceptions," and thereby to use an individualistic framing to justify their adverse feelings about blacks as a group. As Jhally and Lewis write, "[Whites] can accept the Huxtables as people who are 'just like us.' Beneath this progressive attitude, however, lies an implicit and unstated rejection of the majority of black people, who are not like the Huxtables and, by implication, not 'like us.'"[44]

Even though this softer racial framing emphasizes individuals and claims to ignore racial characteristics, it is important to note that some of the harsher elements of the white racial frame are here as well, for this framing only views certain assimilated-to-whiteness people of color as acceptable. Typically, these are people of color who do not openly discuss or emphasize their and others' racial oppression, so that those whites who accent a soft frame can "forget" these individuals are black. Indeed, viewers applauded *The Cosby Show* for its depiction of a family that was visibly black, but not "too black." One respondent remarked thus:

> [*The Cosby Show*] is not like a jive show, like *Good Times*. I don't think it's aimed at, I think those other shows are more jive, more soul shows, say as far as the way the characters are with making you aware that they are more separate from . . . Where Cosby is more of American down the line thing, which makes everybody feel accepted and being a part of watching it.[45]

This soft version of the dominant frame reveals that certain people of color and their individual stories and actions are acceptable to most whites, but only as long as those people of color do not highlight their racial status in ways that are threatening and discomfiting.

Researcher Eduardo Bonilla-Silva has described a similar process in his analysis of the color-blind perspective held by many whites. The color-blind ideology is comprised of four key dimensions: Abstract liberalism, minimization of racism, biologization of culture, and naturalization of effects.[46] Today, many whites employ this color-blind perspective in order to avoid a discussion of racism issues and to conceal their highly racialized views, which they still hold, but tend to express in more subtle and covert ways. Employing color-blind rhetoric, then, enables contemporary whites to proclaim that "they do not even see color," and to suggest that racism has disappeared, that race-based disparities are a consequence of individual choice, and that institutional racism is nonexistent.[47] Thus, this color-blind ideology informs their public defense of their actions, including discriminatory actions, in most social spheres. If whites profess that they do not "see" race, then they also do not have to "see" their own privilege, the discriminatory actions they and their peers actually engage in, or the ways in which institutional structures routinely advantage whites and disadvantage people of color.

These color-blind-ideology dimensions accent important cognitive aspects of contemporary white thinking. But there is a question of how these cognitive views translate into everyday actions. How do individuals who operate out of the color-blind ideology respond to people of color in everyday life? How do they interact with members of other racial groups? The color-blind ideology suggests that they strive not to notice race, but do they in fact act that way in interracial interactions?

In public settings, whites usually operate with a racial framing that reveals much more than just this color-blind ideology. Operating out of a soft racial framing, many whites will accent individualism and thus view some people of color as acceptable if they have assimilated well to whiteness. We will see this view come into play several times in later chapters, as whites evaluate black Americans such as Senator Barack Obama from this framing. From the point of view of people of color, such "exception" framing is not in fact subtle or emotionless, for whites usually make clear that *they* are determining what is acceptable and white-like. Significantly, people of color must downplay racial identity and any important markers of racial status that whites consider undesirable in order to be welcomed and viewed positively by whites. Thus, the soft racial framing is emotion-laden and encompasses much more than a color-blind ideology, and it allows us to understand the difficulties of much white–nonwhite interaction better. This soft racial framing also highlights the ways in which individuals of color often must reconstruct themselves in order to be acceptable to those whites operating out of this version of the old white-racist frame.

The soft racial framing with its typical color-blind ideology is just one aspect of contemporary racism. A great many whites, as well as others, regularly transition between a soft racial framing and a hard racial framing whenever and wherever it is expeditious. Much data show that a soft racial framing accenting color-blindness is only one part of a particular person's repertoire. Depending on the setting and circumstances, they may also operate out of a harder racial framing. Evidence for this behavioral shifting with settings can be seen in one major study of 626 white college students at numerous colleges and universities across the country. The researchers asked these students to keep diaries of any racial events that they observed or participated in over part of one college semester. In relatively brief diaries, these educated whites reported some 7,500 overtly racist events, including racist joking, games, commentaries, skits, and discriminatory actions. In a great many cases, however, the overtly racist events that these well-educated whites participated in or observed took place "backstage" in spaces where only whites, especially friends, acquaintances, or relatives, were present. In the private backstage spaces, these well-educated, mostly younger whites regularly resorted to the hard, old-fashioned racist stereotypes, language, and emotions of the white racial frame and expressed it in backstage performances and behavior as a way of passing along and maintaining the white frame and thereby preserving their white privilege, status, and identity.[48]

Strikingly, many white students also claimed that they or their white friends would not usually act in these blatantly racist ways in public or multiracial "frontstage" settings. In the more public places, as they made clear in these diaries, they and their friends and relatives assert or signal (falsely) that they are color-blind and operate out of a soft racial framing—that is, that they do not notice or care about racial differences. Our conceptual framework, thus, emphasizes the reality of a broad and old white racial frame from which whites can and do choose elements for everyday behaviors, with both the operational framing and everyday behaviors frequently varying substantially according to the specific social settings and circumstances.

We want to be clear about our terminology here. Both the "soft" framing and the "hard" racial framing draw elements out of a broad and old white racial frame to suit the interpretive needs of particular places and moments. Thus, while the soft racial frame eschews the overt and blatant stereotypes of the hard frame, both variations on the white racial frame still rely on racial stereotypes, sincere fictions, cultural imagery, racialized emotions, and hoary narratives to reinforce ideas of whiteness as dominant and normative while simultaneously marginalizing blacks, Latino/as, Asians, and other people of color. In addition, while the soft racial frame may often be construed as less offensive than the hard framing, it still has clear disadvantageous, often painful impacts and consequences for people of color who must confront it. Recall the example of the white male executives from Feagin and O'Brien's study who immediately equate the hypothetical presence of blacks in a jewelry store with criminal proclivities, or who assume black workers are less qualified and intelligent. Neither of these executives uses blatantly racialized terms to categorize blacks in these fictional real-life-type scenarios, but they both still rely on soft racial framing as a rationale for their discriminatory behavior. In real life, their soft-frame motivated actions might well have painful consequences for the targets of their racial framing.

Conclusion

White racial framing is a key aspect of maintaining systemic racial inequalities across all sectors of U.S. society, from educational and economic institutions to legal and political institutions. In contemporary society, the softer versions of this racial framing typically call for as little public and overt discussion about "race" and racism as is possible. Indeed, part of how the white racial frame functions is by downplaying discussion of or attention to the still widespread racial discrimination and inequality in this society. For those who operate out of the soft version of the frame, avoiding discussion of racism becomes a convenient way to emphasize supposedly color-blind individualism, rather than directly addressing the continuing and painful realities of white-on-black oppression.

In this book, we argue that Barack Obama's two campaigns for the presidency and his presidency provide a unique and quite historic lens through which to examine systemic racism as well as the white racial frame that legitimizes it. Thus, Obama's first campaign, presidency, and re-election bid forced recurring discussions of numerous aspects of racism into the public mainstream, and likely generated a great many analyses and debates in backstage, private settings across the country as well. As we will show, much of the language, framing, and interpretations of the race-related campaign issues has been, and continues to be, communicated through some version of the dominant racial frame.

Furthermore, there are ways in which the Obama campaign officials chose to work within this white racial frame in order to appeal to a broad array of voters and thus to win the election. We argue that the Obama campaigns reveal not only the pervasiveness of the old white racial frame, and the underlying reality of systemic racism, but also the complexity and variations of this frame and the ways that it is differentially utilized depending on the contexts, settings, times, and actors in question. Using selected key events from the two Obama campaigns as case study data, we explore the ways white racial framing and systemic racism shaped these historic presidential campaigns and have thus persisted well into the 21st-century United States.

2

"TOO BLACK?" OR "NOT BLACK ENOUGH?"

Unsurprisingly, one of the earliest issues that arose in Barack Obama's historic 2008 presidential campaign was the issue of "race." During the early stages of the 2008 Democratic primaries, many people raised questions as to how racial views and issues would impact Senator Obama's ability to gain support from white, black, and other Americans. Many of these questions stemmed from the fact that he embodied an important new shift in political goals and style among black politicians, and as a result, he stood to become the most famous black politician to adopt and benefit from this new direction in politics.

Blacks in Politics

In electoral politics, black Americans have always faced enormous challenges gaining the groundswell of support necessary for election to most offices. For most of this country's history, black citizens were almost entirely excluded from the political process as voters and as elected officials. During the centuries-long period of legal slavery, the racially segregated political process prohibited blacks from voting in the South and, for the most part, in the North. Simultaneously, legal and political rules upheld the slave system and counted an enslaved black person as the infamous "three-fifths of a person," ensuring that white southern slaveholding politicians could benefit from the greater representation the larger population count brought them—even as they denied the substantial black part of their state's population the right to vote and hold office. Starting in the 1790s, large numbers of those enslaved in the major slaveholding states were counted by the new federal government but not conferred with any legal, social, economic, or political rights. Under this system, African Americans were systematically excluded from any participation in the political system as voters or political representatives.[1]

During the brief Reconstruction era after the 1860s Civil War, numerous black politicians were elected at local, state, and federal levels. For the first time, some African Americans served in the U.S. Congress. Often, these politicians represented black communities and their political interests. They sought congressional positions as a way to draw attention to, and hopefully rectify, the many racial inequities and injustices that newly freed black Americans faced. Yet, black politicians such as Senators Blanche Bruce and Hiram Revels, mentioned in the last chapter, were few and far between. As the short decade of Reconstruction ended and whites ensured that the Jim Crow era would replace the slavery era, black citizens experienced stark segregation and legalized inequality. Strict policies of racial separation were regularly enforced by official and Klan-type violence. This meant that it was extremely dangerous for blacks to express interest in the political process, let alone attempt to vote or run for elected office. In many places during this Jim Crow period, blacks who attempted to register to vote were assaulted, killed, or driven out of town. Hence, very few black officials held elected office once Reconstruction ended and Jim Crow began, and then only in all-black towns.[2]

After long decades of bloody segregation, the 1960s civil rights movement finally brought down Jim Crow, and black citizens began again to run successfully for public office. The post-civil rights era saw the first of several noteworthy, although ultimately unsuccessful, black presidential campaigns. In 1972, Shirley Chisholm (D-NY) was the first African American to run as a major-party candidate for the U.S. presidency. Though Chisholm knew her chances for winning were virtually nonexistent, she ran for the office in order to make a point that African Americans should not accept the political status quo. In 1984 and 1988, Reverend Jesse Jackson became the second African American to seek his party's nomination. Jackson was supported by a broad coalition that included voters of color as well as some white progressives and members of other disadvantaged groups. Though, like Chisholm, observers considered it all but impossible that he could win the nomination, Jackson won 20 percent of the popular vote in the 1984 primaries and some five Super Tuesday Democratic primaries in 1988. Given Jackson's involvement in the 1960s civil rights movement as an associate of Dr. Martin Luther King, Jr., it was not surprising that a major component of his platform involved drawing attention to the civil rights and socioeconomic issues faced by marginalized and oppressed social groups, especially Americans of color.[3]

Since the attempts of Chisholm and Jackson, other black candidates have attempted to win their party's nomination for the presidency.[4] Yet, most of these candidates followed one of two models. Some drew on their affiliation with and involvement in the civil rights movement in order to shape their candidacy. In his 2000 presidential bid, for example, the Reverend Al Sharpton emphasized social inequalities and used the resulting political debates as a way to bring critical issues affecting communities of color to center stage. Sharpton argued that certain issues—such as racial profiling, disparate racial sentencing, and dwindling jobs in predominantly black communities—were usually ignored or downplayed by both Democratic and Republican political candidates who worked within the mainstream political establishment. By focusing on these enduring racial inequalities and the policy changes necessary to redress these issues, Sharpton became an example of a mainstream-media-named "Old Guard" of black politicians whose credibility and platform stem mostly from their work in the black civil rights movement, in the past and present.[5]

The other model available to black politicians has been to embrace a very conservative agenda, typically in the hope of seeking the Republican Party's nomination for president. Former U.S. Ambassador Alan Keyes is an example. Keyes attempted to become the Republican nominee in 1996, 2000, and 2008 by running on a platform that ardently opposed gay rights and abortion. In contrast to the "Old Guard" model, Keyes fashioned his candidacy as one that rejects the argument that black Americans are oppressed in U.S. society. Instead, he emphasized an arch-conservative agenda in attempts to appeal to a right-wing constituency. Taking a much less conservative position, the former head of the U.S. armed forces, and one-time Secretary of State, Colin Powell also let himself be considered for the Republican presidential nomination in recent decades, yet he never actively campaigned for that position.[6]

Senator Barack Obama, then, represented a very important shift away from these two existing models of black politicians with an eye to the U.S. presidency. Unlike Keyes, Obama refused to pitch himself to a right-wing constituency. Yet he also differed from politicians such as Jackson and Sharpton whose credibility and influence have stemmed substantially from their participation in the civil rights-era movement activity and more recent civil rights protests. Obama is unlike those black politicians and is in fact a younger beneficiary of the national gains that the civil rights movement produced for African Americans. Like former D.C. mayor Adrian Fenty, Newark mayor Cory Booker, and Massachusetts governor Deval Patrick—fellow black politicians to whom he is often compared—Barack Obama represents a member of a new generation of black politicians who have grown up after the civil rights movement and have experienced racially integrated schools (at least after high school), workplaces, or, less often, communities. This more integrated racial context has significantly shaped their outlooks, perspectives, and political platforms, and contributed to the sense, especially among white observers and voters, that they are "new" black politicians for whom racial issues and civil rights are not central factors in their candidacies for political office.

A "Post-Racial" Politics?

Senator Obama's candidacy was heralded by many observers as the beginning of a new era in politics, one in which black politicians can now shed what whites have perceived as the negative "baggage" of the civil rights-era leadership in order to become "post-racial" or "color-blind." For example, Deneen Borelli, a fellow at the National Center for Public Policy Research, a conservative think tank, assessed the election in this way:

> This was a color-blind election. Obama's success certainly makes the case for any race-based preferential treatment a weak

argument. You may still have individuals out there who will try to uphold that 1950s and '60s argument that blacks still need such treatment, but his personal story proves otherwise.[7]

A conservative *Washington Times* report put it this way:

> Political analysts have called Mr. Obama's political style "postracial," a far cry from the explicit, race-conscious campaigns of Mr. Jackson and the Rev. Al Sharpton. Mr. Obama supported affirmative action while in the Illinois state legislature, but did not highlight the issue at all during his run in the Democratic primaries or in the general election with Republican Sen. John McCain.[8]

By using the white-created terms "color-blind" and "post-racial," many in the political punditry and the mainstream media have repeatedly suggested that black politicians no longer need to align themselves with civil rights platforms geared primarily to African Americans or to messages about ending discrimination and gaining equal opportunity. In contrast, from this viewpoint, contemporary black politicians can now seek to, as whites have often said, "transcend race"—they can be visibly black but at the same time have a broad, mass appeal to a multiracial coalition of voters. By attempting to transcend race, however, these black politicians face the paradoxical dilemma of positioning themselves as people who are "black enough" to win votes from African Americans, but are not "too black" for most white voters.[9]

Obama himself actively utilized this approach of playing down or ignoring racial issues. Though he never explicitly identified himself as post-racial or color-blind during the campaign, and in fact has always self-identified clearly as black, he has to this day carefully avoided casting himself as a politician who places civil rights issues at or near the center of his political goals. During the 2008 campaign, Obama's oft-quoted statement was that there are no "red states, no blue states, just the United States." This signaled his universalist message, as did his efforts to avoid being pigeonholed as just a Democratic Party candidate or just a black candidate. During most of his long campaign and much of his first term,

Obama avoided talking specifically about important racial issues. He often evoked his white mother and grandparents as important influences in his early development, thereby signaling to whites his partially white ancestry and "safe" racial status. Indeed, some of his own campaign workers in the field used the point that he was mainly raised by a white mother and white grandparents, and thus "did not think from a black perspective," to try to convince undecided whites to vote for him.[10]

Importantly, Obama's multiracial heritage has been a key factor in his ability to embody the image of a post-racial politician. Obama's family tree includes his Kenyan father, aunts, and cousins, white mother and grandparents, Indonesian stepfather, Indonesian and white half-sister, and African American wife and daughters. His clear links to a multitude of racial and ethnic groups clearly establish his credentials as a member of this supposedly "post-racial" cadre of black politicians. To emphasize this, Obama has frequently commented that "nowhere else in the world is my story possible," and has often stressed that his multiracial heritage puts him in a unique position to understand and empathize with the experiences of many diverse groups in the United States. Additionally, as the son of an African immigrant father and native-born white mother, and having grown up in Hawaii, Obama has a family background that is very different from that of most African Americans. Indeed, he does not have even one (known) African American ancestor, whereas the typical African American has many African American ancestors, usually going back nine to 15 generations in the United States. Unlike the Old Guard of black politicians, then, Obama has taken great pains to present himself as an African American who is proud to be African American and is part of an African-American family and community, but whose life and outlook are directly shaped by the people from several different racial and nationality groups, especially including white Americans.

In our view, the terms "post-racial" and "color-blind" are quite inappropriate for describing the Obama campaign and election, and in fact the terms reflect the racialized views and needs of those whites who created them. These terms represent one more attempt by many whites, and a few conservative nonwhite allies, to again play down the significance of white racism in U.S. society. This ideological perspective has been used to shape perceptions of U.S. racial realities. Thus, while the history and reality of Obama's life, experiences, campaign, and election have been anything but "post-racial" and "color-blind," that type of language has been widely employed by hundreds of media pundits and commentators. Indeed, as we will see, Obama himself expertly used this imagery to his advantage in the campaign.

Challenges of Reaching Black Voters

Obama's label as a new type of black politician who played down issues of racism generated numerous questions about whether this factor would potentially alienate black voters during his long election campaign. From early 2007 to early 2008, before any primaries had been conducted, Senator Obama faced a particular challenge as a black politician seeking the presidency who was largely unknown to black voters nationally. Unlike black politicians and activists such as Jesse Jackson and Al Sharpton, who are household names in black America, Senator Obama was largely unknown to most black audiences, except for those who had watched him deliver his powerful keynote speech at the 2004 Democratic National Convention.[11] At this stage in the preprimary process, Senator Hillary Clinton was the Democratic frontrunner, leading by wide margins in opinion polls and generally expected to win the nomination. Capitalizing on the reputation of her husband, former President Bill Clinton, Hillary Clinton enjoyed widespread support among African Americans. Obama thus faced the daunting task of becoming a recognizable, trusted figure among African Americans in a short period of time, and persuading these voters to support him instead of Clinton, a more familiar face with visible ties to prominent black public figures such as Reverend Jesse Jackson, business leader Vernon Jordan, and Representative Maxine Waters (D-CA).

During these early days of the Obama campaign, it was not a given that most black voters would support Obama. As a newcomer to the national political stage, he lacked the visibility of several other candidates seeking the presidential nomination. Furthermore, with less than three years' experience in the U.S. Senate, he had yet to build a national reputation. Unlike black public figures such as D.C. Councilwoman

Eleanor Holmes Norton, former NAACP Chair Julian Bond, or Reverend Al Sharpton, Senator Obama had not been present at, or spoken out in support of, the numerous civil rights marches and protest meetings that sought to turn public attention to issues dealing with continuing racial discrimination and inequality. Consequently, being black did not guarantee that he would earn many black votes. Several major concerns were raised during this time about Obama's ability to gain support from this important political constituency. Some media voices questioned whether Obama was truly "black enough" to gain the necessary groundswell of support from African Americans.[12]

Commentators raising such questions pointed to aspects of Senator Obama's background that they felt might distance him from many black voters. Specifically, they raised questions about his biracial heritage, Ivy League education at Columbia University and Harvard Law School, and dissimilarities with the "Old Guard" black politicians. In short, those who voiced this concern argued that these distinctive markers might render Obama unfamiliar and unpalatable to most African Americans.

Nonetheless, Obama did occasionally and carefully acknowledge certain racial issues during the campaign. One example was the written reply he made to an NAACP questionnaire for presidential candidates. Responding to a question about affirmative action, he wrote: "We shouldn't ignore that race continues to matter. To suggest that our racial attitudes play no part in the socio-economic disparities that we often observe turns a blind eye to both our history and our experience—and relieves us of the responsibility to make things right."[13] He also made comments in this questionnaire indicating his opposition to racial profiling and his support for ending discriminatory sentencing. His racial commentaries, however, were not made in a public speech, and got remarkably little attention later on in the mainstream media.

Significantly, among Obama's top campaign staffers there was only one African American, Valerie Jarrett of Chicago, now a senior advisor at the White House. Reportedly, Jarrett was the only top staffer who occasionally pressed the Obama campaign to be more open in discussing racial matters and more conscious in publicly relating to African Americans. In contrast, as we will show in detail in Chapter 5, the other handful of top staff members, all white, sought to play down his racial characteristics and to accent him as all-American. They saw his being black as "mostly a distraction," and his campaign manager, David Plouffe, reportedly did not want his candidate "to be defined by racial politics" in any manner.[14]

Among African Americans, moreover, there were concerns that rarely crossed most white minds. They worried less about Obama's biracialism and relatability and more about his and his family's personal safety. Most black Americans are aware of this country's many militant white supremacists (estimated to be at least 100,000 activists and 400,000 followers) and the presence in most regions of Klan-type, violence-oriented white groups. They worried greatly about Obama's safety as a black man seeking such a visible and powerful political position, and felt that his nomination or election would place him at great risk for assassination. For some black Americans, this was even a reason not to vote for Obama.[15] In the cases of some older African Americans, having witnessed the assassination of black male leaders, such as Dr. Martin Luther King, Jr., and Malcolm X, who had worked to initiate major social changes, made them reluctant to support Senator Obama for fear this white violence would be repeated. Given these realistic concerns—which indeed persisted when he became President Obama—they argued that it might be better not to vote for Obama in order to avoid the possibility of witnessing the murder of another talented black leader.

Very rarely did whites express such fears during the campaign, but we heard numerous ordinary African Americans frequently express such views, especially as the November 2008 election got closer. Black fears about Senator Obama's safety, and also about the safety of his family, clearly revealed how differently the white and black communities saw Senator Obama and his lengthy presidential campaign. We will see these contrasts demonstrated repeatedly in later chapters, but here we can note several key variations in political perspectives. In addition to realistic fears over Senator Obama's safety, which white observers mostly ignored, African Americans had much more of a personal stake than others in emphasizing the great political significance of a black man seeking the presidency in what is still a white-run nation.

White Reactions to Senator Obama in 2008

Although Senator Obama needed to win support from black voters, his status as a new model of a black politician also meant that he had the opportunity to generate substantial support from white voters as well. Consequently, in the early days of his campaign, Obama's differences from preceding black politicians generated various reactions from whites. For many, the fact that Obama did not pattern himself after the "Old Guard" of black politicians was alternately a source of concern, speculative intrigue, or suspicion.

The presence of significant numbers of black elected officials is new in the United States. In the mid-1960s, there were only about 70 black elected officials in all the southern states, and no more than that in the North. With the passage of the 1965 Civil Rights Act, however, the opportunity to be elected to local, state, and federal offices slowly increased, so that by the early 21st century there were more than 9,000 black elected officials in all states. Today, however, black officials represent only a modest percentage of the number they should be, for they are still less than two percent of all U.S. elected officials. Today, in 2012, there are 42 black voting members of the U.S. House, all but two Democrats, and not even one black senator in the U.S. Senate. Significantly, among the more than 9,000 black elected officials, only a few hundred have run political campaigns playing down or ignoring civil rights issues. And Obama's self-presentation as a different sort of black politician who did not accent civil rights issues meant that many whites in 2008 responded to him more favorably than they did to other well-known black political figures.[16]

These different reactions were often manifested in positive comments and other noteworthy remarks from various white public figures, and in the responses such statements generated. For example, in launching his own campaign for president in February 2007, Senator Joe Biden (D-DE)—who would later become Obama's running mate—awkwardly offered what were intended to be praiseworthy words about Obama's style and charisma: "You got the first mainstream African American who is articulate and bright and clean and a nice looking guy . . . I mean, that's a storybook, man."[17] In his racialized, white-framed comment

Biden underscored the idea that Obama was a different type of black politician, one that did not fit conventional white racist stereotypes.

On the other end of the political spectrum, the conservative radio commentator Rush Limbaugh referred to Obama as "halfrican American" in an attempt to parody and emphasize his biracial background.[18] For many whites, Obama's biracial background rendered him a different type of black politician. Limbaugh's stated perception that Obama chose to identify himself as black suggested that, like other black politicians, Obama was still suspect and possibly untrustworthy. Limbaugh's view that individuals can choose their racial status regardless of physical appearance is unsupported by much research that demonstrates that white outsiders, especially those with some socioeconomic power, generally determine an individual's racial status in U.S. society.[19]

As we see here, and will see in later chapters, Obama's biracial background makes him part of a growing group of Americans who publicly and assertively acknowledge their biracial heritage. Their contemporary experiences underscore the fact that in the United States, racial identities are socially, not biologically, constructed. Recent studies of biracial and multiracial Americans, such as that by Kerry Rockquemore and David Brunsma, have shown that being categorized in an intermediate status between white and black on the U.S. racial continuum does not mean equality in rights and privileges. Their interviews of mostly younger people with a white parent and a black parent as President Obama found that the majority did not choose a single racial identity, but did accent a border or biracial (white and black) identity in their minds regardless of how they were viewed by others. Yet, the identity imposed on most of them by outsiders, especially whites with power over them, was, or soon will be, just "black."[20] This imposed identity is what President Obama himself has accented in regard to his own experiences growing up.[21]

White Racial Framing and "Post-Racial" Politics

As Senator Obama became classified as a different type of black politician, he became subject to questions of how this distinctive political identity would appeal to black and white voters. These issues were presented in terms of whether he was "black enough" for black voters or "too black" for white voters. This forced him to make a choice.

Obama's choice to represent himself as a mostly non-racial politician to the general public plays into the soft version of the white racial frame in many ways. By emphasizing his biracial status, refusing to identify any more closely with African Americans than was absolutely necessary, and portraying himself as someone who was not overly concerned with civil rights issues, Obama reinforced the idea that racial characteristics are something to be casually observed at most, but are no longer significant factors that concretely shape various aspects of social life. Because this soft framing suggests that racism has ceased to be a major societal reality, Obama's decision to capitalize on it has reinforced among whites (and others) the damaging idea that societal racism matters less today than the personal choices of African Americans and other Americans of color.

Obama's stance on affirmative action in particular revealed the utilization of the soft racial frame. When asked about affirmative action programs in the campaigns, Obama backed off from supporting traditional programs redressing societal racism to a position of supporting class-oriented remedial programs that would benefit all economically disadvantaged people. In doing so, he managed to use soft racial framing to position himself as a black individual who would be palatable to most whites, given his lack of support for racially based affirmative action. Many whites view these programs as offering unfair assistance to people of color and thus see no need for continued affirmative action; hence, Obama's unwillingness to align himself with such a program offered him an opportunity to show white voters that he was one of the more "acceptable" black Americans who would not agitate for racial causes. He also operated within the "post-racial" ideology, which suggests that racial matters are of little importance in shaping educational, occupational, and other outcomes. As a result of his downplaying racial issues, especially racial inequality, there were far more analyses by pundits, commentators, and media analysts on how "race" was shaping his presidential campaign than there were statements from Obama and his team on Obama's understandings about racial matters, including the large and unjust racial inequalities, in the United States. Obama attempted to minimize racism issues in a manner that was very much in line with the soft racial frame's ideas about the diminishing power of racism in shaping socioeconomic opportunities and outcomes.

Public reactions, especially white reactions, to Obama reveal the fluidity between the hard and soft versions of the white racial frame. Discussions about the perceived difficulty that white voters in 2008 might have in relating to this "different" (they meant black) politician were typically grounded in a hard version of the white racial framing. These public discussions often argued that white and other voters alike might be uncertain about what to expect from a President Obama because he was "post-racial" and thus a new type of politician, at the same time implicitly foregrounding his blackness in a conventional framing. Consequently, mildly stated questions of how whites might relate to Obama were themselves examples of a soft racial framing. Yet, these same questions implicitly built on hard racial framing to show how he was different from other black politicians—who are defined, through hard racial framing, as too overtly racialized, less formally educated, and less "articulate" than Obama. The early debates over whether Obama was "too black" or "black enough" thus show that hard and soft frames are not mutually exclusive, but are often overlapping and related.

During the campaign, numerous media commentators and political pundits suggested early on that Obama might not relate well to everyday African American voters because he was too different from them. Major newsmagazines ran articles with titles such as "Is Obama Black Enough?" The implication was that because of his Ivy League education and white mother and grandparents, or other distinctive aspects of his background, Obama was unlike most black Americans and thus might be perceived by them as "not black enough." However, this line of (usually white) thinking relies on a hard racial framing that emphasizes stark racial differences and highlights stereotypical depictions of black men and black masculinity. The hard racial framing of a great many whites associates black men as a group with negative physical and cultural characteristics—criminality, lack of intelligence, laziness, and immorality. Yet, other white negative framing targets black men such as the Reverend Al Sharpton as "bad blacks" because they often protest white racism.

Thus, from the perspective of such white framing, Obama ran the risk of failing to be "appropriately" black because he did not meet such negatively stereotyped criteria. Hard racial framing thus characterizes most blacks as people who are starkly different from Obama, while soft racial framing is evident in the tamer language that euphemistically asks whether Obama is "black enough" to relate to these apparently uneducated, inarticulate, criminally inclined masses. However, over the progress of a long campaign, it became clear that Obama was indeed "black enough" as African Americans overwhelmingly came out to support him in later primaries and the general election.[22]

Significantly, many of the political comments and commentary that erupted during the early stages of Obama's presidential campaign relate to this issue. When then-Senator Joe Biden commented awkwardly that Obama was neat, clean, and articulate, his statement highlighted the ways in which Obama did not reflect the conventional white-racist framing of black men as overtly threatening, unsavory, and unintelligent. When this revealing comment made national news and generated a great deal of media attention, many African American professionals noted that their own eloquence and achievements are often met with similar surprise and astonishment by many whites, and they spoke of how these reactions reveal white Americans' amazement to learn that many blacks do not conform to the conventional stereotyped representations of the hard racial frame.[23]

Still, Obama did not use his candidacy to openly challenge the hard-racist framing that posits black Americans as inherently unintelligent, criminal, or lazy. Rather, he utilized certain elements from the soft racial frame and emphasized his biracial-ness and personal ties to several racial and ethnic groups, as well as his commitment to a united America. In doing so, he worked within the soft frame, particularly its suggestion that some people of color are acceptable as long as they minimize their racial status and implicitly reinforce the message that racism is declining in societal significance. At no point did Obama aggressively confront the hard-racist framing that casts black Americans in such a negative light that intelligent, well-spoken African Americans come as a shock and a surprise to whites. Instead, he accented his multiracial roots and positioned himself as one of the more "acceptable" African Americans—

that is, one who is visibly different, but not in ways that make whites uncomfortable. This approach was not accidental. In 2008, Obama's political team was quite aware of the "exception to his race" principle and made use of it as the campaign progressed. For example, Cornell Belcher, who did polling for Obama, made this comment: "It would be difficult for an African American to be elected president in this country. However, it is not difficult for an extraordinary individual who happens to be African American to be elected president."[24] This suggestion clearly underscores key ideas of soft racial framing: that racial characteristics have become so unimportant in shaping life chances that for an exceptional black American, his or her uniqueness so trumps racial stigmas that being elected president is not difficult. In other words, a unique black American running for president should find that his or her exceptional nature enables race-related challenges to recede into the background.

Ironically, the continuing debates over the long campaign about whether Obama would remain too black for whites actually spoke to the pervasiveness of the hard racial framing. Within the hard racial frame, blacks are cast as inherently and obviously unequal to whites. Unlike the soft racial frame, the hard frame is explicit and overt about its hoary racial stereotypes and related emotions. Thus, when media and academic analysts debated whether Obama was too black to win the general election—or, as this question was more commonly framed, whether America was "ready" for a black president—the underlying issue here was whether a majority of white Americans were locked into hard-racist framing that renders black Americans as always less qualified, intelligent, and desirable than whites. (Once again, "America" meant "whites.") As Obama began his candidacy, one of the major questions surrounding his quest for the presidency was whether these white voters would continue to view the election through the lens of a hard racial frame that routinely associates blackness with negativity.

Conclusion

The primary and general election debates over whether Senator Barack Obama was "too black" for white voters or "black enough" for black voters unmistakably reveal the continued existence of the old white frame, both in its hard and soft versions. Obama's Ivy League education, his obvious high intelligence, his personal bearing, and his studied professionalism meant that he did not easily fit into the hard racial framing's customary depictions of black Americans as lazy, unintelligent, and immoral. Viewed by whites from this white-racist perspective, his supposedly unique characteristics should have made him unfamiliar to African Americans as well. This harsh framing is so pervasive and well-entrenched that a great many white voters operated out of it in both the primaries and the general election, no matter what evidence there was to the contrary. White voters who opted for white candidates in the primaries led many commentators to debate, albeit often in mild or disguised language, whether a hard racial framing would prevail and render Obama "too black" for white voters to feel comfortable voting for him.

Rather than directly address the hard racial framing and the systemic racism it represents, Senator Obama mostly chose to work within the limits of the soft racial framing. He did not openly challenge the age-old assumptions that pervade whites' hard racial framing—that African Americans are inherently unintelligent and uncouth such that well-educated, well-spoken black Americans appear a novelty. Instead, he emphasized his white family members and biracial background to position himself well within the soft racial framing that establishes some "good" black Americans as acceptable and tolerable, as "exceptions to their race." Significantly, within the soft racial frame, those black Americans are the ones who do not focus on or highlight the continuing racial divide in America, or perhaps most importantly, on the ways in which white racism remains embedded in all societal institutions. By casting himself as a new type of politician with personal ties to several racial and ethnic groups, Obama could become an "acceptable" African American who made some white voters (though, as it turned out, still a minority) feel comfortable voting for him—even as they continued to rely on the racial images, ideologies, emotions, and assumptions of the soft version of the white frame.

As we will show in later chapters in some detail, this issue continued to persist once Obama took office as president, as he continually struggled to avoid being overly identified with black communities and interests. We can illustrate this point here with one brief example—the

2010 firing of Department of Agriculture (USDA) employee Shirley Sherrod. In the summer of 2010, the National Association for the Advancement of Colored People (NAACP) argued that conservative groups collectively known as the Tea Party should denounce the racist behavior and actions of those affiliated with the group. In response, far-right activist Andrew Breitbart (now deceased), argued that the NAACP was itself a "racist" organization that should do the same. As evidence, he posted a video to his right-wing website that purported to show Sherrod giving a talk to NAACP members who listened politely as she acknowledged that she did not do as much as she could to help a white farmer she was tasked with assisting. As the story generated controversy, Sherrod was quickly fired from her post at the USDA and denounced by the NAACP. However, as Sherrod defended herself, further review revealed that the video on Breitbart's website had been selectively edited, her remarks had been intentionally taken out of context, and that she had ultimately helped the family to whom she referred and was actually making a point about the importance of racial reconciliation. Indeed, she became friends with them and learned a valuable lesson about forgiveness and unity.

Once the truth of the video surfaced, Secretary of Agriculture Tom Vilsack publicly apologized and offered Sherrod her job back. She received a conciliatory phone call from President Obama and an offer to work with the White House as a consultant. Sherrod declined both and filed suit against Andrew Breitbart, the conservative activist who had posted the deceptive video.[25]

While there is no conclusive evidence that Obama ordered Sherrod to be fired, his Agriculture Secretary's hasty actions suggest that her immediate dismissal before all facts were heard and known plays into a broader narrative of Obama's efforts to avoid the difficult work of challenging implicit assumptions of black immorality and inferiority that underlie both the hard and the soft racial framing. Breitbart's duplicitous video was carefully edited to depict Sherrod as someone who took pride in treating whites inequitably. Additionally, his accompanying written commentary suggested that Sherrod's audience for her talk—mostly black members of the NAACP—supported and encouraged this type of behavior; it stated that "Sherrod's racist tale is received by the NAACP audience with nodding approval and murmurs of recognition and agreement."[26] As such, Breitbart utilized a common trope in whites' soft racial framing that racial inequality is more a matter of personal preference and individual behavior that can be exhibited by anyone, and less a sweeping structural mechanism that has for centuries benefited whites at the expense of people of color. Within this framework, any racial minority person can be construed as racist for identifying racist practices, reacting to them, or, as in Shirley Sherrod's specific case, acknowledging the ways that ongoing racial discrimination may—even temporarily —have a negative impact. Breitbart thus employed a soft white racial framing that allowed him to ignore the systemic processes that largely disadvantage black Americans as a group and to cast black audience members—and the NAACP at large—as morally questionable.

It is important to note that President Obama took virtually no steps to challenge this white racial framing. Though there is no evidence to prove that he ordered her dismissal, it is unlikely that Sherrod's firing was done against his wishes. Additionally, once the entire story surfaced, Obama made no efforts to criticize or call attention to the racial framing that underscored Breitbart's analysis, or to provide his own interpretation of events through a counterframe. As Emory University political scientist Andra Gillespie stated:

> I don't know [Sherrod's] motivations, but the reality of it is that they screwed up. They apologized, but the decision to fire her is the sort of knee-jerk reaction that people get concerned about with deracialized candidates, such as Obama. The administration overreacted in the Shirley Sherrod case to prove that they don't always side with the minorities, but they were wrong.[27]

Working within the soft racial frame, then, limited Obama from using a strong antiracist counterframe when racial issues arose, and in this case put him in a position where he was complicit in Shirley Sherrod's unfair termination from her government job.

3

FROM SUSAN B. ANTHONY TO HILLARY CLINTON

The 2008 Democratic primary contest was an historic event. By February of that year, the field of nine Democratic Party challengers had diminished to just two: Senator Hillary Clinton (D-NY) and Senator Barack Obama (D-IL). After that month's Super Tuesday primaries, Senator John McCain (R-AZ) had secured a majority of Republican Party votes and pledged delegates and was considered the presumptive Republican nominee for president. Three members of a very elite political body, the U.S. Senate, had made the final leg of this long electoral journey, and the narrowing of the Democratic Party choices meant that for the first time in U.S. history, the November general election would include a presidential candidate who was not a white male. Senator Hillary Clinton, long considered the Democratic Party front-runner, spoke in several early debates of how honored she felt to share the stage with Senator Obama, and of the importance of the Democratic Party taking this important and past-due step to break the racial and gender glass ceiling. While Senator Obama almost never discussed publicly his thoughts about being the first African American widely considered to have a viable opportunity to secure the nomination, he frequently complimented Senator Clinton as an admirable opponent, a savvy politician, and one with whom he, too, was honored to compete.[1]

However, as the primary season continued longer than many political experts, politicians, and voters expected, the discussions about how the primary candidates were evidence of U.S. (and the Democratic Party's) gender and racial progress quickly became less celebratory. Instead, these laudatory remarks gave way to increasingly contentious, often bitter arguments about the relative roles of sexism and racism in both campaigns, in the media coverage, and in the larger society. As the nature of the public discussion changed from one that highlighted the major changes in the Democratic Party and in national politics to one that heatedly debated the ongoing nature of gender and racial inequalities, both the hard and soft racial frames were, once again, summoned in order to shape and contextualize these debates and structure related campaign events.

Systemic Sexism: Women in Politics

For many women, Clinton's candidacy and run for the Democratic nomination represented an important corrective to centuries of gender oppression and political marginalization. For many others, it was simply time to see a woman in the White House. In the contemporary political scene, men are very disproportionately represented among the highest levels of politicians. Though women are about 51 percent of the U.S. population, they comprised only 16.4 percent of the 112th Congress (2011–2012), with just 17 women serving in the Senate (17 percent) and 71 serving as full members of the House of Representatives (16 percent). Of the women in the House, 27 percent are women of color. No women of color currently serve in the Senate. Women of color constitute only 4.5 percent of the current Congress. Over the last decade, however, some important barriers have been broken as Condoleezza Rice, first as National Security Advisor (2000–2005), then as Secretary of State (2005–2008) rose to one of the highest-ranking positions in the U.S. government. Additionally, during her tenure as Speaker of the House from 2007–2010, Nancy Pelosi (D-CA) became the first woman in this position and, thus, the highest-ranking person in Congress and next in line for the presidency after the Vice President. If Senator Clinton had secured the Democratic nomination and possibly the presidency, those achievements would have further brought important changes in the way that U.S. politics is gendered.

Women's advances in the political sphere have been a long time in the making, and have occurred against a history of tremendous odds. Women of all racial groups have historically had a fractured relationship with the political arena. From the 1600s to the early 1900s, all women in the colonies, and later the United States, were limited in their legal and political rights in what was a highly patriarchal society. They were for the most part denied the right to vote, campaign, or hold political office. Conventional wisdom of the day argued that white women did not need to vote or to concern themselves with political matters at large. In order to justify this gendered exclusion, elite white men instituted and perpetuated the emotion-laden sexist framing known as the "cult of true womanhood." This perspective decreed that "real" women concentrated their energies on home and family. In order to adhere to the dictates of this rigid patriarchal perspective, women were expected to stay out of the public sphere, confine themselves to the home, and show no interest in politics, education, the economy, or other "masculine" endeavors. Women who conformed to this framing could establish themselves as worthy of being placed on a pedestal, protected, and cherished. Those who violated these normative ideals were considered unfeminine and thus undeserving of the special protections and safeguards afforded to their more decorous counterparts. Well beyond the political sphere, the colonial and early U.S. laws on things such as inheritance and contracts were explicitly aimed at firmly keeping white women in their place as daughters, wives, and mothers.[2]

While the standards of the cult of true womanhood were supposedly applied to all women, they were in fact overtly racialized. For black women, it was nearly impossible to achieve the particular behaviors this ideal standard of "true womanhood" required. As a result of slavery and its legacy of continuing impoverishment and great racial inequality, black women had always been a part of the country's labor force, even when, most of the time, they were unable to earn fair compensation for their hard work.[3] After slavery, most black women remained in the labor force as paid workers in Jim Crow or de jure segregation systems, in the South and the North, in order to ensure their families' very survival. As black men were employed primarily in the few low-wage jobs available to them, many black families found it impossible to exist on just one meager wage. Thus, black women mostly had to work outside their homes to help provide for their families. Most could not confine themselves to the home and adhere to the idealized standards of "true" femininity. Importantly, black women's labor force participation served to reinforce the white-racist framing of their inferiority and lack of femininity, most especially for whites. Because they worked, they were not really "ladies," and therefore did not deserve to be treated with the reverence and care usually afforded to the white women who behaved "appropriately."[4]

In this context, gendered and racial messages intersected so that only white men were guaranteed the right to vote. Black women and men were denied the right to vote during slavery, and institutionalized sexism in the laws and informal practices usually precluded white women from voting as well. Some visionary white women realized that there were commonalities between their fight for equal rights and that of black men and women, and joined with black activists during slavery to support the abolitionist cause and eventually to advocate for a universal right to vote. In the mid-1800s, these causes led white women such as Susan B. Anthony and Elizabeth Cady Stanton to join forces with legendary black writer and public speaker Frederick Douglass, black orator Sojourner Truth, and black underground railroad hero Harriet Tubman in supporting an end to slavery.[5]

After slavery, blacks were no longer subjected to this system of chained servitude, and many black speakers and public figures argued that the right to vote was a necessary step towards full emancipation. In the mid- and late-1860s, after the Civil War, the "Radical Republican" members of the U.S. Congress succeeded in passing the 13th amendment, which officially prohibited slavery, and the 14th amendment, which officially granted those formerly enslaved full citizenship rights. As white members of Congress began to debate a 15th amendment that would grant newly freed black men the right to vote, white feminists such as Stanton and Anthony forcefully argued that it was critical that this amendment guarantee women the right to vote as well.[6] However, not only were the white male congressional representatives unresponsive, even most fellow black and white male abolitionists dismissed these white women's concerns, suggesting that their right to vote could wait, but that this was "the Negro's hour." Of course, they meant the "Negro man's hour," and black women were also denied the vote.[7]

Frederick Douglass, one of few black or white men of the day to support feminist causes openly, agreed that Stanton and Anthony should temporarily table the issue of women's right to vote. Given that white women maintained a more secure position in that they were not subject to lynching or other forms of overt racial harassment, Douglass believed that his white female allies did not need the right to vote as urgently as black men.[8] However, Stanton, Anthony, and many of their feminist contemporaries vehemently disagreed. After having offered much financial, emotional, and social support to the abolitionist cause, they understandably felt angry that their male allies did not reciprocate when it came to their efforts to secure the right to vote. For many of the feminist women involved in this voting rights cause, it likely seemed that men of all racial groups refused to take them seriously and honor their rights as equal citizens.

Though the interracial ties that arose out of the efforts of the abolitionist movement were not idyllic, black men, black women, and white women had for a time been able to work together with some degree of efficacy towards their common goal of eradicating slavery. There were some fissures in this movement, as some white female abolitionists expressed discontent and unwillingness to share facilities with black women whom they openly considered racially inferior.[9] Hence, it is unsurprising that when white male elites held out the possibility of suffrage rights to black men and not white women, white women who had previously considered themselves allies in the antislavery movement accented their already held racist stereotypes and framing to demonstrate why black men did not deserve the right to vote. The same women who had organized for an end to slavery and championed black men's freedom now argued that white male elites had

> lifted up two million black men and crowned them with the honor and dignity of citizenship [and] they have dethroned fifteen million white women—their own mothers and sisters, their own wives and daughters—and cast them under the heel of the lowest orders of manhood.[10]

Relying on such overtly racialized imagery, numerous white feminists changed their position and argued for the defeat of the 15th amendment on the grounds that it would enfranchise "degraded, oppressed" men "over the daughters of Jefferson, Hancock, and Adams."[11]

In this racialized hubbub, however, most white women and black men just ignored the fact that in the debates over which group would get the vote (and ultimately over whether racism or sexism was the more significant societal barrier), *black women* were overlooked by both parties. Sojourner Truth, a black woman and leading abolitionist, was one of the few voices who argued that "if the colored men get their rights and not colored women theirs, you see the colored men will be masters over the women, and it will be just as bad as it was before."[12] Black men sought the vote on the grounds of racial empowerment without attempting to challenge gender discrimination, and white women believed that gender was the key factor inhibiting political progress. Discussions of sexism and racism as intersecting forces rather than as separate "silos" were rare, except among African American women.[13]

Gaining the Right to Vote: Still More to Do

The 15th amendment was ratified in 1870, guaranteeing the right to vote without regard to a citizen's "race, color, or previous condition of servitude."[14] The wording of this amendment meant that gender was still a disqualifier that could legally be used to prevent women of all backgrounds from voting. Not until the 19th amendment was ratified in 1920 did all women get the right to vote. By that time, however, the groundwork had been laid for future debates on the ills of racism versus those of sexism.

Gaining the right to vote did not guarantee women full participation in the political arena. Women in all racial groups still had to fight the strong framing that it was unladylike and inappropriate for women to work outside the home, much less in the public sphere as elected officials. While women occasionally held appointed or elected offices during the early to mid-20th century, the women's movement of the late 1960s and the 1970s helped to change this negative framing of women's political capabilities and thus created many new opportunities. Since this period, women have increasingly moved into professional occupations including those in government, which were previously unavailable, and have enjoyed official protection from discrimination by the 1964 Civil Rights Act.[15] This large-scale shift in public attitudes and consciousness is credited with creating greater outside-the-home opportunities for women in all racial and ethnic groups.

Nonetheless, women still face great challenges and obstacles that stem from institutionalized, ongoing gender discrimination. Although women, on paper, have access to better-paying professional and managerial occupations, most women remain concentrated in a limited array of "feminized jobs" that are generally lower in status, wages, and prestige than the jobs predominantly filled by men. Women also must still contend with stereotypes that they are less intelligent, focused, rational, and analytical than men, and these images often disadvantage them in the labor market and in other important institutional settings. Women also remain at high risk for acts of sexual violence inside and outside the home. Statistics suggest that one in six women will be sexually assaulted in her lifetime.[16]

For women of color, the overlapping effects of racism and sexism continue to create particular employment and other economic challenges. Women of color as a group are overrepresented in numerous low-wage service and other blue-collar jobs and are disproportionately represented among the ranks of the country's poor. This is especially true for African American, Latina, and Native-American women workers. Asian-American women, who are somewhat overrepresented in professional and managerial positions held by women, still face controlling images of themselves as "Dragon Ladies" and "Lotus Blossoms," and contend with a docile "model minority" stereotype that masks their ongoing experiences with racism.[17] In the political sphere, not until 1968 was the first black woman, Shirley Chisholm (D-NY), elected to the U.S. House of Representatives—many generations after the United States was created. In 1993, the first black woman, Carol Moseley Braun (D-IL), was elected to the U.S. Senate. To date, Braun remains the only woman of color who has ever served in what is likely the world's most powerful political body since the country's first elections in 1790. It was not until 1989 that Ileana Ros-Lehtinen (R-FL) became the first Latina ever elected to Congress, and to date there have been only seven other

Latinas to serve in the House of Representatives. For Asian-American women, the numbers are even smaller. Only five have served in Congress since Patsy Mink (D-HI) became the first Asian-American woman elected in 1965. Moreover, more than half of all the 44 women of color ever elected to Congress are currently serving there.[18]

In this country, most discussions of women's issues have often been oriented to the needs and goals of women who are white and middle class. Historically, women of color have been very critical of some white feminists' tendencies to emphasize issues that have particular salience to middle-class and upper-class white women, while ignoring the ways that the joint effects of sexism and racism create specific challenges for millions of women of color. For instance, the mainstream feminist movement has often focused heavily on access to abortion, while ignoring the reality that poor and working-class women, especially women of color, must confront other women's issues such as forced sterilization and the effects of raising children in poverty.[19] In particular, women of color have argued that white feminists are eager to emphasize gender discrimination, but usually remain silent about their white privilege and the ways it enables their complicity in maintaining the racial and economic discrimination faced daily by women of color.[20]

These racial and class issues have always been present in feminist discussions of gender inequality, particularly in the ways these conversations play out in the U.S. political arena. Not surprisingly, thus, these issues resurfaced during the 2008 Democratic primary as it became clear that the nomination would be won by either Hillary Clinton, a white woman, or Barack Obama, a black man. As the Democratic primaries continued and the delegate counts of the two candidates remained for a time rather close, many discussions and claims about sexism and racism took center stage in ways that were quite reminiscent of past debates on similar issues.

Sexism in the Democratic Primary

Because U.S. political arenas are still mostly dominated by men, women candidates face particular challenges when they run for most political offices. Often, women must confront stereotypical perceptions that they are too emotional, indecisive, or passive and do not manifest the characteristics of assertiveness and dominance seen by many voters as essential for political or economic leadership. Not coincidentally, these are characteristics typically associated in this society with the dominant masculinity, and white men are of course the ones who created these primary norms of our established political institutions. Indeed, when women in public service display these traits, they are often seen as too aggressive, unladylike, and unfeminine.[21] Women politicians also face heightened scrutiny over their appearance, hair, clothing choices, and level of attractiveness—factors that are rarely mentioned or given serious consideration when it comes to male politicians.[22] All in all, these various factors create additional difficulties for women seeking elected office.

The array of reactionary critiques of Hillary Clinton were revived during her 2008 primary campaign for president. Several were extraordinarily superficial and blatantly sexist. For example, the mostly male media commentators and pundits derided her laugh, nicknaming it "the Clinton cackle." Other public discussions, with barely concealed disgust, highlighted speaking engagements where she appeared to show cleavage.[23] Amazingly enough, arch-conservative commentator Rush Limbaugh openly questioned how both gender and age would impact Senator Clinton's candidacy, asking "whether Americans will want to watch a woman get older before their eyes on a daily basis."[24] This statement was particularly ironic, given that Limbaugh had never raised such issues for men such as former President Ronald Reagan or for Senator John McCain, the two oldest presidential candidates in U.S. history.

For some women, this discriminatory treatment generated renewed attention to the ways that women as a group are treated unequally in the political and economic realms. Some highly visible white feminists, however, took this observation a step further and argued that the way Clinton had been treated was indicative of the reality that today sexism is a greater societal evil, is more entrenched, and is thus a bigger problem than racism. Some argued that the overt hostility and discrimination to which Senator Clinton was subjected—such as nutcracker dolls made in her image and a voter who asked John McCain, "How can we beat the bitch?" and was not criticized for this sexist epithet—would never have been directed to Senator Obama. Early in the primary season, several well-known white feminists openly attested that Hillary Clinton's treatment by the mainstream media was evidence that sexism remained a greater evil than racism. In January 2008, *Ms.* magazine founder and noted feminist author Gloria Steinem remarked in a *New York Times* op-ed piece about the 2008 primary that "gender is probably the most restricting force in American life," and went on to question "why the sex barrier [is] not taken as seriously as the racial one."[25] Although Steinem later acknowledged that she was not "advocating a competition for who has it toughest," the wording of her piece clearly suggested that being a woman was a more significant factor in limiting advancement than being black, and that sexism is more likely and overt in society than is racism.

Similarly, in March 2008, former vice presidential candidate Geraldine Ferraro generated much media attention when she commented that

> if Obama was a white man, he would not be in this position. And if he was a woman of any color he would not be in this position. He happens to be very lucky to be who he is. And the country is caught up in the concept.[26]

While Ferraro subsequently indicated that her words had been taken out of context, and that her original statements were in response to the question of why Senator Obama's campaign generated such public attention, she later defended her remarks by stating, "Every time that campaign is upset about something, they call it racist . . . I will not be discriminated against because I'm white."[27] Like Steinem, Ferraro suggested that gender plays a greater, more significant role than racial characteristics in limiting opportunities and advancement. Unlike Steinem, however, Ferraro also contended that the public criticism she received for her controversial statements was tantamount to racial discrimination because of her whiteness.[28]

The widely circulated statements made by Ferraro and Steinem echoed the responses of many other white women who argued that the media's sexist treatment of Senator Clinton justified not voting for Senator Obama, or voting for Senator McCain—even with his past record of minimal support for women's issues such as equal pay and reproductive rights—as an act of protest against that anti-Clinton sexism. For many women, the mass media attacks against Clinton were concrete proof of Ferraro's and Steinem's strong assertions about the centrality of gender discrimination and inequality. From their observations, as Clinton attempted to claim the Democratic Party nomination, commentators and pundits in the predominantly male-controlled mainstream media engaged in sexist stereotyping and coverage that resulted in the Democratic nomination going to yet another male politician. In their view, male privilege and institutionalized sexism worked to Senator Obama's benefit as he gained the nomination in the midst of the unchecked and ceaseless attacks on what they viewed as his better-qualified female competitor.

Hillary Clinton—Racial and Gendered Rhetoric

For her part, Senator Clinton actively participated in these dialogues and conversations about gender inequality. Early in her primary campaign, when she was widely considered the front-runner and inevitable party nominee, Clinton frequently stated how proud she was to be a woman running for the highest office in the country and discussed her efforts to break this long-standing glass ceiling. Thus, in her June 2008 concession speech, in which she urged her supporters to back Senator Obama, Senator Clinton accented this view strongly:

> From now on, it will be unremarkable for a woman to win primary state victories, unremarkable to have a woman in a close race to be our nominee, unremarkable to think that a woman can be the President of the United States. And that is truly remarkable, my friends.[29]

Still, as her 2008 campaign neared its close, Clinton had acknowledged that sexism had hindered her efforts. As such, she openly drew attention to the continued existence of gender inequality and the ways that it affected her as a visible, politically powerful woman.[30] In her effort to secure the Democratic Party nomination, Senator Clinton and others associated with her campaign got involved in public discussions that included covert and overt references to Obama's racial status. In January 2008, when Obama won the South Carolina primary by a large margin, former President Bill Clinton likened Obama's victory to Jesse Jackson's win in that state's primary in 1984 and 1988. Many pundits and media commentators interpreted Bill Clinton's comments as a way to emphasize Obama's standing as "the black candidate," thereby highlighting South Carolina's large African American population and Obama's support among this overwhelmingly Democratic group.[31] This statement was widely interpreted as part of a racialized strategy intended to minimize Obama's growing momentum by casting him as the black candidate who operated in relation to, and thus largely for, an African American base. In offering this description of Obama and his campaign in such a pointed way, several observers contended, former President Clinton intended to reinforce Obama's racial identity in a way that would make him less appealing to potential white voters.[32]

As the primary season continued longer than most expected, Senator Clinton found herself in the position of needing to quickly develop a better political strategy for the now prolonged battle for the party nomination. Unfortunately, Clinton's tactics in this case involved efforts to play into racial and religious stereotypes in order to shape the course of the continuing primary elections. One of the earliest examples of this involved Clinton supporters' attempts to circulate or fan erroneous rumors that Senator Obama was actually a Muslim. In December 2007, a junior staffer in the Clinton camp resigned after circulating an email that made that claim.[33] Shortly after the Super Tuesday primaries, the Clinton campaign leaked a photo of Senator Obama in Somalia wearing ceremonial Muslim dress to the Drudge Report, a major conservative internet website that often indulges in such rumors.[34] Clinton supporter Rep. Stephanie Tubbs-Jones (D-OH) argued on MSNBC that she "had no shame, or no problem, with people looking at Barack Obama in his native clothing, the clothing of his country."[35] (Ironically, since Obama's father was Kenyan, he has no direct or indirect links to Somalia, and thus was in no way photographed wearing clothing that can be interpreted as representative of "his country.") Although the Clinton campaign argued that the Obama photo was not intended to be a smear, its leak at this particular time was widely interpreted as intentional and designed to stoke existing white fears and rumors about Obama's religion.[36] For many observers, these instances were overt attempts to reinforce the negative white-generated framing of Obama as a Muslim, and therefore, in the minds of many voters who hold negative stereotypes and prejudices about Muslims, as yet more untrustworthy and dangerous. And just beneath the surface was the centuries-old imagery of the "dangerous black man."

Towards the end of her campaign, Clinton began to speak openly about the U.S. racial divide and its importance in the Democratic primaries. Despite the fact that at this point, most political experts and politicians openly conceded that it would be mathematically impossible for her to secure the number of elected and super delegates necessary to win the Democratic nomination, Clinton argued that it was actually Obama who would have serious problems being electable in the general election. In several cases, she attributed this to the fact that he was not winning large numbers of votes from working-class whites. In contrast, Senator Clinton sought to posit herself as the candidate who could win many votes from this white constituency, and thus as the better candidate to go forward for the November general election.

One particular comment in this vein generated much attention. In May 2008, Senator Clinton referenced an Associated Press report, which she described thus: "Obama's support among working, hard-working Americans, white Americans, is weakening again, and [that] whites in both states who had not completed college were supporting me."[37] Clinton continued on to say that her words were not racially divisive but rather were a description of the reality of U.S. electoral conditions. Many people disagreed. Some argued that her choice of words reinforced racist stereotyping of white Americans as being more hard-working and industrious than people in other racial groups.[38] Though many commentators doubted that Clinton meant to be racially inflammatory and immediately absolved her of any intentional wrongdoing, her words were seized upon for reinforcing racial divisions. By openly evoking and highlighting Obama's relatively low numbers of support among working-class whites, Clinton sought to position herself as the primary candidate for this group and to employ a discursive framework that cast Obama as the othered black candidate who had limited appeal to many white Americans and thus would be hindered in the general election.

Others in the Clinton camp wanted to take this strategy even farther in order to emphasize the perceived difficulties Senator Obama would have commanding votes from white citizens during the general election. During the primary season, Clinton strategist Mark Penn strongly encouraged her to highlight Obama's "lack of American roots." In an internal campaign memo, Penn shared his sense that Obama's multicultural background "exposes a very strong weakness for him—his roots to basic American culture and values are at best limited." This extreme conclusion about a man who had lived in the United States for more than four decades was generally excluded from media stories that quoted this memo. These media accounts accented instead Penn's next comment in the memo that all articles about Obama's

> boyhood in Indonesia and his life in Hawaii are geared toward showing his background is diverse, multicultural and putting that in a new light. Save it for 2050 . . . I cannot imagine America electing a president during a time of war who is not at his center fundamentally American in his thinking and in his values.[39]

In addition, in the memo Penn argued, somewhat contradictorily, that Obama's being "black" was an advantage, as one of the things that "holds Obama up." Clearly, Obama's blackness was in Penn's eyes somehow an advantage, yet he suggested that this blackness might be made a liability if the Clinton campaign framed it aggressively as signaling a lack of roots in "real" American values and, thus, as showing he was not "fundamentally American."

Note again the implications here. If Penn had actually viewed "Americans" as including people of many different racial groups, then his argument that Obama's blackness and multiracial-ness prevented him from being fundamentally American made no logical sense. Clearly, to Penn, and probably others in the Clinton campaign, "basic American culture and values" were viewed as mostly white. Penn's proposed political strategy might not have openly discussed racial matters in the same manner as Senator Clinton's comments about "hard-working Americans," but it would have ultimately reinforced the same argument

—the idea that Obama would not be electable by mainstream (white) Americans because of the potential liability of his "diverse, multicultural background." Indeed, Penn was arguing that Obama could be portrayed as un-American, a political strategy that the John McCain campaign would later actually employ. While Clinton elected not to pursue Penn's deceptive political strategy to the extent that he suggested, she continued to rely on hard racial framing during her campaign as a means of discrediting Obama, particularly as she began to lose momentum.

Ultimately, during the primary season both racial and gender issues became important as it became clear that the Democratic Party would, for the first time in history, nominate someone other than a white man as its presidential candidate. Unfortunately, these issues were all too often framed as mutually exclusive forms of oppression wherein either racial disadvantage or gender disadvantage would "win out" as the bigger liability. This thereby contributed to the continued marginalization of women of color, for whom both forms of inequality operate as inter-secting phenomena. Thus, various media depictions of Michelle Obama as an "angry black woman" aptly highlighted how both vectors of oppression simultaneously impact upon women of color.

Given that Hillary Clinton was the presumptive front-runner, initially much attention focused on her and her status as a woman with a strong chance of securing the presidential nomination. Unfortunately, however, much of this attention came in the form of sexist stereotypes and gendered insinuations that undoubtedly hurt Clinton's political efforts. As Obama's numbers began to rise and he began to secure more primary wins, caucus wins, and super delegates, Clinton herself turned to racial imagery from the white racial frame as a strategy for securing the nomin-ation. Simultaneously, as sexist attacks against Clinton continued, many white women responded by identifying with Clinton, criticizing the rampant sexism they observed, and in some high-profile cases like those of Ferraro and Steinem, suggesting that this was evidence that sexism was a greater inhibiting political factor than racism. Although these cases ostensibly focused on gender and sexism, they simultaneously incorp-orated significant racial framing as well.

Gender Dynamics: The Use of White Racial Framing

One major argument that explicitly emerged during this primary season was whether sexism was now a greater evil than racism. White feminists such as Gloria Steinem and Geraldine Ferraro, as well as CBS network news anchor Katie Couric made this case unequivocally in numerous public statements. Yet, their arguments often relied on the soft version of the white racial frame in order to make their major points.

Making the claim that sexism is more accepted, widespread, restrictive, or prevalent than racism relies on a soft racial framing that minimizes the continuing and ongoing significance of racial barriers in shaping numerous aspects of this society. In order to argue that sexism is a more pervasive force, those who make this argument often have to rely on a racial framing that publicly argues that white-generated racial inequality is no longer a major societal issue and that ignores the subtle, covert, and complex ways that racial disparities are still perpetuated and reproduced by recurring discrimination in this society. Thus, when Clinton supporters and other feminists suggested that sexism was now more acceptable than racism, they relied on a racial framing that enabled them to ignore ongoing racial inequalities in educational attainment, omnipresent residential segregation, major racial inequalities in health care, racial disparities in the criminal justice system, and numerous other racial inequalities—all generated by past and present discrimination by many white Americans.

Significantly, this softer version of the white racial frame acknowledges, even emphasizes, the existence of serious societal inequality. However, this inequality is seen mostly through the lens of gender imbalances, so that patriarchy and male domination are highlighted while racial inequality and white-on-black oppression are downplayed. In practice, this means that the mostly white women who contended that the primary season proved sexism was a greater hindrance than racism could focus on the explicit or implicit sexism of media pundits and other commentators who derided the "Clinton cackle" while ignoring the overt racism of the 5–20 percent of white voters who openly declared in an array of 2008 opinion polls that they would not vote for a black candidate. Thus, one *New York Times*/CBS poll asked the 5 percent of whites who publicly admitted they would not vote for a black candidate whether most people they knew "would vote for a black candidate." Nearly a fifth said most would not.[40]

These white women also remained silent about the fact that even while she was besieged by sexist stereotyping and gendered attacks, Hillary Clinton still periodically sought to emphasize Obama's racial characteristics in an effort to gain leverage and discredit him with white voters. Relying on a soft racial framing that minimizes the extent and nature of racism, they instead prioritized the sexism faced by white women as the most significant, dangerous form of oppression that exists in U.S. society. Notably, these white women also chose to ignore or overlook the ways that Michelle Obama was routinely disparaged and subjected to both sexist and racialized imagery and language.

This racial framing is rather similar to the framing that surfaced in the late 19th and early 20th centuries among white women suffragists. When these women were denied the vote in the 15th amendment, they subsequently vented their frustrations by articulating racist stereotypes of black men who they believed had undeservedly secured greater rights than they. (Importantly, even though black men had officially been granted the right to vote, this right was usually denied in practice due to massive white discrimination. Most resided in southern and border states where white officials openly violated the 15th amendment and blocked black male voters with discriminatory laws and overt violence. In the North, there was also significant discrimination against these black male voters.) Many suffragists of that time emphasized the "undue" advancement black men would experience at their expense, and thus accented their racial connections with powerful white men.

Like their 19th-century feminist counterparts, thus, contemporary white feminists accenting sexism over racism have regularly overlooked the ways their white privilege within the racially stratified U.S. system has regularly minimized their ability to develop organizational solidarity with millions of women of color. Such solidarity would enable them to challenge the sexist inequalities of this country much more comprehensively and effectively. Instead, when they have not achieved their political objectives, they have too often taken refuge in the old white-racist framing and in their white privileges. While contemporary white feminists with qualms about supporting Senator Obama in 2008 did not publicly use racist slurs and blatant stereotyping like their 19th and early 20th century forerunners, they did engage in a similar pattern of emphasizing their racial allegiance to whiteness and white privilege as a way of allegedly protesting societal sexism.

White feminists who emphasized sexism but ignored racism were not the only ones who employed this binary either/or framing to understand inequality. Most mainstream news stories and media accounts of the primary race between Clinton and Obama emphasized her gender or his race, but failed to consider their other characteristics. In other words, very few mainstream media stories talked about the ways Clinton's position as a *white* woman influenced her campaign's use of racial framing in a way that would likely not have been possible were she a woman of color. Similarly, media accounts of Obama focused on his racial characteristics without considering how his position as a black *man* shaped the types of racialized imagery and stereotypes applied to him.[41] In both cases, a candidate's other important category (Clinton's race, Obama's gender) went unmentioned—further reinforcing the ways in which these categories were made to seem so natural and normative that they did not require substantive attention.

Given this common use of the white racial frame by white women and men, women of color have often employed a counterframe to challenge the white-framed notion that forms of societal oppression are best understood as separate phenomena that can be pitted against each other. Many feminists of color and white feminists who use a critical intersectional perspective have pointed out the ways in which systems of oppression are frequently overlapping, so that white women who suffer from sexism can simultaneously enjoy the benefits that accompany their racial position.[42]

Over the course of the Democratic primary season and the general election campaign, some women writing from this perspective emphasized the fallacy in believing that feminist movements can succeed if they ignore the ways gender inequality intersects with racism, classism, heterosexism, and other oppression. In an online article, black female law professor Kimberle Williams Crenshaw and white playwright Eve Ensler insightfully critiqued what they described as "either/or" feminism that simplistically suggests that sexism is the greater evil—hence, "voting for Clinton is the only sensible thing for women to do." Crenshaw and Ensler wrote: "For many of us, feminism is not separate from the struggle against violence, war, racism and economic injustice. Gender hierarchy and race hierarchy are not separate and parallel dynamics. The empowerment of women is contingent upon all these things."[43] By focusing on the overlapping and interrelatedness of sexism and racism, Crenshaw and Ensler deployed a major counterframing that refused to minimize the pervasiveness of racial oppression in order to emphasize the seriousness of political sexism.

Senator Hillary Clinton's Own Racial Framing

While the responses of many white feminists reveal hard racial framing, they were not alone in employing this perspective. Senator Clinton and others associated with her campaign also relied on white racial framing to bolster her position and increase her chances of winning the Democratic Party nomination, particularly through the use of its most emotionally grounded stereotypes. In an era where national security concerns are still paramount, operating within the context of a hard racial frame depicting certain racialized "others" as dangerous threats to U.S. security and stability was a strategy that likely appealed to numerous white voters. In several cases, Senator Clinton and members of her campaign chose to capitalize on this by casting Obama as a racial "other" in an attempt to limit his chances for securing the Democratic Party nomination. Similarly, the previously noted internal memos by Mark Penn, which argued that Obama's multiracial, diverse background prevented him from being "fundamentally American," highlighted this conceptualization of Obama as too different to appeal to many white voters. Yet again, we see the use of a hard racial framing that casts black Americans as too different from a supposed mainstream, too racially self-interested, and fundamentally unlike most whites.

Recall that Senator Clinton used the hard racial frame explicitly in her statement that "Obama's support among working, hard-working Americans, white Americans, is weakening again."[44] As some commentators noted, Clinton's conflation of hard work with white Americans reflected thinly veiled racist stereotypes that posit whites as hard-working and industrious, while certain other racial groups are conversely assumed to be lazy and lacking ambition. (However, the fact that many of these same commentators rushed to absolve Senator Clinton of any bad intent in making these statements was consistent with a soft racial framing that downplays racism.) Senator Clinton's comments certainly resonated with the pro-white imagery of the hard racial frame that routinely casts whites in this positive light and that thereby denigrates working people of color. Furthermore, Clinton's comments came late in the primary season when it was mathematically impossible for her to secure the presidential nomination, and much of her support was then coming from working-class, non-college-educated white Democrats. Senator Clinton thus relied periodically on a racial framing to strengthen her new base among this constituency and simultaneously to highlight how Senator Obama, as a racialized other, could not relate well to this important white group of voters.

Conclusion

During the long Democratic primary season, Senator Hillary Clinton experienced numerous examples of blatant and subtle sexism. Vicious sexist commentaries could be found thousands of times across many internet websites and in the mainstream mass media. In addition to the many sexist commentaries from (white) male analysts, these attitudes were also evidenced in statements from voters and other ordinary people. As the tide of sexist comments and media coverage became increasingly pronounced, prominent white women feminists concluded that this public barrage proved that sexism had greater significance and staying power than racism. In this context, and as it became increasingly apparent that she was losing the primary contest, Clinton and her advisors and supporters frequently relied on hard racial framing to depict Senator Obama as a racialized other fundamentally outside the mainstream, unable to relate to most (white) voters, and ultimately incapable of winning the general election in November 2008. In doing so, Clinton periodically attempted to posit her own whiteness as an electoral advantage and to cast it as something that made her familiar and relatable to white voters. Though Senator Clinton has had a long history of working on behalf of women and all racial groups, when it came down to gaining access to power, she chose to emphasize her whiteness as an ascendant feature and a characteristic that supposedly made her more deserving of the political rewards she sought—just like the white women abolitionists of the 19th century.

Not surprisingly, thus, during the Democratic primary elections, there was among white voters a strong correlation between the strength of their antiblack views and the likelihood they would vote for Hillary Clinton. Researchers have found that this relationship holds up even when they have controlled for factors of gender, age, and income. Working-class white Democrats in midwestern states such as Ohio, Indiana, and western Pennsylvania were much more likely to support Senator Clinton than Senator Obama.[45]

In the primary campaign, we observe Hillary Clinton deploying the hard version of the white frame to offset Senator Obama's attempts to define himself within the soft racial frame in a way that would be more appealing to many white voters. For Obama, operating within the context of the soft frame's color-blind imagery allowed him to escape some of the negative associations of blackness of the hard frame. Obama strove to construct himself as a person of color who fits within the acceptable boundaries defined by the soft racial frame—that is, as well-spoken, different from the negative stereotypes whites associate with African Americans, and, perhaps most importantly, unwilling to engage in significant public discussions of racism and racial inequalities. In contrast, Senator Clinton took opportunities to depict Obama using the hard version of the old racial frame, particularly by emphasizing what she perceived as a disconnect between his blackness and ability to connect with white working-class voters.

During much of the primary season, however, Obama and/or his top advisors generally chose to respond to these attacks within the context of the racial frame rather than overtly challenging this frame itself. For example, shortly after the primaries ended, during a June 2008 campaign stop in Detroit, members of Obama's staff refused to allow women wearing traditional Muslim headscarves to sit behind him on the stage where he would speak because they would be visible on television. One of the women denied a seat was quoted as saying that Obama's desire to distance himself from Muslims served to perpetuate "this attitude towards Muslims and Arabs—as if being merely associated [with] one is a sin."[46] Instead of addressing the dominant framing that connects racialized others to terrorism and danger, these Obama staff members played into it by distancing the senator from potential Muslim supporters, of whom there were many in the Detroit area.

Interestingly, while Obama responded to Clinton's early attempts at hard racial framing by relying on soft racial framing, once he took office the questions related to gender and race hardly abated. Obama selected former rival Hillary Clinton for his Secretary of State and appointed a number of other women to important administrative positions— Anita Dunn as a communications director, Christina Romer as chair of the Council of Economic Advisors, and Valerie Jarrett as a senior advisor. Obama also established a White House Council on Women and Girls and soon nominated two women to the Supreme Court, bringing the total of women there to three, its highest number in history. Yet, in his book *Confidence Men*, journalist Ron Suskind reported critiques from many women who worked in the White House and cited it as a hostile work environment for women. They described it as one where their contributions and efforts were routinely ignored or derided by men such as Larry Summers, Rahm Emanuel, and Peter Orszag.[47]

This description of gender bias within an administration that, on paper and in its hiring decisions, was committed to advancing women's presence in spheres where they had been previously underrepresented indicates some of the gender privileges that were overlooked due to a focus on racial framing. When, during his 2008 campaign, analysts emphasized Obama's race and Clinton's gender, there was little discussion of other intersecting factors that helped inform their abilities to use and be subjected to various types of stereotypes and framing. However, it is entirely possible that the emphasis on Obama's racial status blinded many observers to ways in which he might replicate traditional gendered patterns that marginalized and isolated the women who worked in his presidential administration. Social science research suggests that informal practices often leave women in male-dominated jobs facing patterns of exclusion and discrimination.[48] The common focus on Obama's race and the attempts to categorize him using various types of white racial framing may have obscured attention to ways that both race and gender allowed Obama to engage in traditional behaviors, personnel choices, and actions that undermined some of the women within his administration.

In the next chapter, we examine in depth yet other ways that the hard racial framing was regularly used to define Senator Obama as politically unacceptable during the 2008 election season.

4

THE COOL BLACK MAN VS. THE FIST-BUMPING SOCIALIST

One major challenge facing Senator Barack Obama over both the primary campaign and general campaign was whites' racist framing and perception of him. As a newcomer to the national political scene, Obama faced the daunting task of establishing an appealing public persona while simultaneously mounting a highly scrutinized push for the country's highest office. Unlike his chief opponent for the Democratic nomination, Senator Hillary Clinton, Obama had not had years in the public eye to restructure and morph his public image into one that already resonated well with a large cross-section of voters. Similarly, unlike his Republican challenger Senator John McCain, Obama did not enjoy a national reputation as a maverick known for his independence and willingness to break with the party line. On the contrary, many voters were unfamiliar with Senator Obama when he launched his historic campaign for the presidency in 2007. On the one hand, this newness enabled Obama to position himself as a presidential candidate who could change Washington, D.C. for the better. On the other hand, however, his lack of long-term national exposure meant that he and his campaign faced the challenge of introducing him to most voters while he simultaneously convinced them that he would be the best choice for president.

As Senator Obama struggled to define himself for voters, various representations of him emerged in the mainstream media and among political commentators. As with most political candidates, there was significant tension between the way Obama sought to portray himself and the way that his opponents and the media commentators depicted him. In this chapter, we examine both Obama's efforts and the mainstream media's attempts to define him politically. We assess the ways that these defining efforts reflect, and in some important cases work within the confines of, the hard and soft versions of the conventional white racial frame.

Obama's Self-Definition: The "Cool" Black Man

From the start of his long presidential campaign, Senator Obama worked very hard at defining himself as a distinctively American candidate, yet one whose distinctiveness represented the best of this country's possibilities and opportunities. Even earlier, in his 2004 keynote address at the Democratic Party's convention, one of his frequently emphasized themes was the rosy claim that the United States has a respected place for everyone, regardless of background or pedigree. This traditional ideal was conveyed in several places in Obama's speech: in his assertion that "in no other country on earth is my story even possible," and in his declaration that the United States held the promise of hope for all, even for the "skinny kid with a funny name who believes that America has a place for him too."[1] Thus, Obama sought to cast his multiracial heritage as evidence of the United States' best possibilities, and the success of his senatorial and presidential candidacies as proof that the country was ready to surpass its tumultuous racial history and contentious divisions.

As his presidential campaign progressed, Obama continued his efforts to position his background and ultimately himself as a different example of the all-American story. This became more of a conscious tactic as the election season progressed. Indeed, one of the key goals of the 2008 Democratic National Convention was to familiarize voters with Obama's "very American" story, focusing on his own prototypical nuclear family and how this enabled him to relate to challenges facing ordinary Americans.[2] By the time of this convention, Obama's strategists knew they were facing one of their last chances to shape the way voters perceived the senator. They realized that, for Obama to have an opportunity to win, he would have to define himself in ways that resonate with general U.S. themes—as someone well within the white-normed mainstream, unquestionably patriotic, and with the capacity and strength to lead the nation.

One way Obama sought to make this impression was by emphasizing his family background, particularly his white mother and grandparents who were primarily responsible for raising him. Doing so undoubtedly provided some reassurance to white voters who may have been uncomfortable with the prospect of a black man as president. However, Obama was able to balance this with the appeal his African American wife and children likely posed to black Americans and other Americans of color. Though major aspects of Obama's background and biography—such as having an African father and being raised by a white mother and grandparents in Hawaii and Indonesia—are not like that of most other African Americans, his visibly black wife and children created a very important link to these voters of color and likely increased their support and comfort with him.

Obama's family structure served another purpose in establishing his identity for many voters of various backgrounds. Obama, his wife, and his daughters conform to the father-dominant, traditional nuclear family that has been the normative paradigm since the first European colonists came to North America. With his "Cosby" family, Obama was able to appeal to most voters' sense that this family type—and he by extension—is "normal." He was able to further this message on several occasions with speeches about the importance of black male responsibility. In these speeches, Obama asserted a patriarchal perspective and admonished black men for too often minimizing the significance and importance of fatherhood. Addressing the congregation at one very large, predominantly African American church in Chicago in June 2008, Obama argued that

> We need fathers to realize that responsibility does not end at conception . . . Too many fathers are MIA, too many fathers are AWOL, missing from too many lives and too many homes . . . They have abandoned their responsibilities, acting like boys instead of men. And the foundations of our families are weaker because of it.[3]

Statements such as these helped Obama to craft his image as a "normal" family man, indeed as part of a patriarchal framing of society. Thus, while his racial status was an issue he would have to address in his efforts at self-definition, his gender enabled him to present himself within the context of patriarchal messages of men as logical authority figures who command respect—an option that would likely have been unavailable to a woman candidate of any racial background. More importantly, he could also portray himself as someone who would be willing to speak to issues commonly perceived among whites (and among some black Americans) to signify personal irresponsibility and family pathology within black communities. Speaking in this manner, Obama chose to highlight black male irresponsibility, while ignoring the fact that white fathers comprise a much larger group of problematical fathers who could also be instructed to take similar moral responsibilities. (Indeed, recent research suggests that, of fathers who do not live in the home with their children, black fathers are more likely than fathers of other racial groups to provide a consistent presence in their children's lives.[4]) His exhortation for "personal responsibility" also managed to ignore the ways significant structural issues (the prison-industrial system, economic restructuring, and educational tracking) greatly exacerbate the serious socioeconomic challenges facing many black fathers.

In a rather lurid case, Obama was inadvertently called on this by Reverend Jesse Jackson shortly after his address to the Chicago church. Speaking with a fellow guest after an interview segment on the Fox News channel, Reverend Jackson—unaware that his microphone was still on—stated that Obama had been talking down to black people and that he wanted to "cut his nuts off."[5] Jackson quickly apologized for his crude remark and attempted to put his comments in context. He added that

> My appeal was for the moral content of his message to not only deal with the personal and moral responsibility of black males, but to deal with the collective moral responsibility of government and the public policy which would be a corrective action for the lack of good choices that often led to their irresponsibility.[6]

In other words, Jackson's frustration came from Obama's willingness to join in the chorus of white voices criticizing black fathers for their perceived irresponsibility without simultaneously addressing the institutional discrimination and public policy decisions that limit the options and opportunities of black men. By framing his comments in the way that he did, Obama could define himself as a presidential candidate who, while undeniably black, would still deliver the tough truths that many, especially whites, felt the black community needed to hear. One white commentator noted the political advantage of this approach: "This helps Obama make the case that he is not a 'black' leader but just a Democratic candidate for president. Some cynics even questioned whether Jackson made this comment on purpose to help Obama."[7]

Senator Obama is not the only Democratic presidential candidate to take this approach. Inasmuch as they are often perceived as too "black oriented," certain political candidates may make public statements and pronouncements to show that they are willing to criticize black communities. Thus, Bill Clinton, who during his 1990s presidential campaigns was viewed as closely associated with black communities because of his extensive civil rights work, took comments about gang violence made by the African American author and activist, Sister Souljja, grossly out of context in a discursive political move that was widely viewed as a means of reassuring the country's white voters that he was "not too black-oriented."[8]

Obama was thus able to define himself as someone who was consistently savvy, poised, and "cool," particularly under pressure. Shortly after his victory in the general election, several media sources referred to him as "No-Drama Obama," in a nod to his tightly and efficiently run campaign and his unruffled, unflappable demeanor. Indeed, as we will discuss later, Obama's reputation for coolness under pressure provided a sharp contrast to his Republican opponent, such as when Senator John McCain grew visibly angry during debates or when he abruptly suspended his campaign in the first major bailout situation of the U.S. economic crisis that developed during the 2008 campaign. While Obama did not seek artificially to present himself as someone who was cool under fire, his obvious self-control and calm certainly became part of the "cool" image he did present.

Given his unusual biography, newness on the political scene, and African-origin (Swahili) name, Obama was well aware that the political odds were against him. He also knew that it was imperative that he present himself in a way that would be palatable to many voters, especially nonblack voters, given that he was not then a familiar figure to most in the U.S. electorate. Obama thus attempted to counter the way that his opponents depicted him using the old hard racial framing. His "cool strategy" enabled him to avoid many of the gendered-racist representations of black masculinity that are part of the white-racist frame—the "angry black man," "buddy," or "sidekick"—because those would render him unpresidential. What he could do was maintain this cool strategy in which he was consistently unruffled, poised, and in control at all times. In this fashion, he could still embody the gendered (and implicitly white) characteristics many people ascribe to presidents—that is, being assertive, in control, and decisive—without crossing the line into being angry or threatening. Establishing himself as someone with a typical American story, with a normal nuclear family, who was cool under pressure and, though he happened to be black, would still echo mainstream white criticisms of black families, was an approach that worked very well for him in the national political sphere despite Republican opponents' occasional attempts during the 2008 and 2012 campaigns to turn Obama's "cool" into a liability.[9]

Obama as Unpatriotic

Nonetheless, numerous media sources and political opponents were painting Obama in a rather different light. During the 2008 primary season, one of the major images that emerged in defining Obama involved the representation of him as quite unpatriotic and un-American. Some mainstream media sources questioned whether Obama was sufficiently patriotic to earn the nomination and ultimately win the general election. Others strongly hinted that he simply was not loyal to his country and lacked the devotion befitting a presidential candidate. Two incidents were frequently cited as the impetus behind these early discussions: Obama's decision to wear a flag pin on his lapel intermittently rather than regularly, and his rumored unwillingness to stand or cover his heart when saluting the flag.

Especially since the terrorist events of September 11, flag pins and accessories have become a common and increasingly popular way of demonstrating nationalist, pro-American sentiments during a time of international tensions and wars.[10] As such, many U.S. citizens have worn them as a way to communicate their patriotism and support for the "war on terrorism." In this context, Obama's refusal to wear a flag pin on a daily basis garnered some scrutiny. News commentators questioned whether Obama's decision not to wear the pin every day demonstrated a lack of support for the Iraq war effort, the troops, or more broadly, the United States generally.[11]

Faced with these criticisms and attacks, Obama addressed the rationale behind his refusal to wear the pin on a regular basis. When questioned, he stated:

> You know, the truth is that right after 9/11, I had a pin . . . Shortly after 9/11, particularly because as we're talking about the Iraq War, that became a substitute for I think true patriotism, which is speaking out on issues that are of importance to our national security, I decided I won't wear that pin on my chest . . . Instead, I'm going to try to tell the American people what I believe will make this country great, and hopefully that will be a testimony to my patriotism.[12]

Based on this argument, Obama claimed that patriotism is demonstrated more convincingly through words and deeds than by fashion accessories. However, Obama's reasoning was not well received by all, particularly conservative voices in the mainstream media. One guest on a Fox News show argued that Obama's refusal to wear the pin on a regular basis hurt the troops. On another episode, a Fox News commentator argued that it was necessary to wear the pin because the country was "at war." Despite Obama's repeated assertions of his love and support for his country, many in the mainstream media took his decision about the flag pin to be evidence of his lack of patriotism and thus of his supposedly tenuous ties to the United States.[13]

Interestingly, an *ABC News* story acknowledged that many other presidential candidates also did not wear the flag pin on a regular basis.

This story noted that of the initial field of nine Democratic and nine Republican contenders for the respective nominations, only former New York City mayor Rudy Giuliani wore the flag lapel pin with any regularity. Senator Hillary Clinton, who would become Obama's primary challenger for the Democratic nomination, stated that "there are so many ways that Americans can show their patriotism." Media-generated controversy over Obama's thoughts about the flag pin persisted to the point where he began wearing it somewhat more consistently. Predictably, this decision sparked media and Republican criticism that Obama was being a flip-flopper in changing his position on the importance of wearing the pin. While other candidates wore the flag pin sporadically with little or no media scrutiny, for Obama this became fodder for media commentators' and pundits' attempts to portray him as unpatriotic. Such treatment strongly suggested a racial component to the media coverage of Senator Obama.[14]

Significantly, this issue of his patriotism may have affected support for Obama among constituencies where he initially had weak poll numbers. In many articles describing voter reactions to these issues, the accent was mostly on white voters in "middle America" who strongly objected to Obama's alleged refusal to wear the flag pin, and also to place his hand over his heart during one flag pledge situation.[15] These articles framed voters in this segment of the population as those most likely to doubt Obama's patriotism.

About this time, in February 2008 in two speeches, including one in Madison, Wisconsin, Senator Obama's wife, Michelle Obama, made a comment that got significant national attention until the November election. She said that

> For the first time in my adult lifetime, I'm really proud of my country . . . not just because Barack has done well, but because I think people are hungry for change. I have been desperate to see our country moving in that direction and just not feeling so alone in my frustration and disappointment.[16]

Conservative pundits and commentators took this to mean that she was not proud of her country. Even though Obama campaign staff pointed out the context of her remarks—her reference to Obama as the first black candidate and to the large-scale turnout of "thousands of Americans who've never participated in politics before"—the conservative media and Republicans insisted that she was indeed unpatriotic if not un-American. They immediately linked her to Senator Obama, and one commentator in *Commentary*, a conservative magazine, asserted what others were saying, that this "gaffe" revealed the "pseudo-messianic nature of the Obama candidacy" and "the way the Obamas themselves are feeling" about saving the country.[17] Her phrase, "for the first time . . . I'm really proud of my country," was repeated in the media literally thousands of times, with very little attempt to understand the historical context of what she was saying, especially as a black woman in a still extensively racist country. This incident revealed more about the white denials of racism that are central to the prevailing white frame than about Michelle Obama's patriotism. It again demonstrated the unwillingness of white media commentators, indeed a great many whites, to even try to look at contemporary U.S. society from a black perspective and to consider why for black Americans national pride might be a complex feeling.

During the campaign against John McCain in the general election, the patriotism theme had other incarnations. Obama was simply cast by Republicans as someone who was obviously unpatriotic and put winning the general election over the best interests of the country. Obama's Republican challenger John McCain, and his ally Senator Joe Lieberman (I-CT), were among those who advanced this oddly warped perspective. Introducing McCain at a campaign event, for example, Senator Lieberman stated bluntly that the election called on voters to decide between "one candidate, John McCain, who has always put the country first, worked across party lines to get things done, and one who has not." This statement was one of the most outright and unequivocal ones that clearly cast Obama as much less patriotic than John McCain and thus represented Senator Obama as someone who had not consistently prioritized U.S. interests. Obama later responded that McCain should stop this line of political attack and warned that he would "let no one question [his] love of this country."[18]

Allegations of a lack of patriotism reached a fever pitch in the final stages of the general election. By late September 2008, the collapse or near collapse of several major financial institutions (American International Group, Fannie Mae, Freddie Mac, and Lehman Brothers) created the biggest economic crisis in the United States since the Great Depression of the 1930s. Many Americans saw their retirement savings adversely affected, many jobs were lost, and an already rocky economy became even shakier. As the George W. Bush administration and Congress worked to partly nationalize many banks and infuse financial institutions with government capital, it became clear that the country was in the throes of a major economic disaster. This crisis facilitated a significant shift in support to Senator Obama, the candidate widely viewed as better able to handle this faltering economy. By late October, Obama held a solid, often double-digit lead in most Democratic-leaning states, and even held a lead or had erased McCain's advantage in several traditionally Republican states. In this context, as it became clear that McCain was likely losing the race, McCain chose to employ a controversial strategy of attacking Obama's character and again attempting to paint him as unpatriotic and un-American.[19]

The speeches, advertisements, and comments that followed were some of the most explicit and overt characterizations of Obama as un-American and unpatriotic. At a campaign fundraiser in Colorado, Republican vice presidential candidate, Sarah Palin, addressed a mostly white audience by describing Senator Obama thusly:

> This is not a man who sees America as you see America, and as I see America. Our opponent, though, is someone who sees America, as . . . imperfect enough that he's palling around with terrorists who would target their own country.[20]

Palin's remarks alluded to modest contacts Obama had had with University of Illinois professor William Ayers (see below), who had been actively involved 40 years earlier with a radical antiwar group. Palin's comments were clearly intended to posit Obama as someone whose sense of patriotism and love for America were lacking. Her statements even incited inflammatory and extreme responses from some crowd members at some of her campaign events. When Senator McCain himself launched a series of speeches beginning with the question, "Who is Barack Obama?" shouts of "terrorist!" and "kill him!" could be heard from the audience.[21] These violently hostile remarks and terrorist imagery overlapped with depictions of Obama as radically different and dangerous, and clearly underscored the successful Republican efforts to paint Obama as someone not fully American.

These examples again demonstrate the great importance of nationalistic symbolism and its associated emotions in U.S. elections. In none of the above cases was there *any* substance to the conservative arguments that Obama was unpatriotic, yet these arguments were powerful because a great many Americans make up their minds about who to vote for in terms of candidates' personalities and images, not in terms of rationally thinking through the key issues.[22] In these examples, moreover, the Obama campaign relied heavily on reasoning and data to counter the Republican attacks and did not call out the right-wing framing as unethical and designed just to appeal to certain emotions. (For example, they could have shown McCain without a flag pin or in similar postures with regard to the pledge of allegiance.) Nor did they introduce their own emotion-centered counter attack that accented Obama's own great patriotism, community service, and high achievements attained against the great odds of racial hostility and discrimination.

Obama as Different and Dangerous

As we noted in Chapter 3, early in the primary season Senator Obama faced media representations that sought to position him as different and implicitly dangerous.

One major incident that revisited these themes during the general election was a July 2008 *New Yorker* magazine cover. The cover art has a cartoon drawing of Senator Obama and his wife Michelle in the Oval Office in the White House. Obama is dressed in the distinctive clothing worn in some Muslim countries and Michelle sports an Afro and has a machine gun strapped to her back, in an image many argued was intended to evoke academic and activist Angela Davis. The two are tapping their fists together in the gesture they exchanged before Obama gave a speech acknowledging that he had won more than the required

2,117 votes and super delegates required for the Democratic Party's presidential nomination. A framed portrait of Osama bin Laden hangs over the fireplace, and a U.S. flag is burning in the fire. The *New Yorker's* cover art thus reinforced many of the basest stereotypes of both the Obamas and Muslims and depicted the fears of many U.S. citizens reflected in national polling data—specifically, that Obama was Muslim and had links to Islamic extremist groups.[23]

The editor of the *New Yorker*, a white liberal, defended his cover as being planned to attack the numerous "lies" and stereotypes that were circulating about Obama and his wife. He and other *New Yorker* staff defended their use of this cartoon as intended to be very satirical and not at all harmful to Senator Obama's family or campaign.[24] However, numerous social scientists and other analysts disagreed with this official explanation, calling the cover a thinly veiled marketing attempt and noting that it would have obvious negative effects. Princeton biology professor Sam Wang has noted that if erroneous information such as that on the *New Yorker* cover is prominently presented again and again, the human brain is likely to eventually interpret that misinformation as fact, effectively forgetting the context in which that misinformation was actually learned.[25] Despite the magazine's claim that the cover art was intended to be satirical and should be viewed as such, ultimately the images of the Obamas as terrorists played into existing white-framed ideas of the Obamas as different and potentially dangerous threats to U.S. national security.

Several conservative white politicians picked up on the closely related theme that emerged during the 2008 primaries about Barack Obama as someone who would give comfort to enemies of U.S. interests. Predictably, these "enemies" were often defined as Middle Eastern terrorists seeking to wreak havoc on the United States. For example, in announcing his candidacy for a fourth term in the House of Representatives, veteran Congressman Steve King (R-IA) discussed his fears about an Obama presidency:

> When you think about the optics of a Barack Obama potentially getting elected President of the United States—I mean, what does that say to the rest of the world? What does it look like

to the world of Islam? ... I will tell you that, if he is elected
president, then the radical Islamists, the al-Qaida, the radical
Islamists and their supporters, will be dancing in the streets in
greater numbers than they did on September 11 because they
will declare victory in this War on Terror.[26]

Here, Representative King engaged in an intentional effort to reinforce
the conservatively framed connections between Senator Obama and
certain dangers to the United States. Citing those who perpetrated or
celebrated the events of September 11, King crudely represented Senator
Obama as a threat to national security and one whose presidency would
undermine U.S. efforts to maintain its safety and stability. Although
King stated that he did not want to "disparage anyone," he did just that
by suggesting that Obama's physical (thus, racial) characteristics and
falsely alleged ties to Islam made him a great risk to the country.

An additional guilt-by-association effort that gained significant
political traction was the effort to link Senator Obama to University of
Illinois professor William Ayers. Ayers and his wife, Bernadine Dorhn,
are former members of the 1960s-era group known as the Weather
Underground. This group was a radical offshoot of the organization,
Students for a Democratic Society (SDS), and contended that the 1960s
nonviolent protests were insufficient for creating significant political,
social, and economic change. The group engaged in symbolic political
bombings and other actions within the United States that were intended
to draw attention to the U.S. government's complicity and role in the
war in Vietnam. (The group generally took steps to ensure that no people
would be hurt by their political bombings, preferring instead to destroy
government offices as a way of protesting what they viewed as the government's immoral war actions.) As leading members of what was labeled a
"terrorist" organization, Ayers and Dorhn were involved with bombings
at several government sites. They went into hiding to avoid prosecution,
but later turned themselves in to authorities. Ayers was never convicted
of these property crimes because of illegal government efforts in gathering evidence against him. Today, Ayers and Dorhn reside in Chicago,
where Ayers is a retired professor of education at the University of Illinois
and Dorhn is a respected law professor at Northwestern University.

The tenuous connection between Obama and Professor Ayers first emerged during the Democratic primary season. Arch-conservative internet websites—several of which targeted the Obamas with detailed accounts of their lives and alleged failings throughout the campaign—were the first to raise the issues of Ayers and Dr. Jeremiah Wright, as well as allegations about Obama's Islamic ties, during mid-2007. By the early spring of 2008, this information had somehow worked its way into Republican operations and into the mainstream media. The links between Senator Obama and Ayers began to get much national media coverage in April 2008 when Republican Party political operative and Bush strategist Karl Rove opined on Fox News that Obama should explain his ties to Professor Ayers.[27] Further, news stories circulated that quoted Ayers as saying that he had "no regrets about setting bombs" and "we didn't do enough."[28] Other sources contended that Ayers and Obama sat on several academic conference panels together at the University of Illinois, that they had worked together on the board of a charitable organization, and that Ayers had hosted a fundraiser for Obama at some time in the past. These formal connections were used as evidence to bolster claims of a strong personal and political link between the two.

For his part, Ayers has argued that his controversial comments have been taken out of context. On his website, for example, Ayers has stated that:

> I'm often quoted saying that I have "no regrets." This is not true. For anyone paying attention—and I try to stay wide awake to the world around me all/ways—life brings uncertainty, doubt, misgivings, loss, regret. I'm sometimes asked if I regret anything I did to oppose the war in Vietnam, and I say "No, I don't regret anything I did to try to stop the slaughter of millions of human beings by my own government." Sometimes I add, "I don't think I did enough." This is then elided: he has no regrets for setting bombs and thinks there should be more bombings.[29]

Other sources also provided a different account of Obama's connection to Ayers. The *Washington Post* reported that Ayers donated $200 to

Obama's campaign for re-election to the Illinois State Senate and cast the relationship between the two as very weak.[30] Furthermore, Chicago columnist Lynn Sweet wrote that Obama's links to Ayers "never bugged anyone" in the course of the city's everyday politics, and that most politicians and citizens in the city considered these old ties unimportant and a non-issue.[31] A *New York Times* article released about a month before the November election—the article that Governor Palin cited in making her assertion that Senator Obama was "palling around with terrorists"—described Ayers as "largely rehabilitated" and concluded that the two men "do not appear to have been close."[32] Finally, we should also note that numerous Chicago politicians, officials, and academics have had, and still have, significant educational and political connections to Professor Ayers.

During the latter stages of the general election, the McCain campaign resuscitated the story of Obama's connections to Ayers and made their "relationship" a major part of an increasingly desperate campaign strategy. As Obama's numbers grew and McCain's declined, McCain's staff engaged in robocalls—automated telephone calls to likely voters in battleground states like Virginia, Ohio, and Florida—stating that "Barack Obama has worked closely with domestic terrorist Bill Ayers, whose organization bombed the U.S. Capitol, the Pentagon, a judge's home, and killed Americans."[33] This misleading phone call implied that Obama worked closely with Ayers when he was engaged in the bombings —an allegation that is patently false given that Obama was eight years old when these events occurred. The calls make no mention of the fact that Ayers has expressed regrets and become a model citizen, obscure the Weather Underground's intentional efforts to bomb only unoccupied buildings to avoid taking lives, and greatly overstate the political relationship between the two men.

Making these connections between Senator Obama and Professor Ayers served a major Republican Party political purpose. By linking Senator Obama to someone widely described as a 1960s-era radical, McCain represented Obama again as dangerous and threatening to national stability and security. Ayers served particularly well in this regard, as he was associated with a time period that had seen significant societal change and upheaval, and with an organization that engaged in symbolic political bombings and refused to repudiate such violence as a tactical strategy. Furthermore, the fact that Ayers' involvement in political bombings occurred when Obama was a child, that Ayers was never convicted of a crime largely because of government misconduct, or that the Weather Underground generally sought not to injure individuals in its symbolic bombings was downplayed by the McCain campaign and other conservatives in favor of heightening the image of Ayers, and by extension Obama, as someone with a "dangerous terrorist" background and anti-American interests.

Finally, during the late stages of the general election campaign, the theme of Obama as dangerous was manifested in charges that he and his policies were socialist in nature. As the large-scale financial crises continued, driving Obama's poll numbers up in the process, McCain and other Republicans stepped up criticisms that Obama's plans to fix the ailing economy amounted to dreaded "socialism." Vice presidential candidate Sarah Palin seized on a statement Obama made during a debate with McCain to make the following claim:

> Senator Obama said he wants to, quote, spread the wealth. What that means is he wants government to take your money and dole it out however a politician sees fit. Barack Obama calls it spreading the wealth. But Joe the Plumber and Ed the Dairy-man, I believe that they think that it sounds more like socialism. Friends, now is no time to experiment with socialism.[34]

The clear implication of these claims was that Obama's policies, and Obama himself, were dangerous for the country and threatened to undermine basic U.S. values and ways of life through the eradication of capitalism and the implementation of a supposedly socialist agenda.

Subsequent events showed that these arguments had an impact on some members of the electorate. In one memorable case, Obama entered a North Carolina restaurant to be greeted by a white woman patron shouting, "Socialist, socialist, socialist—get out of here!" The speaker refused to shake Obama's hand when he offered it, and later added, "I still think he's a closet Muslim."[35] Clearly, branding Obama with the label of socialism, which few Americans actually know much about, had a strong negative effect on some voters.

Obama as Unqualified, Naive, or Unprepared

A third definition of Obama that surfaced during the primary and general election involved depictions of him as unqualified, unprepared, naive to the ways of politics, and basically "not ready to lead." According to this representation, Obama was rather patronizingly defined, mostly by whites in the political and media elites, as a person with good intentions and a skilled politician, but ultimately not one who was fully prepared or experienced enough for the rigors of the country's highest office. To bolster these claims, his opponents cited his short service of three years in the U.S. Senate, minimal experience in foreign policy, and few examples of sponsored congressional legislation, especially bipartisan legislation.

These arguments surfaced from Obama's political challengers in the primaries and the general election. His Republican opponent John McCain emphasized Obama's lack of bipartisan legislation, and his one-time Democratic rival Hillary Clinton echoed the claim that Obama was too inexperienced to be "ready to lead on day one."[36] While Obama did have significantly less experience with national politics than either Clinton or McCain, this charge of inexperience was made to suggest that Obama was not truly qualified for the office of the presidency. Thus, when Obama discussed the possibility of meeting with foreign leaders in countries considered by many to be U.S. enemies without preconditions (as many past U.S. presidents have done), his opponents denounced this as evidence of the poor judgment typical of someone who did not comprehend the complexities of the presidential office. To wit, Senator Clinton labeled this idea "irresponsible and frankly naive."[37] Overall, the argument that Obama was simply not yet ready for the presidency was one of the key tropes his political challengers deployed.

In his turn, Senator Obama defended himself by pointing to the fact that former president Bill Clinton was similarly cast as too new to succeed in Washington politics when he mounted his ultimately successful campaign for the White House. During the Democratic Party primaries, Clinton countered that he had been a senior state governor and had headlined many national organizations, which offered him more hands-on preparation than that to which Obama could lay claim. Moreover, Obama replied to his critics by noting that his real-life experience living in and visiting several foreign countries added an important chapter to his ability to understand and craft foreign policy. He further suggested that his lack of immersion in traditional Washington politics actually was an advantage to a citizenry hungry for major political change.[38]

This idea that Obama was not ready for the presidency was linked to charges that he became "too arrogant" when he saw some success in the national polls. In late July and early August of 2008, Obama embarked on an international visit that took him to various countries in the Middle East and in Europe. Obama visited the Western Wall in Jerusalem and gave a speech in front of the Brandenburg Gate in Germany, a site with important historical significance.[39] This trip was met with mixed political results. He avoided making any of the mis-steps or inaccurate statements that traveling politicians sometimes make. However, as time passed, many in the mainstream media questioned whether Obama's trip rendered him presumptuous and arrogant. Republican strategist Karl Rove stereotyped Obama in this way very early in the general election season, characterizing him as "the guy at the country club with the beautiful date, holding a martini and a cigarette that stands against the wall and makes snide comments about everyone."[40] *Washington Post* columnist Dana Milbank disdainfully chided Obama for changing from the "presumptive nominee" to the "presumptuous nominee."[41]

Moreover, during an interview with *The Hill*, the major Washington, D.C. newspaper covering Congress, when asked to compare Michelle Obama to Republican vice presidential candidate Sarah Palin, Representative Lynn Westmoreland (R-GA) stated, "Just from what little I've seen of her and Mr. Obama, Sen. Obama, they're a member of an elitist class individual that thinks they're uppity."[42] Historically, Westmoreland's word "uppity" has long, and frequently, been used by racist whites to describe African Americans who "don't know their place"— that place typically being one of racial subservience, humility, and service to whites. Westmoreland denied that he was aware of any racial implications, although in the South where he was raised this adjective has been widely used to describe black Americans who do not appear appropriately deferential to whites.[43] Another Congressional representative, Geoff Davis (R-KY), argued that Obama was unprepared for the presidency by stating, "That boy's finger does not need to be on the button."[44] Like using "uppity," referring to a grown black man as a "boy" is racialized rhetoric intended to reinforce the idea that African Americans should be appropriately subordinate and submissive to whites.

Collectively, these recurring white representations of Obama cast a very different picture of Obama than the one he sought to promote. Throughout the primary and general election, Obama worked carefully to operate within soft racial framing and depict himself as someone whose story was uniquely American, who was a candidate who happened to be black rather than a black candidate. He presented his multiracial background as a particular advantage that lent itself to unifying the country and argued that his background and history would enable him to be a force for change in a country where people were overwhelmingly dissatisfied with the political path the country was following. Further-more, he was willing to chastise black Americans in ways that evoked stereotypical ideas of black male irresponsibility, even as he sought their votes and their support. Yet, white political opponents and media figures cast Obama as alternately unpatriotic, different, dangerous, unqualified, and arrogant.

Racially Framing President Obama

Despite Obama's attempts at self-presentation, this hard racial framing did not cease once he took office in 2009. Shortly after his election, groups loosely organized as the Tea Party (after the famous Boston Tea Party in which colonists protested the British government's decision to tax tea in the absence of any governmental representation) mobilized in opposition to Obama's stimulus package. Early Tea Party members' concerns also included a perception that their taxes were being raised (despite the fact that the Obama stimulus plan included middle-class tax cuts) and that the proposed health care reform was an example of government overreach.

In several cases, Tea Party protests and causes for concern included issues that reflected aspects of racial framing. Indeed, shortly after his election and inauguration, a new controversy began to garner steam and traction in some Tea Party and mainstream Republican circles. Beginning before his election, but gaining increased attention shortly after he began his first term, rumors began to circulate widely that Obama's birth certificate was a forgery, and thus that he was legally unable to hold the office of the presidency.

Despite being categorically disproven with documentary evidence, this highly dubious cause became central in some political platforms advocated by the Tea Party and eventually was articulated or implied by mainstream Republicans such as business leader Donald Trump, Rep. Jean Schmidt (R-OH), and House Majority Leader John Boehner (R-OH). Indeed, in April 2011 a CBS poll reported that nearly a quarter of Americans believed that Obama was not born in the United States.[45] While controversy died down somewhat after Obama released his long-form birth certificate, as recently as spring of 2012 Arizona sheriff Joe Arpaio (known for his outspokenness against and deportation of illegal immigrants) revived the issue by recasting doubt on whether the certificate was real and accurate.[46]

The questions about Obama's birth certificate perhaps more clearly than any others evoke the idea that he is not qualified for the presidency. Were Obama to have been born in another country, clearly he would not possess one of the most basic qualifications for this office. Thus, the contention that Obama was born outside of the United States is one of the most overt ways of raising doubts about his qualifications.

The birth certificate issue, however, raises other racialized issues as well. Alluding that Obama was not born in the United States serves to cast Obama as someone not only unqualified for the Presidency, but as different and unfamiliar to "mainstream" Americans. The birth certificate issue thus implies Obama's lack of qualifications, but also involves the issues of Obama being different and dangerous that we raised in the previous section.

Finally, following Obama's 2008 election, representations of Michelle Obama also revealed the ways that hard-racist framing was still present in gender-specific ways. One obvious case of this came in reactions to Michelle Obama's "Let's Move" campaign, in which the first lady advocated healthy eating and strategies that families could take to minimize obesity, one of the leading public health challenges facing the country. However, despite the innocuousness of this initiative, critics found various ways to deride the First Lady, often in ways that relied on gender-specific hard racial framing.

In perhaps one of the most noteworthy cases of this, Representative Jim Sensenbrenner was overheard—and later apologized for—commenting that while the First Lady advocated healthy eating and exercise, she has a "large posterior herself."[47] Additionally, radio host Rush Limbaugh called her a hypocrite, stating:

> it doesn't look like Michelle Obama follows her own nutri-tionary, dietary advice . . . I'm trying to say that our First Lady does not project the image of women that you might see on the cover of the *Sports Illustrated* swimsuit issue or of a woman Alex Rodriguez might date every six months or what have you.[48]

It did not escape commenters and observers that both men themselves are overweight, yet their critiques of Mrs. Obama centered on aspects of her physical characteristics.

This commentary reflects a gendered case of hard racial framing because of the ways that black women's bodies have historically been objectified and often commodified as well. Black women have routinely been aggressively stereotyped as overweight or obese, and as far back as the case of Sarah Baartman (an African woman racialized as the "Hottentot Venus," caged, and displayed in Europe so whites could ogle her backside and genitals), black women's behinds have been subjected to intense scrutiny and hypersexualization.[49] Thus, Sensenbrenner's crude objectification of Michelle Obama's backside is consistent with gendered hard racial framing that sexualizes black women's physicality.

Limbaugh's remarks, too, display aspects of hard racial framing. In his assertion that Mrs. Obama does not resemble *Sports Illustrated* cover models or baseball player Alex Rodriguez's girlfriends (who have included actresses Minka Kelly, Cameron Diaz, and Madonna), he implicitly endorses a traditional, predominantly white feminine standard of beauty. It was not until 1996—a full 32 years after the first swimsuit issue was published—that model Tyra Banks became the first black woman ever featured on the cover; and even in this case she was featured with a white model. Moreover, Banks's long hair and light skin reflected a certain type of black beauty that is still grounded in European ideals. When white conservatives glorify this as an ideal type of beauty and femininity, they are grounding their analysis in gendered hard racial framing that emphasizes women's physical features as important, significant characteristics, and suggest that the basic standard of beauty is measured by ideals that are easier for white women to fit than women of other racial groups.

Black Men and Women as Unpatriotic

Let us now consider some historical context for the array of political attacks on Obama and his family in the 2008 election and following years. The repeated assertion that Obama was unpatriotic gained traction and remained a key device that Republicans—especially John McCain—used to define Senator Obama during the course of the 2008 primary and general elections. Indeed, it remains commonplace today on arch-conservative websites. Coupled with Obama's distinctive African name, family ties to other countries, and familiarity with Islam (a religion cast by many Americans as implicitly dangerous and a threat to "real" U.S. values), the depiction of him as insufficiently patriotic seemed an easy charge for his political opponents to level. However, this representation substantially relies on the hard version of the white frame that had long depicted African Americans as "others" who are outside the (white) U.S. mainstream.[50]

There is a long historical context that accents a racial framing of African Americans as a group whose loyalty and patriotism is in doubt. While African Americans have historically played a very central and integral role in establishing and maintaining the country's wealth and prosperity, they have primarily done so as racialized workers and outsiders. Black labor during slavery dramatically facilitated the country's economic growth, and much white wealth and prosperity. In order for the slave system to work effectively, African Americans were stripped of their basic human and legal rights, as well as socioeconomic resources to pass along to their descendants. After the slavery era ended in 1865, African Americans were forced into the near-slavery of Jim Crow segregation, which continued the process of unjust impoverishment for them as individuals and as communities. During the long Jim Crow apartheid era, African Americans served in agricultural jobs such as farmworkers and sharecroppers, work which was poorly and discriminatorily compensated and thus contributed greatly to the country's continuing economic prosperity, especially white prosperity. However, African Americans were still denied full citizenship rights and benefits.[51]

This history is part of an oppressive long-term situation where black labor is essential for U.S. stability and prosperity, yet black workers are simultaneously denied all the benefits of full U.S. citizenship. In this context, historian Paula Giddings' observation that "American citizenship has always been racialized as white" helps explain the old racial framing of African Americans as unpatriotic. Giddings asks, "Who is a true American? Are African Americans true Americans? That has been the question."[52] In part, the hard racial framing of black Americans as "inferior beings" who are not really citizens and are thus unpatriotic has for centuries been linked to policy, legal, and other institutional decisions that have made full U.S. citizenship the province of whites only.

The U.S. legal system long reserved full citizenship for whites alone. During this country's era of slavery, from 1789 to 1865, each enslaved African American was famously counted (thanks to the U.S. Constitution) as only three-fifths of a person for the purpose of bolstering southern white politicians' power, while at the same time providing a continued rationale for African American enslavement. For centuries, the slavery system denied enslaved African Americans the citizenship rights guaranteed to whites: the right to vote, own major property, and other basic freedoms guaranteed by the U.S. Constitution and subsequent amendments. Although the 14th amendment established that all people born in the United States were automatically endowed with full citizenship rights, black Americans were still denied these rights after slavery ended in 1865 through extensive, often violently enforced, legal segregation laws and by informal segregation norms up until the 1960s.[53]

From the time of the U.S. Constitution in the late 1780s to the 1950s, numerous Supreme Court rulings, all made by elite white male judges, further established that the full benefits of U.S. citizenship were intended for whites only. For example, in various Supreme Court cases deciding who could be a citizen, the high court decisions sought to "distinguish white from nonwhite, to deny those whom the white-controlled courts deemed as racial 'others' the privileges associated with whiteness."[54] Cases involving Asian, Mexican, and Native American plaintiffs seeking full citizenship mostly ruled that because of their racial status, they were excluded from numerous legal protections and rights afforded white citizens. For the U.S. courts, the language of individualism has long masked the fact that group rights—particularly the rights of white citizens to maintain dominance over people of color—were of primary salience to the white judges:

> The process of racialization and racial "reasoning" employed by the courts often situated African Americans as the archetypal "other" against which to measure both whites and other racialized groups. When the "white gaze" turned upon people of color who attempted to assert their individuality within the U.S. legal frame, the courts repeatedly confirmed that the language of individualism was merely rhetorical and that group-based concerns, specifically the protection of white power and privilege, were the primary focus of the courts.[55]

Thus, many federal court decisions established a decades-long tradition of people of color being denied full U.S. citizenship—and, thus, that certain basic rights guaranteed by the U.S. Constitution were usually read by elite white judges and legal scholars as applicable to whites only.

Legally excluding people of color from the basic rights and privileges of U.S. citizenship helped to bolster their image in the hard white racial frame as "others" who were not really Americans. As the deep racial frame legitimizes ongoing racial subordination, depicting people of color as outside the mainstream and as those who are somehow not real U.S. citizens serves important purposes. Specifically, it provides a dominant rationale for denying people of color specific citizenship rights and reinforces whites' privileges and undue enrichment over the others. Most relevant for our analysis here, moreover, is that this view forms a basic component of a hard racial framing that posits people of color as inherently un-American and as physically and culturally different.

Based on this omnipresent racial framing today, African Americans' patriotism is often still questioned. Inasmuch as they are described as racial "others" who are not really Americans, the hard framing portrays them as Americans who do not maintain the appropriate loyalty to their country. African Americans are quickly, if subconsciously or half-consciously, viewed through a hard racial frame suggesting they are "inferiors" whose nationalism can be easily questioned, and who therefore are not to be trusted. Feagin terms this process white-frame resonance.[56]

Emotion-laden, antiblack stereotypes have been central to the white racial frame since the 1600s, and it is easy to call them up in white minds by direct reference to them or by alluding to closely related ideas or images that induce old stereotypes. In this way, frame resonance reinforces the impact of the contemporary attacks, even as those who are affected may not be fully conscious of why there is such influence on them. In contrast, there is no such frame resonance for a white political candidate, since there is no dominant background frame in which whites are seen as un-American and problematical in terms of values. For example, there was no widespread frame of the "dangerous white man" among whites to resonate when Senator McCain was criticized for his various moral and political failures. Such attacks on him just did not persist the way they did for Senator Obama. There is no pervasive and deep framing of white men or women as racially othered, unpatriotic, and dangerous, so that even if political opponents question their patriotism, such questioning does not resonate and thus does not echo across the society.

Furthermore, the hard racial framing of black Americans as unpatriotic relies on the insistent downplaying of the manifestations and results of institutionalized and everyday racial inequality. The idea that black Americans do not "love America" contends that they do not appreciate or value the opportunities and liberties that the United States has to offer. Several right-wing websites that criticize President Obama still contend that despite the great opportunities the country has offered them, both Barack and Michelle Obama really "hate America."[57] Such claims obviously ignore the vast and well-documented encounters with white racism that black Americans face—harassment in social spaces, discrimination in the workplace, police and other state-sanctioned forms of brutality—that explain their reluctance to praise the United States uncritically and without qualifiers.

Furthermore, this white-only framing assumes a very narrow conceptualization of patriotism wherein national pride is implicitly defined as refusing to question, disagree with, or critically analyze any of the social, political, or economic practices that might be problematic for certain racial groups. This particular version of hard racial framing thus ignores many other demonstrations of patriotism—for instance, black Americans' high rates of military service, or their insistence (demonstrated through numerous social movements intended to abolish institutional inequality) that the United States live up to its stated ideals of liberty and justice for all. Hard racial framing denies the patriotism of figures such as Fred Hampton, Angela Davis, Leonard Peltier, Yuri Kochiyama, Russell Means, Dolores Huerta, and many other Americans of color who over the decades have worked to highlight the necessity of social change and progress. In a sense, then, the hard racial framing of black Americans as "unpatriotic" is not only ignorant of U.S. history, but rests on a racialized conception of patriotism that refuses to acknowledge the oppressive realities facing people of color—as well as the well-honed and experiential perspectives on U.S. society of those people of color.

Hard Racial Framing of Blacks as Dangerous

During the 2008 primary and general elections, many subtle and overt images, comments, and analyses were grounded in the white framing that posits African Americans, and most especially black men, as implicitly or explicitly dangerous. We have already discussed obvious examples of this (the *New Yorker* magazine cover, various remarks by Republican members of Congress) as well as more insidious cases such as attempts to tie Senator Obama to Professor William Ayers and to label Obama as a socialist. Though the specifics vary, such incidents make use of the hard racial frame and its attendant emotion-laden stereotypes and images of African Americans as dangerous, criminal, and threatening. In each case, the fact that this recurring stereotyping and imagery resonated with the old racist framing in most white heads, and that this is not possible with similar political assertions about whites, is central to our analysis of the chronic racialization of once Senator, and later President, Barack Obama.

Negative emotion-laden images of black Americans have a four-centuries-old heritage in the white racial frame, which evolved out of the specific historical circumstances of extreme racial oppression, out of slavery and Jim Crow segregation. During the period of intense and legalized slavery, black Americans were often depicted as happy-go-lucky, lazy, slow-witted beings who needed the stabilizing influence of enslavement and white "masters" to tame their inherently "savage" and "uncivilized" natures. White-racist framing suggested that slavery was beneficial for African Americans inasmuch as it civilized them and provided them with much-needed social order—an argument, unfortunately, still echoed by some contemporary analysts who accept this white supremacist perspective.[58] Racist framing of African Americans as people who "needed" slavery provided a justification for continuing this extremely oppressive system and the unjust economic enrichment and high racial status it offered for whites.

This situation changed with the end of slavery. At the end of the Civil War, with the passage of the 13th amendment outlawing slavery, the United States underwent significant cultural, social, economic, and political changes. Consequently, the white racial frame shifted, but in many ways only modestly, in order to accommodate the Jim Crow society that was emerging. Whites could no longer legally force blacks into enslavement. However, whites still sought to maintain their positions of socioeconomic power and racial privilege relative to African Americans by means of the extremely hierarchical and exploitative Jim Crow system in the South and by the equally stratified de facto segregation in the North. In both regions, the white-racist framing persisted to explain continuing white privilege and justify the oppressive treatment of black workers and their families in the legal segregation system.

In this era, whites in the South established a near-slavery system of Jim Crow, with its social, economic, legal, and political norms that maintained whites' great socioeconomic advantages and racial privileges over African Americans, as well as over other people of color now coming into the United States (such as Asian and Mexican immigrants). These laws and informal norms had many similarities to those of slavery:

withholding the right to vote, severely constrained job opportunities, and strict residential and other legal segregation. In order to provide a rationale for oppression, the images, stereotypes, and common-sense assumptions grounding the old white racial frame of slavery days continued. Under slavery, whites' framing of black Americans accented the view of the latter as happy-go-lucky individuals who needed and were happy with slavery, but it also included images of them as sometimes dangerous and rebellious, and thus in need of strict discipline and punishment. With the rise of legal segregation, this latter imagery of them being dangerous and threatening was continued, even accentuated, in the blatantly racist framing of the Jim Crow era, with its extensive racial etiquette.[59]

This "dangerous black" representation built on several related depictions that helped to legitimize continuing structures of racial oppression and inequality. From the first days of North American slavery, whites viewed themselves as quite virtuous, and blacks as lacking in such virtue. Over centuries of slavery, and especially during legal segregation, black men in particular were cast as lustful, oversexed beings driven by their baser physical impulses. According to images of the dominant frame, the greatest danger was to white women. The emotion-laden stereotypes and everyday assumptions of the white frame contended that white women were the epitome of purity and ideal womanhood; consequently, they were at great risk of rape and sexual assault from ever-threatening black men. In contrast, and also within the centuries-old racist frame, black women were depicted as highly licentious, which justified their sexual assault at the hands of white men and helped to establish a contrast with pure, virginal white women. As such, this white-racist framing of black Americans as dangerous and threatening was explicitly gendered inasmuch as it cast black men, in particular, as those who posed a particular threat to white women—and, as whites saw it, to the foundation of U.S. society.

Far from being coincidental or random, these emotion-laden images—and the emotion-laden racist framing in general—served a very important societal function. With representations of dangerous black Americans a central part of white framing, whites thereby could justify strict racial segregation as an everyday necessity. After all, if blacks posed a clear hazard to whites, then this threat legitimized whites' efforts to curtail blacks' civil liberties and to maintain the latter's position as, at best, third-class citizens. Furthermore, if black men were predisposed to attacking white women, this provided a justification for the increase in lynchings that took place in the post-slavery days and reached heightened numbers in the years between the Reconstruction of the 1860s and the civil rights era of the 1960s (an estimated 6,000 for the entire era). Indeed, black men were frequently the target of lynch mobs, and the reasons given were often that they had menaced or otherwise threatened white women. In most cases where rape was charged against black men, the evidence was non-existent or questionable. (Though less often, black women and even children were also lynched.) The real reason for most of the thousands of lynchings was to keep black people "in their place" and "under control"—that is, from protesting their oppressive conditions individually or collectively.[60]

Currently, though the specifics of whites' discriminatory practices have changed in significant ways—segregation is no longer legal, lynching is rare—the image of black Americans, especially men, as dangerous and threatening has remained a core component of the dominant white framing. This is evident in commonplace stereotypes and controlling images of black men as criminals, including in the media, and exists on a more micro level in gut reactions of irrational fear and obsessive panic that many whites and other nonblacks have in response to even the presence of black men of most any size and dress.[61] Because this image is such a core and pervasive aspect of the hard version of the white racial frame, it was easily manipulated and used in shaping various political depictions of Senator Obama.

This old negative framing of black men was a key background factor in many negative representations of Senator Obama during the primary and general elections as somehow dangerous or threatening. It is perhaps most clear in the framing of his allegedly dangerous and threatening associates such as Dr. Jeremiah Wright (see Chapter 5). When Representative King argued that Obama's election would leave the United States more vulnerable to overseas terrorist attacks, he relied on the hard white framing of black men resonating in white heads to make a supposedly good case that Senator Obama's election would bring catastrophic results nationally. King explicitly began his discussion of the pitfalls of an Obama presidency by emphasizing his racial charac- teristics and arguing that his "optics" (skin color) supposedly placed citizens in danger. He openly evoked the old frame's images of black men as threatening to suggest that Obama's election would place the country at risk. Hard racial framing is also present in King's implied assumption that Muslims are inherently unsuited for the presidency, a belief that relies heavily on stereotypes. The fact that a U.S. representative could use this old racist framing so overtly and successfully—and without significant media or public backlash—revealed its deep, insidious, and ubiquitous presence.

By linking presidential candidate Obama to Professor Ayers and emphasizing the latter's decades-past tie to the 1960s protest era, Obama's white opponents created resonance with the old white framing and thereby evoked conscious and unconscious images of Obama as the dangerous black man. Despite the fact that, as Obama argued, he was only eight years old when Ayers was involved with the Weather Under- ground and did not agree with Ayers' views or actions, this dominant white framing nonetheless helped in portraying him as an angry black man with links to past eras of radicalism. Connecting Obama to a "'60s radical" evoked imagery of black men associated with that time period—men such as Malcolm X, Black Panther Party cofounder Huey Newton, and Student Nonviolent Coordinating Committee leader Stokely Carmichael (Kwame Ture). The white-racist framing of these men, during the 1960s and today, has intentionally and simplistically depicted them as belligerent, enraged radicals who had no real cause to protest but who sought to destroy the country because of exaggerated racial grievances. Thus, when Obama was connected with Professor Ayers, it served to link him to specific depictions of certain "dangerous black men" frequently associated with social upheaval and unrest.

Finally, the depiction of Obama as a "socialist" late in the Republican campaign also resonated with the old racist framing of black men as dangerous and threatening. This socialist label hearkens back for decades, as blacks who advocated for equal rights and ending segregation have often been branded socialists or communists. Early on, Dr. Martin Luther King, Jr., was regularly labeled a socialist or communist (a charge one still finds on some conservative websites) because of his work with the civil rights movement, his embrace of nonviolent philosophies for social change, and his often scathing critiques of the impact U.S. capitalism had on the poor. As with Dr. King, the "socialist" label is often affixed to African Americans who have sought to create fundamental changes in this country's status quo regardless of their actual political views or platforms. Such terms have long been shorthand for negatively describing black Americans who challenge the traditional structures of U.S. society, either implicitly or explicitly. As Senator Obama came to lead in the opinion polls and appeared headed towards the U.S. presidency, he fit clearly this white-generated political criterion. Consequently, labeling him a socialist fit into a harsh racial framing of threatening black Americans who upset the racialized status quo. This campaign attack presaged similar attacks accusing him of being a socialist that he continued to face once he became president. In Chapter 10, we will discuss the ways that this "threat" issue continued to resurface during the 2012 campaign.

The Hard Framing of Blacks as Unqualified, Naive, and Uppity

The hard version of the white racial frame could also be seen in the depiction of Senator Obama as unqualified, naive, or unprepared for the rigors of the top executive office. In the dominant racial framing, black men and women are typically depicted as less competent, capable, and skilled than their able and knowledgeable white counterparts. This framing is especially common in predominantly white, professional workplaces where African Americans may be the first, or one of few, high-status white-collar workers. Research on black employees in these settings regularly shows that they face a great deal of discrimination, marginalization, and stereotyping. These factors often give rise to challenges and difficulties that negatively affect promotion, job stability, or the ability to perform workplace tasks successfully.[62]

In these work environments, whites' framing of black employees as "not quite ready," "unprepared," or "unqualified" helps to limit or curtail their occupational ascension and upward mobility. In research on the experiences of white women and black men attempting to rise in the legal profession, Jennifer Pierce has described the experiences of

Randall Kingsley, a black lawyer who worked at a firm that enjoyed a reputation for being a diverse and welcoming environment.[63] However, Kingsley found that most of his white male colleagues held the opinion that as an African American, he was unqualified for the rigors and challenges of work in the legal field. These perceptions that he was unsuited for litigation contributed to his difficulties in finding adequate mentorship and support at the firm, and ultimately led to his departure. Although Kingsley met all the stated qualifications for work at his firm, the widespread perception that as a black lawyer, he was not really adequately prepared for the work proved an insurmountable barrier. In numerous research studies over the last two decades, many black men and women have experienced similar discriminatory treatment.[64]

In a study of white men in the U.S. elite, Feagin and O'Brien found that these whites' framing of black men and women as less qualified and competent often clouds white employers' decisions about hiring and promotion in ways that advantage an array of white workers. One white business owner tellingly revealed that when faced with a choice between a black candidate with more experience and time on the job than his white counterpart, he wrestled with the question of whether to promote the black worker:

> Even though I felt that the white male was more qualified than the black male, but not by much, I was sort of at an impasse, it took me about two weeks, but I decided to give the black guy a shot, and give him a chance . . . And everything turned out to be fine. In fact, he's still with me today . . . that and the fact that he was there a couple years more, although I felt that the white man was more qualified, was better qualified is what I should say. I gave the shot to the black guy because he was with me for a few years.[65]

This white employer acknowledged that the black candidate had more experience and seniority (and on those measures was actually more qualified), but somehow the white candidate was viewed as meeting an abstract and undefined standard more clearly. As was the case for Randall Kingsley, the belief that African American professionals are, often by some vague or intangible measure, less qualified than their white counter-parts is a key part of much white racial framing and one that often serves to restrict black workers' employment or upward mobility.

Discussions of Obama's lack of readiness are an example of similar stereotyped framing. As virtually all of Obama's political competitors took pains to paint him as "too unprepared" and "not ready to lead on day one," they invoked a key component of contemporary white framing—the image of black Americans as unsuited, unprepared, and unqualified for high-ranking and powerful positions.[66] Although Obama did have markedly less experience with national politics than his major competitors, this did not necessarily render him "unqualified" for the presidency. Ironically, despite his relatively short time in national politics, he was widely regarded as running a much better political campaign than his Democratic primary and Republican general election opponents. While success on the campaign trail is not necessarily a predictor of success once in elected office, it is worth noting that someone both Hillary Clinton and John McCain asserted was "unprepared" ran a campaign generally considered to be far superior to those run by these seasoned political veterans. As white opponents declared themselves ready and prepared for the presidency, and as they argued that Obama was not, their statements often resonated with the old racist frame asserting that blacks are less competent and less capable than their white counterparts.

Hypocrisy was evident too. When Senator John McCain selected Governor Sarah Palin (R-AK) as his running mate, a woman whose little experience in state and national political arenas was widely acknowledged, McCain argued that her short time as governor did not render her unqualified to assume the presidency if need be, and contended that she had 16 years' worth of history on the political stage. Interestingly, this history included less than two years as governor of the least-populated state in the country, time as mayor of a town with a population of less than 10,000 people, and work in a school PTA. Yet, McCain considered this background more relevant preparation than Obama's eight years in the Illinois state Senate and three and a half years in the U.S. Senate, as well as his earlier years as a Chicago community organizer and constitutional law professor.

As we have seen, some white critics of Senator Obama also accented what they viewed as his "presumptuousness." Like the image of black Americans as unqualified for high-ranking positions, the idea of them as "not knowing their place"—in southern white jargon, "uppity"—has a long history within the old racist frame. Historically, in the South and in the North, black Americans have had to present the appropriate veneer of submission, docility, and complacence. In many historical cases, a failure to show this deferential demeanor resulted in injury or death. At the turn of the 20th century, Ida B. Wells' research into lynching uncovered that in many cases black men were murdered not because they had assaulted white women, but because they insulted or otherwise affronted whites who took issue with their attitudes, economic prosperity, or pride. Black men and women thus faced serious risk and the possibility of death for infractions such as looking whites in the eyes, failing to step off sidewalks when whites approached, or even generally appearing too self-confident or self-assured. It is important to underscore that for a significant period in this country's history, blacks could be killed for showing any visible indications of pride, autonomy, or most dangerous of all, revealing that they considered themselves equal to whites. In later decades, and even in many cases to the present day, black men and women have continued to conceal their emotions of frustration, anger, or annoyance, and even intelligence, from whites in order to avoid significant reprisals. Historically, if they did not do this convincingly enough, the results could be fatal.[67]

This dimension of the hard racial framing has long included a specifically gendered component. For black men, it has often been especially important to avoid displays of many "white masculine" characteristics—independence, assertiveness, and forthrightness. Historically, exhibiting these traits suggested to whites that black men were stepping out of the defined boundaries for black masculinity, an action that was usually punished, sometimes by death. As such, many black families faced the daunting task of socializing their sons to dissemble and be subservient when in the presence of whites, and to be sure to hide any hint of attitudes, behaviors, or characteristics that whites might find unbefitting black men. A contemporary variation on this family instruction is still conducted by many black parents concerned with how white authorities, especially police officers, might treat their sons negatively in public places.

As Senator Obama made key campaign decisions, he was frequently labeled as "presumptuous" or "arrogant." These usually white-generated claims were consistent with the hard racial framing that suggests that African Americans should present a general image of deference and contentment. Importantly, this framing is specifically gendered, in that it depicts black masculinity as ideally subservient and passive in public places—at least, outside sports arenas and music studios. (Black athletes and some musical artists typically do not have to be subservient in these arenas, but they often face censure if this persona leads them to question racial inequality elsewhere.) Thus, when Senator Obama attempted to prepare for the possibility of winning the 2008 election, he violated the widely held views whites have about black men and was once again asserted to be arrogant and overconfident. This election imagery underscored the ways that multiple images of black masculinity are filtered through the hard version of the old frame; when Obama did not behave in accordance with the preferred stereotypes, he was depicted through alternative ones. When Obama came across as proud and confident, even some of his congressional colleagues resorted to calling him "uppity" and labeling him a "boy" so as to reconfigure him into old images of appropriate black masculinity.[68]

This presented a persistent political dilemma for then-Senator Obama. He had to show that he was "presidential"—that is, to project an image of being confident, prepared, even-handed, and decisive. Yet, these particular traits are ones that are incompatible with the hard framing's images of black men as lazy, unintelligent, and appropriately subservient. They are traits that have conventionally gotten black male leaders categorized as militant, ominous, or dangerous. In other words, showing traits associated with the presidency too convincingly meant that Obama ran the risk of being racially framed in negative ways. He had to walk a fine line between showing that he could be presidential and carefully avoiding being so aggressive in his demeanor that he could be constructed through the old racist framing's negative depictions of black men.

For the most part, Senator Obama managed to achieve this by appearing consistently unflappable and steady. After several presidential debates, many political pundits and media commentators noted that Obama's calm, relaxed demeanor—what we call his "cool strategy"—provided a sharp contrast to McCain's visible agitation and annoyance.[69] Additionally, several important political figures, including former Republican Secretary of State Colin Powell, criticized McCain's erratic responses to the growing economic crises and argued that Senator Obama presented much more stable, measured leadership.[70] In a *New York Times* op-ed piece written shortly before the election, even the conservative columnist David Brooks wrote thus:

> We've been watching Barack Obama for two years now, and in all that time there hasn't been a moment in which he has publicly lost his self-control. This has been a period of tumult, combat, exhaustion, and crisis. And yet there hasn't been a moment when he has displayed rage, resentment, fear, anxiety, bitterness, tears, ecstasy, self-pity, or impulsiveness.[71]

Even though he was still labeled by many as arrogant and with other pejorative labels, Obama's unflappable cool enabled him to appear presidential to growing numbers of white pundits and voters without seeming angry or threatening.

This self-presentation was likely necessary for Obama's presidential aspirations, but it also highlights both the complexity and gendered nature of the images in the centuries-old white frame. Because this racial framing usually depicts assertive black men as angry or militant, Obama could never display any behaviors or attitudes that approximated these sentiments. While Republican vice presidential candidate Sarah Palin could make numerous negative comments about Obama, and presidential candidate John McCain could frequently and openly show irritation and annoyance with Senator Obama during the debates, Obama's range of emotional expressions had to be severely restricted. Like many black men who are employed in occupations where they must appeal to whites, he faced a difficult choice of avoiding certain tropes of black masculinity while appealing to others.[72]

Newsweek columnist Jon Alter described this by suggesting that white voters watching the presidential debates expected to see Jesse Jackson, but instead got Will Smith, and probably thought, "I like Will Smith."[73] By carefully and studiously projecting this image, Obama engaged in the cool strategy of aggressive impression management and presented a presidential figure that allowed him to avoid, to a significant extent, certain adverse stereotypes of black masculinity.

As we have discussed previously, however, the consequence of creating and adhering to this image was that Obama could rarely talk about racial issues of any kind. In some of the rare cases where he chose to introduce issues of "race," such as in his Father's Day speech, he chose to do so using a discourse that emphasized erroneous stereotypes about black fathers. Indeed, for many white voters, this was part of his political appeal. In some cases, white Obama campaigners overtly and aggressively sold reluctant white voters on the candidate by downplaying his blackness and emphasizing him as more white than black in his early rearing and values.[74] In these examples, Obama's reluctance to focus even moderately on the severe consequences of racial inequality for black Americans was a selling point. His emphasis on black men's need for individual and personal responsibility, coupled with his silence about the ways social, governmental, and economic policies create conditions that disproportionately affect black men and their families, helped him construct a more or less deracialized persona and to operate using the soft racial frame. At the same time, Obama chose to court black voters surreptitiously in ways that let this community know he valued their support, without broadcasting these efforts publicly.[75]

Summary

In this chapter, we have demonstrated a number of ways in which a very hard racial framing was frequently used to define and categorize Senator Obama during the primary and general elections in 2008. His vocal opponents, Democratic and Republican, as well as media figures and ordinary white Americans, alternately labeled him unpatriotic, too different, dangerous, unqualified, and presumptuous. These negative images shaped the ways he was constructed through the mainstream media and how he was perceived by many voters, because they appealed to the hard racial framing that is still prevalent in society.

Significantly, Obama for the most part utilized a soft racial framing to define himself and to respond to critics' attempts to depict him using the lens and language of the hard framing. A rather bland color-blindness was central to the campaign and was likely even necessary to secure significant numbers of white voters. While Obama emphasized his biracial background and presented it as an advantage in creating national unity, he almost always stopped well short of explicitly criticizing or challenging the openly racist framing some whites used to define him as "too different." Obama doubtless perceived that this option was unavailable to him as a black man running a national campaign in a still highly racist United States. It may have been his sense that attacking the hard-racist framing depicting black Americans as different, and by extension too dangerous for the presidency, might cost him the 2008 election. In this regard, he was probably correct. It is telling that the dominant white racial framing greatly shaped the extent of his presidential run such that using a traditional black counterframe, such as one accenting civil rights, as a major part of his political approach appeared to be a losing proposition. It is also noteworthy that racial framing so infused this campaign that there were times when Obama himself chose to talk about social issues such as fatherhood in ways that evoked racialized stereotypes of black male irresponsibility and unreliability. By refusing to counter the racist attacks, and indeed by infrequently articulating racial stereotypes, he let them have their still-pervasive impact. This type of pattern continued into Obama's presidency and throughout his re-election campaign. In cases that we discuss in Chapters 9 and 10, Obama continued to rely on soft racial framing in response to opponents' efforts to define him through hard racial frames.

Over the course of the primary and general elections in 2008, there was only one incident that forced Obama to confront the issue of U.S. racism head-on. Though he attempted to run his campaign operating largely within the soft racial frame that ignores or minimizes whites' privilege and unjust enrichment—and the consequential unjust impoverishment this visits upon people of color—Senator Obama's relationship with his longtime pastor, Dr. Jeremiah Wright, eventually forced this issue to the forefront. In the next chapter, we discuss yet more hard and soft racial framing, as well as the important counterframing, that arose in this very important case of a black minister "speaking truth to power."

5

THE DR. JEREMIAH WRIGHT CONTROVERSY

Senator Barack Obama's personal relationship with his longtime pastor, Dr. Jeremiah Wright, surfaced as a potentially problematic issue early in the 2008 Democratic primary season and continued to shadow Senator Obama throughout the 2008 general election. This issue proved one of the most controversial of Obama's campaign, gaining significant traction early and adding fuel to opponents' claims that Obama was unpatriotic and associated with the "dangerous black men" of the old white frame. Additionally, the controversy about Obama's relationship with Wright was significant in that it prompted Obama to make his most detailed statements about racism and racial inequality in the United States. In this chapter, we discuss the contexts of Obama's relationship with his now former minister, Dr. Jeremiah Wright, as well as how this issue reflected tensions between a hard white racial framing and the strong counterframe against racism often used by African Americans to survive and thrive in this still-racist society.

Senator Obama, Dr. Wright, and the Trinity United Church

In his personal memoir *Dreams from My Father*, Senator Obama describes his journey to the Christian faith. Raised in a household with no exclusive religious faith, Obama began seeking organized religion in his twenties while he was working in Chicago, Illinois. In this search, he encountered a Christian church that promoted a liberal Protestantism and black uplift, with an emphasis on the traditions of black self-help and individual accountability. Obama made an appointment to meet with the pastor and to learn more about the church. That pastor was Dr. Jeremiah Wright, who would become Obama's spiritual mentor for the next two decades of his life. This church, Trinity United, would become the Obama family's place of worship until early 2008, when it ended under the racialized political circumstances discussed below.

In this discussion we will mostly use the more appropriate educational title for Obama's minister, which is Dr. Jeremiah Wright. Dr. Wright not only has an earned doctorate, but also is a much-published author and the recipient of numerous honorary doctoral degrees. Very few in the white-run media or white punditry have ever acknowledged Dr. Wright's outstanding professional achievements and distinctions or his extensive public service over many decades.

Consider, for example, the Trinity United Church that Dr. Wright pastored and that Senator Obama and his family long attended. This particular church is part of the United Church of Christ (UCC) denomination, a Protestant denomination created in 1957 by a merger of the old Evangelical and Reformed Church and the very old Congregational Christian Churches. Interestingly and ironically, this denomination traces its roots to the earliest white European colonists in North America, the Pilgrims who located in the Plymouth, Massachusetts area. Dr. Wright was, and still is, a minister in the oldest white-created Protestant denomination in North America, one that is today overwhelmingly white in national membership. This is hardly a religious organization that would allow a truly "extremist" and un-American minister to lead there for several decades. In addition, we might add that Dr. Wright's books of sermons are studied by ministerial students in numerous prominent divinity schools.[1]

Trinity United Church has taken a somewhat different course from other churches in the denomination, but it has mostly done so with the support of UCC leadership. It bills itself as both "unashamedly black" and "unapologetically Christian."[2] Founded in 1961, its members are predominantly, though not exclusively, African American. The church was led for nearly three decades by Dr. Jeremiah Wright, who retired in 2008 and was succeeded by Dr. Otis Moss, III. Under Wright, the church developed important ministries, outreach programs, and missions that speak specifically to issues facing African Americans in cities. These have been sustained by a ten-point vision that includes a congregation "with a non-negotiable commitment to Africa" and to the "historical education of African people in the diaspora." Several outreach ministries, thus, have been given names from Swahili, an African language.[3]

In order to get a sense of Trinity United's mission and character, it is important to contextualize it in the history of black liberation theology. Historically, the black church has been a very important institution for African Americans. During slavery, African Americans were encouraged by white slaveholders to embrace Christianity in place of their "heathen" African religions. In the post-slavery Jim Crow era, black churches provided some of the few sites where African Americans could hold positions of significant community power. In the church, thus, black men could become preachers and deacons and fill other important roles that provided a stark contrast to their subordinate racial status in the larger society. (Such leading roles, however, were usually not open to black women, though they did become leaders in an array of church-related women's and community groups.) Certain religious doctrines of the Christian church, specifically the ideas of deliverance and the promise of a better life in the hereafter, were appealing to black Americans who faced brutal oppression under slavery and legal segregation in the here-and-now. Moreover, given the bleak societal realities facing black Americans in the Jim Crow period after slavery, the black church, thus, rose in power and prominence as a location that continued to offer them hope, temporary respite from white oppression, and—especially for black men—some community leadership opportunities.[4]

During the 1960s civil rights era, the political power of the African American church became even more evident and significant. Sociologist Aldon Morris has documented the primary role that African American churches in the South and the North played in organizing and providing spiritual and monetary sustenance that was critical to the eventual successes of the 1960s civil rights movement.[5] During this time, both black men and women played important, though divergent, roles in the church and community organizations that drew large numbers of African

Americans into the movement and eventually led to its success. Religious figures such as Dr. Martin Luther King, Jr., Dr. Fred Abernathy, Rev. Jesse Jackson, and Dr. Fred Shuttlesworth relied on their leadership positions within black Christian churches, as well as the religious messages of uplift and the social gospel, to mobilize black parishioners and generate support for activism in the movement. Black women such as Ella Baker, Fannie Lou Hamer, JoAnn Robinson, and Daisy Bates received much less attention for their movement activities, but also worked within and outside the context of the black church to help facilitate and maintain the extensive grassroots activity that was the foundation of the civil rights movement.[6]

As time passed and the social mood of the country changed, so too did the role of the church in motivating and grounding black Americans' theological orientations and desire for social protest. While the efforts of those involved in the civil rights movement created significant changes in Jim Crow segregation, this movement did not provide the comprehensive egalitarian changes that many sought. The civil-rights movement is to be lauded for changing societal norms that confined black Americans to legally segregated neighborhoods, schools, and facilities, and left them with no power whatsoever at the southern ballot box. However, many African Americans grew disillusioned by the slow pace of the educational, political, and economic changes they sought, and the larger white society's unwillingness to, in the words of the Supreme Court's 1954 decision in *Brown vs. Board of Education*, desegregate "with all deliberate speed." As African Americans began to question whether appealing to whites' morality and better natures would ever result in a truly equal social, economic, and political status, many began to ponder whether more decisive and confrontational action needed to be taken. These questions and debates gave rise to a very important "Black Power" movement.

Although this black movement has been widely misrepresented and misunderstood, especially by whites and certain other people of color, the goal of black power, as it was originally defined by activist Stokely Carmichael (later known as Kwame Ture), was simply for black Americans to have much greater economic and political control over their own neighborhoods, communities, and institutions—something that they had never had.[7] Carmichael and other advocates of black political power believed that once black Americans controlled the social institutions and organizations that had the most power over their lives, they would be better able to escape much racial oppression. This goal, and the aggressive black counterframing that generated it, became central for several African American organizations that sprouted in or followed the civil rights era. One example is seen in the leftward antiracist shift in policy and strategies taken by the Student Nonviolent Coordinating Committee when, in 1967, it became the Student National Coordinating Committee (SNCC).

Accompanying this important social and political shift towards Black Power was a complementary theological development called black liberation theology. Introduced by theologian James Cone, this perspective drew on the liberation theology movements among Catholic priests working with the poor and oppressed throughout Latin America. In two important books, *Black Theology and Black Power* (1969) and *A Black Theology of Liberation* (1970), Dr. Cone developed a sustained critique of the white racism to be found in most white Christian theology and white religious organizations. Dr. Cone and those he has influenced emphasize Christianity's potential for reaching and uplifting African Americans. Specifically, black liberation theology argues that inasmuch as the religious and political radical Jesus Christ highlighted the plight of the most oppressed groups in society, in modern times African Americans are in fact this oppressed group and must use Jesus's more revolutionary teachings to fight for their social, economic, and political liberation from white oppression.[8] Black liberation theology, thus, offers a strong Christian religious grounding for mobilizing black Americans to work towards racial equality and ending white racism.

Importantly, the interpretation of the more radical Christian teachings as a mandate for racial equality is only one part of black liberation theology. This critical theological perspective also stresses the importance of challenging and undermining societal messages about black inferiority and white superiority. Specifically, black liberation theology recognizes well that in a racially stratified, and thus racially immoral, society such as the United States, African Americans are routinely devalued and depicted as unintelligent, weak-willed, and lazy, among many other elements of the old racist framing.[9] This critical theology emphasizes not only racial equality, but also the importance of self-love and acceptance as a means of enhancing self-esteem and countering negative depictions of black Americans that abound in society. Black liberation theology thereby tries to make contemporary Christianity more relevant and liberatory for African Americans and, more generally, to help the Christian faith speak to the racialized challenges and difficulties African Americans face in U.S. society.[10]

Chicago's Trinity United Church is only one of numerous African American churches that are significantly grounded in black liberation theology. Cone himself has identified Trinity United as one of the churches that exemplifies the theological ideals of promoting justice and equality for African Americans.[11] This theological grounding informs Trinity's many field ministries and outreach programs, many of the sermons given, and numerous other aspects of church life. The church has had dozens of ministries intended to help the poor who, in this country, are disproportionately African American.[12] Several of these outreach programs work with those infected with HIV, prison populations, domestic violence survivors, and drug and alcohol recovery programs. In effect, this often pioneering Protestant church "puts its money where its mouth is."[13]

This was the context in which Dr. Jeremiah Wright gave sermons that, when taken out of context and attacked in the white-controlled mainstream media, attracted much attention and controversy. Wright is a staunch proponent of black liberation theology, having been influenced by Dr. Cone's writings. For example, after the terrorist attacks of September 11, 2001, he delivered a prophetic sermon that reflected his grounding in black liberation theology and thus cast the attacks in the context of U.S. complicity in racial and other oppression across the globe. Here, we quote Wright's widely cited words about "chickens . . . coming home to roost," but unlike the mainstream media we quote them here in much more of their sermonic context:

> We took this country by terror away from the Sioux, the Apache, Arikara, the Comanche, the Arapaho, the Navajo. Terrorism. We took Africans away from their country to build our way of

ease and kept them enslaved and living in fear. Terrorism. We bombed Grenada and killed innocent civilians, babies, non-military personnel . . . Blessed are they who bash your children's head against the rock. We bombed Iraq. We killed unarmed civilians trying to make a living. We bombed a plant in Sudan to pay back for the attack on our embassy, killed hundreds of hard-working people, mothers and fathers who left home to go that day not knowing that they'd never get back home. We bombed Hiroshima. We bombed Nagasaki, and we nuked far more than the thousands in New York and the Pentagon and we never batted an eye. Kids playing in the playground. Mothers picking up children after school. Civilians, not soldiers, people just trying to make it day by day. We have supported state terrorism against the Palestinians and black South Africans, and now we are indignant because the stuff that we have done overseas is now brought right back into our own front yards. America's chickens are coming home to roost. Violence begets violence. Hatred begets hatred. And terrorism begets terrorism. A white ambassador said that y'all, not a black militant. Not a Dr. who preaches about racism. An ambassador whose eyes are wide open and who is trying to get us to wake up and move away from this dangerous precipice upon which we are now poised. The ambassador said the people we have wounded don't have the military capability we have. But they do have individuals who are willing to die and take thousands with them. And we need to come to grips with that.[14]

Notice that Wright cites here a white ambassador who also uttered strong words about oppressive U.S. actions overseas having serious blowback in the United States. He is referring to Edward Peck, a white former U.S. ambassador to Iraq and cabinet member for President Ronald Reagan, who criticized the Iraq War and argued that the September 11 terrorist attacks likely occurred because of Osama bin Laden's and other Middle Easterners' intense opposition to U.S. foreign policy in the Middle East, not because bin Laden is just a deranged "evildoer" who "hates our freedom."[15] When Wright's "chickens coming home to roost" words are set in their sermonic context, it becomes clear that his grounding in black liberation theology shaped his interpretation of the September 11 terrorist attacks and motivated him to quote as evidence a white Republican ambassador who is similarly critical of the role that U.S. foreign policy—an interventionist policy that violates some Islamic religious understandings—may have played in these tragic U.S. events.

In addition to media criticisms of this then-seven-year-old sermon, Wright was even more heavily criticized for his prophet-like statements made near the end of another sermon on a biblical text that he delivered in 2003, some five years before the 2008 primary and presidential elections:

> Where governments lie, God does not lie. Where governments change, God does not change . . . Governments fail. The government in this text comprised of Caesar, Cornelius, Pontius Pilate—the Roman government failed. The British government used to rule from East to West. The British government had a Union Jack. She colonized Kenya, Ghana, Nigeria, Jamaica, Barbados, Trinidad and Hong Kong. Her navies ruled the seven seas all the way down to the tip of Argentina in the Falklands, but the British government failed. The Russian government failed. The Japanese government failed. The German government failed. And the United States of America government, when it came to treating her citizens of Indian descent fairly, she failed. She put them on reservations. When it came to treating her citizens of Japanese descent fairly, she failed. She put them in internment prison camps. When it came to treating citizens of African descent fairly, America failed. She put them in chains. The government put them on slave quarters, put them on auction blocks, put them in cotton fields, put them in inferior schools, put them in substandard housing, put them in scientific experiments, put them in the lowest paying jobs, put them outside the equal protection of the law, kept them out of their racist bastions of higher education and locked them into positions of hopelessness and helplessness. The government

gives them the drugs, builds bigger prisons, passes a three-strike law, and then wants us to sing God bless America? No, no, no. Not God bless America; God damn America! That's in the *Bible*, for killing innocent people. God damn America for treating her citizens as less than human. God damn America as long as she keeps trying to act like she is God and she is supreme![16]

Once again, when Dr. Wright's prophet-like statements are placed in their larger context, which is near the end of a long sermon on societal injustice, one sees clearly that he is arguing that in contrast to the power of God, even powerful governments such as that of the U.S. are fallible and transitory and in his view this is especially true of those that fail to treat all citizens equally. Using examples of government-sanctioned oppression in numerous countries as he did in the previous sermon, Wright operates substantially within the framework of black libera-tion theology to offer a religious contextualization of the subordinate and oppressed position of African Americans and some other people of color.

Unsurprisingly, in 2008, most white-controlled mainstream media outlets only quoted a few words from the last sentences of this portion of Dr. Wright's long sermon, and thus quoted it out of context. As such, hundreds if not thousands of news stories and commentators' sound bites intentionally decontextualized and emphasized Wright's words, "Not God bless America, God damn America," and drew unreflective and uninformed conclusions from this rather brief phrase. Even conservative white evangelical Christians have likely heard their ministers speak in this type of prophetic, condemn-evil voice numerous times in their own churches, though the latter probably do not rely on black liberation theology to critique U.S. foreign and domestic policies. In other words, while the specific language and focus may be different, the tone may be quite similar. The media's white-racist framing, however, presented this sermon as extremely radical and distinctive from those presented in similar ways in many white churches.

We might note too that while mainstream media outlets only reported this story of Dr. Wright's sermons in early spring 2008, the story had been on far-right internet websites—along with stories about Obama's alleged Muslim connections and alleged connections to William Ayers and the Weather Underground—some months before it was used by the mainstream media.[17]

Responses to Dr. Wright's Sermons

Once these brief phrases from rather old sermons were aired in an intentionally distorted fashion, the mainstream white reaction was negative, immediate, and intense. Dr. Wright was accused of being anti-American, antiwhite, separatist, and divisive, among other things. Because it was widely known that Obama attended Trinity United Church and considered Dr. Wright a spiritual mentor, Obama faced criticism of being similarly anti-American and divisive. Questions were raised about Obama's personal judgment. Many media commentators and viewers took issue with Obama's judgment in choosing—and remaining under the influence of—a spiritual advisor who critiqued U.S. society so vociferously and pointedly. Democratic and Republican challengers started attacking him for this association. In a press conference, Obama's then-rival for the Democratic nomination, Senator Hillary Clinton, stated that "I think given all we have heard and seen, he would not have been my pastor . . . You don't choose your family, but you choose what church you want to attend."[18] At the time, many voters, especially white voters and other nonblack voters, were beginning to question Obama's specific beliefs, his judgment, and how he truly felt about what they considered to be incendiary, inflammatory, and unpatriotic comments. The mass media distortions, thus, had a large-scale effect.

As a result, the Wright controversy forced the 2008 Obama campaign to confront racial matters—according to his top staff for the first time in a serious and planned way. In an interesting CBS television interview right after Obama won in November 2008, his four top, all white, campaign officials—David Axelrod (chief strategist), David Plouffe (campaign manager), Robert Gibbs (senior aide), and Anita Dunn (communications and research), faced a question from a CBS reporter getting at whether the Obama staff had planned for racial issues that would inevitably arise with a black presidential candidate. David Plouffe, Obama's campaign manager, responded with this unexpected answer:

Honestly, you had to take a leap of faith in the beginning that the people would get by race, and I think the number of meetings we had about race was zero . . . Zero. We had to believe in the beginning that he would be a strong enough candidate, that people of every background and race would be for him.[19]

Plouffe, thus, claimed that Obama and his advisors had not met in advance and planned on how to deal with racial issues that might arise in the 2008 campaigns. However, some other media reports contradicted Plouffe's and others' responses in this post-election CBS interview. According to a *New York Times* report, while the Obama team was surprised by the media excerpts from old Dr. Wright sermons, the team had from the beginning sought to avoid campaign efforts "focused on race. From polling and interviews, the campaign concluded from the outset that it was imperative to define Mr. Obama's candidacy in terms that would transcend skin color."[20] This suggests some early planning on how to deal with at least a few important racial matters. In addition, a *Newsweek* journalist reported that Obama himself had told the journalist that he knew before he began the campaign in 2007 that Dr. Wright's sermons and public comments might be problematic. Obama said at that time that he did not want to disown Dr. Wright because he regarded him as a close friend and his minister.[21]

After a *Rolling Stone* article, "The Radical Roots of Barack Obama," was published in February 2007, Obama also told the *Newsweek* reporter that he decided not to have Dr. Wright give the invocation at the official announcement of his candidacy for president in Springfield, Illinois. (Later, Wright said that an advisor had talked Obama out of allowing the invocation, and that Obama told Wright that this would be best because of his outspoken sermons.) Obama also told the *Newsweek* reporter that he had cautioned his team early on to "pull every single sermon that Wright made, because it could be an issue, and it could be attributed to me, and let's at least know what we're dealing with." But, according to Obama, "That never got done." In addition, at this early point in time, David Axelrod, Obama's chief advisor, told a *Newsweek* reporter that he had sought a "readout of all his sermons," but never got it, and thus was surprised when *ABC News* aired video clips of Wright with the famous "God damn America" language.[22]

Clearly, given that Obama and his team were early on trying to research Dr. Wright's sermons and expecting that they might be a problem, they did indeed see the importance of racial issues for his 2008 campaign. This reality belies their later claims that they never thought or planned in regard to racial issues arising. Otherwise, Dr. Wright's sermons would not have been seen as a potential problem. Certainly, it is unlikely that Axelrod, Obama's chief strategist and a veteran of Chicago politics specializing in getting black politicians elected, had never thought about or talked openly about how Obama's being black might have impacted his chances. His team may not have had specific meetings to talk about particular racism issues and to specify that they thought the best way of dealing with him being black was to minimize it, but according to the early *Times* and *Newsweek* interviews it is clear that some top aides did think considerably, and early on, about how racial issues might affect his candidacy and what to do about them.

In the November 2008 CBS group interview, Axelrod replied to a question about Jeremiah Wright in what seems a rather naive way:

> Well, the Jeremiah Wright affair was probably a pivotal moment in this whole campaign ... We'd all acknowledged that we should have been aware of some of, you know, these tapes were available. We didn't review all of the tapes of Jeremiah Wright as we should have. And as a result we were kind of caught flat footed on some of these tapes. But ... we should have recognized that once that happened that race is such a fascination of the political community and the news media that it would take off as it did, and it did.[23]

Such comments suggest not only significant unawareness about how white racism generally operates in U.S. society among the top white staff, but also that they were thinking out of a soft version of the white racial frame, evinced by their choice to base campaign decisions on the assumption that racism is receding as a significant factor and thus would not matter much to the electorate.

Senator Barack Obama's March 2008 Speech

Initially, Obama himself had no public comments about the growing controversy in response to Wright's pointed sermons. Later, he stated simply that he disagreed with the controversial aspects of Wright's speeches. He noted that Wright was "like an old uncle who says things I don't always agree with" and added that the words generating attention were an example of things with which he disagreed.[24]

However, when the issue continued to fester in increasingly obsessed, white-framed mainstream media discussions, Obama concluded that he needed to address it directly and on his terms. He got his staff to clear time on his campaign schedule for a speech on the Wright videos and racial matters. Axelrod described him as saying, "You know what? I'm going to make a speech about race and talk about Jeremiah Wright and the perspective of the—of the larger issue." Significantly, his top staff reported in the CBS interview that there was no discussion of whether Obama should make such a speech. Anita Dunn, the communications advisor, noted that "probably most of the people in the campaign would have advised against it."[25]

Reportedly, Obama himself worked on his bold speech and created a text that was mostly in his own words. Entitled "A More Perfect Union," he presented the speech on March 18, 2008 in a symbolic political setting, the museum celebrating the U.S. Constitution in Philadelphia, near the old Independence Hall.[26] In his speech, Obama managed to deliver on important objectives. After first speaking about the making of the U.S. Constitution that had once taken place nearby, he made this strong assertion about how Americans had organized against past racial oppression:

> And yet words on a parchment would not be enough to deliver slaves from bondage, or provide men and women of every color and creed their full rights and obligations as citizens of the United States. What would be needed were Americans in successive generations who were willing to do their part—through protests and struggle, on the streets and in the courts, through a civil war and civil disobedience and always at great risk—to

narrow that gap between the promise of our ideals and the reality of their time.

He accented here a recurring theme in his speech and campaign about ongoing efforts to achieve certain American ideals. After some biographical comments about his biracial background, he began some commentary condemning sermon remarks made by his pastor, Dr. Jeremiah Wright. This was a major purpose of his speech:

> Did I ever hear him make remarks that could be considered controversial while I sat in church? Yes. Did I strongly disagree with many of his political views? Absolutely—just as I'm sure many of you have heard remarks from your pastors, priests, or rabbis with which you strongly disagreed ... [His remarks] expressed a profoundly distorted view of this country—a view that sees white racism as endemic, and that elevates what is wrong with America above all that we know is right with America.

After condemning the sermon snippets the media had presented—but not their biased media analyses—Obama added the accurate point that most people have sometimes disagreed with what their religious leaders say. Next in the speech, he noted that Pastor Wright had strengthened his faith and baptized his children and that Wright had never in his presence spoken of any "ethnic group in derogatory terms" or treated "whites with whom he interacted with anything but courtesy." At this point in the attacks on Pastor Wright, Senator Obama showed loyalty to the man who had stood beside him over the years. He then moved to a general point about racial matters:

> But race is an issue that I believe this nation cannot afford to ignore right now. We would be making the same mistake that Reverend Wright made in his offending sermons about America —to simplify and stereotype and amplify the negative to the point that it distorts reality.

Although starting with an important point about not ignoring racial matters, Obama then retreated to the white-framed position that

Wright's critical assessments in his sermons of negative features of U.S. government actions were much too negative.

A little later, he moved to assess the impact of racism by accenting the past. Discussing the burdens of slavery and legal segregation, he made this point:

> Legalized discrimination—where blacks were prevented, often through violence, from owning property, or loans were not granted to African American business owners, or black home-owners could not access FHA mortgages, or blacks were excluded from unions, or the police force, or fire departments— meant that black families could not amass any meaningful wealth to bequeath to future generations.

Following on this discussion of the severe effects of legal segregation, he accented how contemporary black anger over past racial oppression, such as that of Pastor Wright, lingers on:

> That anger is not always productive; indeed, all too often it distracts attention from solving real problems; it keeps us from squarely facing our own complicity in our condition, and pre-vents the African American community from forging the alliances it needs to bring about real change. But the anger is real; it is powerful; and to simply wish it away, to condemn it without understanding its roots, only serves to widen the chasm of misunderstanding that exists between the races.

For Senator Obama, the real anger of African Americans about racial discrimination, while genuine, is contextualized as more a matter of significant past discrimination than a reaction to present-day white discrimination.

Next, Obama tried to balance this comment about black anger over oppression with a statement about contemporary white resentment. After discussing white resentments over job losses, busing for education, affirmative action, and crime, he added this:

Just as black anger often proved counterproductive, so have these white resentments distracted attention from the real culprits of the middle class squeeze—a corporate culture rife with inside dealing, questionable accounting practices, and short-term greed . . . And yet, to wish away the resentments of white Americans, to label them as misguided or even racist, without recognizing they are grounded in legitimate concerns—this too widens the racial divide, and blocks the path to understanding.

The discussion of white distractions is accurate, but somehow legitimate black anger over four centuries of racial oppression, including current discrimination by whites, was counterposed to white resentment over attempts to remedy that discrimination, such as affirmative action. This white-oriented statement played down the continuing reality of racial hostility and discrimination targeting African Americans. As he neared his conclusion, Obama picked up on his major campaign theme of socio-political change, first by again charging Pastor Wright unfairly:

The profound mistake of Reverend Wright's sermons is not that he spoke about racism in our society. It's that he spoke as if our society was static; as if no progress has been made.

Actually, Wright was (and is) quite aware that change is possible and has happened, having been in the civil rights movement himself as a young man.

Somewhat belatedly, Obama then added his only strong statement about contemporary racial discrimination:

In the white community, the path to a more perfect union means acknowledging that what ails the African American community does not just exist in the minds of black people; that the legacy of discrimination—and current incidents of discrimination, while less overt than in the past—are real and must be addressed. Not just with words, but with deeds—by investing in our schools and our communities; by enforcing our civil rights laws and

ensuring fairness in our criminal justice system; by providing
this generation with ladders of opportunity that were unavailable
for previous generations.

This precise commentary would have been much stronger if he had put
it earlier and more forcefully in the section on black anger. Still, Obama
did briefly note the reality of current discrimination, but then played
that down a bit with the "less overt" phrase. (Research shows there is
still much overt racial discrimination targeting Americans of color
today.)[27] Obama did call here for action, not just words, phrasing the
need very much in the tradition of Dr. Martin Luther King, Jr. Yet,
candidate Obama then moved away from this point about discrimination
to reject the view of people who are "breeding division," by which he
meant people such as Dr. Wright, and to emphasize his oft-repeated
option of national unity: "At this moment, in this election, we can come
together and say, 'Not this time.'" And soon he added this point too:
"This union may never be perfect, but generation after generation has
shown that it can always be perfected."

Reactions to Obama's Major Speech

Clearly, Senator Obama presented a courageous speech that dealt more
centrally with racial issues than any major candidate for U.S. president
ever had. He offered the country the kind of optimism most voters wanted
to feel. MSNBC did a nonscientific survey on its website right after the
speech. Some 80,000 people had responded within a day, and two-thirds
thought the speech was honest and dealt with the important societal
issues.[28]

In its presentation, Obama's speech marked a major point in the
presidential campaign where he was able to deal openly with U.S. racial
issues, yet in a way that positioned him as a foil to the typical black
leader who speaks out aggressively against contemporary racism. That
is, he contrasted himself with Jeremiah Wright. A *Newsweek* report put
it in this way:

> But it was a blessing in disguise. Wright gave Obama a chance
> to deal directly with issues that had been the source of whispering

or underhanded attacks in the lower precincts of politics, to take the high road on a matter of pressing national importance but on a subject that can be difficult to honestly discuss. He had shown calm good judgment.[29]

These *Newsweek* reporters, thinking out of a white framing, saw him as acting with "calm good judgment" and thus not acting like the militant black leader that many whites fear. The *Newsweek* reporters also had this to say about the speech:

> He had the ability to empathize with both sides—to summon the fear and resentment felt by blacks for years of oppression, but also to talk about how whites (including his grandmother) could fear young black men on the street, and how whites might resent racial preferences for blacks in jobs and schools.[30]

Again thinking from a white-framed perspective, Obama had properly *balanced* racial matters—that is, four centuries of brutal white racial oppression, on the one hand, with current white fears of black men on streets and with modest affirmative action affecting a few whites, on the other. Candidate Obama himself had played into a soft version of the white frame and recognized that whites are frightened by black leaders such as Dr. Wright talking about white racism. He did not support Wright's accurate and reasoned arguments about contemporary racism and thus again appeared as a "cool" leader to many whites, including influential media reporters. The great weakness of the speech lay in its failure to address head-on the deep structures of racial hostility and oppression that still undergird and pervade all major U.S. institutions. However, it is also noteworthy that neither Senator Hillary Clinton nor Senator John McCain ever touched on these matters of racism. To his great credit, Obama did conclude with a call to U.S. citizens to take this opportunity to tackle racial matters head-on.

"A More Perfect Union" has been widely regarded as a successful political gamble. Many commentators, pundits, and viewers were impressed with Obama's speech and his courage and nuance in addressing a complex hot-button issue. He had taken a political risk by refusing to completely denounce Dr. Wright in the speech, and instead had attempted to humanize him and to put his experiences and words in a historical context that would be more understandable to white media commentators and ordinary white voters.

Even some political opponents agreed that Obama had done an admirable job of this. Former Arkansas governor Mike Huckabee, a former minister and conservative Republican candidate for president, praised Obama's speech and contended that many pastors say things in the heat of the moment that may be considered inflammatory:

> Many times those were statements lifted out of the context of a larger sermon. Sermons, after all, are rarely written word-for-word by pastors like Rev. Wright, who are delivering them extemporaneously, and caught up in the emotion of the moment. There are things that sometimes get said, that if you put them on paper and looked at them in print, you'd say, "Well, I didn't mean to say it quite like that."[31]

Huckabee went on to consider Dr. Wright's racialized experiences while growing up in the very segregated South and how that may have shaped his outlook on racial matters. Though he too stated that he disagreed with Wright's specific statements, Huckabee was one of very few whites who publicly and honestly explored how past and present experiences with racial discrimination and inequality may have contributed to Wright's realistic worldview.[32]

Significantly, as it turned out, this was the only major speech that Senator Obama made over 18 months of campaigning in which he focused on matters of race and racism, yet another signal of his cool strategy of running so as to not contradict the soft version of the white framing that accents color-blindness and the demise of racism in the United States.

Dr. Wright Defends Himself: Further Controversy

Though his historic speech seemed to quell the issue, Obama's public interactions with Dr. Wright were not yet over. In April 2008, Wright gave a speech on the importance of the black church at the National

Press Club and answered questions about his controversial sermons and Senator Obama's reaction. Wright stated that Obama "had to distance himself, because he's a politician, from what the media was saying I had said, which was anti-American."[33] He described the controversy that ensued in response to his sermons as "an attack on the black church," and suggested briefly that:

> Black learning styles are different from European and European-American learning styles. They are not deficient; they are just different. This principle of 'different does not mean deficient' is at the heart of the prophetic theology of the black church. It is a theology of liberation.[34]

These provocative statements reinflamed the controversy, and numerous mainstream media commentators raised anew questions about the extent to which Obama was connected to and influenced by a "radical" Dr. Wright.

This time, however, in the wake of the media uproar and commentary on Wright and others, Senator Obama chose to resign from Trinity United Church. He stated that this was not an easy decision, but that the rash of media attention indicated that certain events at the church would be linked to him, and that his presidential campaign was placing the church and its members under unnecessary scrutiny.[35] He portrayed this decision as the only way to distance himself effectively and unequivocally from comments and attitudes with which he disagreed.

Other Political Candidates and Controversial Religious Figures

Although during the campaign Senator Obama received by far the most public attention for his religious ties, he was not the only candidate who had to negotiate a relationship with a minister or pastor whose controversial views were the subject of media attention. For example, Obama's Republican opponent for the presidency in the general election, Senator John McCain, had close ties to controversial religious figures.

During an earlier (2000) Republican primary, John McCain had once referred to the far-right evangelical leader Jerry Falwell and other comparable leaders as "agents of intolerance."[36] This comment came partially in response to Falwell's many vitriolic statements condemning gays, feminists, and other pro-choice Americans. In one later example of this perspective, Falwell, along with evangelical leader Pat Robertson, argued that these particular groups were actually responsible for the September 11 terrorist attacks. Falwell stated that:

> The abortionists have got to bear some burden for this because God will not be mocked. And when we destroy 40 million little innocent babies, we make God mad. I really believe that the pagans, and the abortionists, and the feminists, and the gays and the lesbians who are actively trying to make that an alternative lifestyle, the ACLU, People for the American Way—all of them who have tried to secularize America—I point the finger in their face and say, "You helped this happen."[37]

However, in a stunning *reversal* of his earlier stance, and one attributed by media sources to McCain's political groundwork for his 2008 presidential campaign, McCain made amends with the religious extremist Falwell, even going so far as to give a commencement speech at Liberty University, of which Falwell was president at the time.[38] Interestingly, although Falwell made very extreme statements about the U.S. government and society in regard to the terrorist attacks, McCain's reconciling with him did not generate nearly the level of negative media publicity that Obama received for the more modest and mostly accurate comments on the United States made by Dr. Wright.

Falwell is not the only controversial figure with whom Senator McCain has been affiliated. Perhaps the most contentious religious leader connected to McCain's campaign was minister John Hagee. McCain openly praised Hagee and welcomed his endorsement, stating, "I am very proud of Pastor John Hagee's spiritual leadership to thousands of people and I am proud of his commitment to the independence and the freedom of the state of Israel."[39] However, Hagee has written that:

> it was the disobedience and rebellion of the Jews, God's chosen people, to their covenantal responsibility to serve only the one

true God, Jehovah, that gave rise to the opposition and persecu-
tion that they experienced beginning in Canaan and continuing
to this very day . . . Their own rebellion had birthed the seed
of anti-Semitism that would arise and bring destruction to them
for centuries to come.

This argument is widely interpreted as a claim that the Jewish people
brought persecutions on themselves. Hagee was also controversial for
statements likening the Catholic Church to a "great whore" and to a
"cult."[40]

McCain initially defended Hagee, but as Hagee's views generated
public scrutiny McCain too had to cut ties with him. Yet, this relationship between Hagee and McCain never generated even 10 percent
of the media attention that ties between Obama and Wright produced.[41]

In addition, Republican vice presidential candidate Sarah Palin
had her own connections to a controversial religious figure. In the intense
media scrutiny that followed Palin's introduction to the national media,
many reports about her family and Christian faith quickly emerged.
One story focused on Palin's pastor at the church she had attended for
most of her adult life. In 2004, during the presidential election between
Republican George Bush and Democrat John Kerry, this pastor
contended that church members who voted for Kerry did so at the risk
of going to hell and stated that he "questioned their salvation." On
another occasion, Palin was in the audience of her church when a guest
speaker stated that Israeli Jews brought terrorist attacks upon themselves
because they had not converted to Christianity, and that these attacks
were appropriate. Video also surfaced of another minister praying over
Palin in her church to protect her from witchcraft.[42] Although for a
brief period her religious ties got some media scrutiny—but far less time
than Obama's religious connections got such attention—Palin was never
pressured to renounce her ties to these religious leaders or to her church.
Indeed, she did not renounce them, despite the ministers' wild and
inflammatory statements about Jewish people, political endorsements
from the pulpit, or offers of protection from witches.

These examples show that over the course of the 2008 election season, Senator Obama was not the only candidate with ties to controversial religious figures. Ultimately, major U.S. politicians are often expected to show that they have some grounding in organized religion, with Christianity being the most acceptable and mainstream connection. Hence, while all the candidates had overt ties to prominent figures in the Christian faith, Obama's ties to Dr. Jeremiah Wright dominated the mainstream media and campaign discussions and became a major issue threatening to derail his run for the presidency.

The Hard Racial Framing of Dr. Jeremiah Wright

The choice of many in the mainstream media to focus on Dr. Jeremiah Wright's statements and his ties to Senator Obama is another example of how the hard version of the old white racial frame regularly shaped Obama's campaign. Both Senator McCain and Governor Palin had strong connections to religious figures who have often done or said very controversial things. All three candidates had ties to religious figures that some people might consider unusual or controversial. However, Senator Obama faced much greater scrutiny for his relationship with Dr. Wright than Senator McCain or Governor Palin did for their relationships with controversial religious figures. This signals the impact of the hard racial framing. Within that commonplace framing, the image of an assertive and angry black male minister is quite strong and negative. Conversely, however, there is no commonplace image within the dominant racial frame of a dangerous, angry, white male religious figure. Thus, Dr. Wright's actions were quickly interpreted by whites through this stereotyped racial framing, and his association with Senator Obama was aggressively questioned as a result. Framed as such, the anti-Wright storyline easily gained traction and prominence in the mainstream media in ways that stories about the ministers associated with McCain and Palin did not.

Much of this focus employed a hard racial framing to characterize Wright's statements. We discussed previously how African Americans are particularly susceptible to a racist framing that casts them as anti-American or dangerous. This aspect of the racial frame was especially pronounced as excerpts from Dr. Wright's speeches became increasingly publicized in the mass media. Conservative commentators such as Bill O'Reilly and Thomas Sowell regularly labeled Wright "anti-American," suggesting that his criticisms of U.S. foreign policy and overseas invasions of other countries indicated a lack of patriotism.[43] Despite Wright's history of heroic military service, his widely studied books of sermons, and his church's deep commitment to social outreach, many people found it easier to ignore the facts and to rely on the old emotion-laden framing of black men and cast him, stereotypically and quite inaccurately, as un-patriotic and anti-American.

In addition, many mainstream commentators argued that Dr. Wright was "rabidly antiwhite," a common accusation against black Americans (and others) who speak out strongly on issues of racism. Once again, a hard framing consciously or unconsciously shaped their analyses. Within this racist framing, as noted previously, African Americans are viewed as deficient, inferior, or morally unsound; and the implicit standard against which they are measured is an idealized whiteness, which has been part of the white frame since the 17th century. In this imagery, whites are more moral, intelligent, kind, and hard-working than their black counterparts. They are generally virtuous as a group, while African Americans are often not. This dichotomy is a major aspect of the dominant racial framing—one regularly echoed by many whites and, sometimes, other people of color.[44] Within this perspective, the idea of whiteness as virtuous, and of other racial groups as lacking, becomes regularized and standardized. Consequently, when individuals of color challenge this notion by taking pride in their racial identity or by asserting self-love, such actions are construed by many whites as antiwhite. When they challenge this norm of virtuous whiteness, people of color are often cast as being antiwhite, rather than viewed as people defying white racist notions that denigrate them. Thus, when Dr. Wright preaches, in accordance with black liberation theology, that black Americans have suffered injustice at the hands of white-controlled institutions and should openly resist, the old white framing portrays this effort to acknowledge the truth of black oppression as something to be viewed as irrationally antiwhite. Once again, unempathetic whites are unwilling to listen to the experienced voices of Americans of color.

African American Counterframing: Resisting Racism

The discussion of Wright as antiwhite raises the issue of whose framing takes precedence and is given more weight in public spheres such as the dominant mainstream media. Although the white racial frame is the lens through which many issues are understood on the public stage, Americans of color, especially African Americans, have developed a strong counterframe that allows them to challenge and question the views and interpretations of the dominant racial frame. For centuries, this counterframe has been necessary for black Americans to offset or oppose the destructive and negative messages about racial matters, as well as the stereotypes, beliefs, and imagery of themselves that abound in the dominant racial frame.

Given the long duration and extensive character of African Americans' oppression in this society, the development of a strong counterframe to challenge old white framing historically emerged as an absolute necessity. White racial framing has been used to justify the enslavement of black Americans, their segregation from white society, violent attacks in the form of lynching and rape, discrimination today in many institutional sectors, and their concentration in prisons, substandard schools, and impoverished and dilapidated neighborhoods. This frame has necessarily included racist stereotypes, sincere racial fictions and narratives, and emotion-laden images of African Americans that are usually negative and very demoralizing. As a result, black Americans have had to create and transmit to new generations a strong counterframe that leads them to challenge widely held beliefs and interpretations that are staples of white-racist framing, one that helps them address and respond to the racialized inequities and discrimination they encounter frequently.

For example, social scientists have observed examples of this counterframe in analyses of black girls' responses to images of ideal femininity in the mainstream media. While white teenaged girls tend to report being negatively impacted by the media ideals of what is feminine, black teenaged girls are largely able to dismiss these media representations as unrealistic and thus average higher levels of self-esteem than their white counterparts. Researchers argue that this stems in part from the fact that black girls rely on cultural standards of beauty that de-emphasize the images that are predominant in the mainstream media and define beauty instead in terms of strength, character, and physical features prevalent among black women. In other words, a strong black counterframe encourages black teenagers to critique the white-centered images of femininity they encounter in the media, while simultaneously developing standards that are more realistic and inclusive. Other research finds that in certain settings, black women also employ a strong counterframe that challenges common notions that black women should compete with one another, that the work they do is unimportant and devalued, and that they themselves are marginal, unnecessary, or peripheral. Moreover, in recent interviews, the First Lady, Michelle Obama, has indicated how she regards these issues from a counterframe as well; she has spoken of how important it has been for her to raise her two daughters with strong positive images of themselves as black girls.[45]

These versions of the black counterframe address gender-specific racial ideas about beauty and femininity that are a key part of the conventional white frame. In its everyday use, the black counterframe challenges numerous other concepts that are central to the dominant white framing. For instance, black Americans often critique the white-proclaimed notion that the U.S. criminal justice system is basically fair, impartial, and infallible. One interview study involving 50 black police officers found that most of them reported racial discrimination as being common both in their own experiences with whites and in their observations of other black Americans who encountered the criminal justice system. They had developed a strong counterframe that saw through the white-racist rationalizations for institutionalized discrimination targeting Americans of color and that recognized their own value and significance. Indeed, such assertive counterframing enables black Americans in various walks of life to see the ways in which criminal justice institutions are pervaded by racial discrimination, and therefore they are often able to develop useful strategies for coping with racial profiling, police brutality, and other white-generated abuses in the U.S. "justice" system.[46]

In addition, the sharp ideas espoused in Dr. Jeremiah Wright's prophetic sermons are yet another example of black antiracist counterframing. Indeed, these sermons were given within the context of a church composed mostly of black Americans and one grounded in black liberation theology, itself a version of a very old black counterframe—a contextual reality rarely noted by the white-run mainstream media. Recall that a key tenet of black liberation theology involves challenging the emotion-laden notion that black Americans deserve the inferior or discriminatory treatment they regularly incur. Because this basic tenet is central to white framing, African Americans have had to develop a strong counterframe that challenges this imagery and draws attention to the deep and lasting structural oppression and inequalities that abound in this society. Black liberation theology draws on an old counterframing that directly disputes these racist ideas and argues that the oppression African Americans suffer on a regular basis can be contextualized and challenged through a countering religious lens.

Given this historical context, it makes sense that Wright would deliberately draw attention to the U.S. government's well-documented imperialist actions across the globe. Viewed through a hard-racist framing, these statements—particularly occurring so quickly after the tragic terrorist events of September 11—are just anti-American and unpatriotic rhetoric. However, when we consider that black liberation theology involves black counterframing against older white-racist framing, Wright's words take on a much different and more realistic significance. Viewed through this historical lens, they can be seen as an accurate testament to the ways in which U.S. foreign and domestic policies have severely impacted all people of color, including those overseas, and thus his words provide a framework for making sense out of the terroristic attacks.

Ironically, however, in his later remarks to the National Press Club, Dr. Wright made statements that were intended to fall within a black counterframe, but in reality seemed more like some of the antiblack framing that whites have used to justify racial inequality. We refer to Wright's statements that "Black learning styles are different from European and European-American learning styles."[47] When viewed in the context of a black counterframing, his statements acknowledging inherent differences were meant to emphasize certain approaches to learning that are often accented differentially in white and black communities. Just because African Americans may utilize some techniques more than whites, he argued, does not mean that these learning approaches are deficient. However, his arguments for significant white–black differences in learning are not supported by social-science research, and he was sharply criticized by white and black analysts for accenting these supposed learning differences across the color line. Furthermore, even though Wright was operating out of a critical black perspective, his point about learning styles appears to parallel the type of argument one finds in the hard version of the white racial frame used to justify racial stereotyping targeting African Americans.[48] Though Dr. Wright adeptly used a black counterframing in his sermons to critique U.S. foreign policy, these later remarks about learning styles serve to reinforce ideas that abound in the white racial frame of innate racial differences.

Most importantly, in challenging the emotion-laden negative ideas of the dominant white frame, such as those suggesting that black people are inferior and deserve substandard treatment, African Americans such as Dr. Wright and their white allies have developed an antiracist counterframe that draws attention not only to structural patterns of discrimination and inequality, but also to white privilege and the nature and mores of whiteness in a racially stratified U.S. society. Black Americans have historically had to know whites and white society intimately just to function in a societal world hostile to their very existence. In contrast, whites have not had to develop a comparable knowledge of African American culture, norms, or society in order to navigate daily life, nor have they had to do this for any other groups of color. For African Americans, then, part of their counterframing involves understanding the ways that most whites view their racial privileges as natural and normal rather than as unearned and unjustified.[49] Understanding the reality of white privilege enables black Americans to engage in a critical analysis of the widespread racial discrimination and inequality that impact them on a daily basis.

In much mainstream media reporting of this issue, however, very rarely did the mainstream commentators and pundits consider that Dr. Wright might have been speaking out of, and in response to, a black counterframe that has been essential for generations of African Americans who must survive daily thousands of onslaughts of racist hostility and discrimination. Instead, the vast majority of mainstream media coverage operated within the context of its own hard-racist framing that cast Wright's words as antiwhite, anti-American, and even in some cases as "racist" towards whites. This last ploy is characteristic of white reactions to challenges to contemporary racism, which is in fact an institutionalized racism cutting across all major sectors of this society. Unlike whites, black Americans as a group have never maintained control of the major social, economic, political, or educational institutions of the United States, nor have black Americans used the power they have had to institutionalize racism and deny opportunities to other groups. Over four centuries, the unjust discrimination and impoverishment that African Americans have experienced has led to the development of a black counterframe that challenges the major tenets of white racial framing by critically examining oppressive racial matters at both the institutional level and the everyday interactive level. In contrast, most mainstream media coverage around these racial issues operated squarely from an old white racial framing and failed to consider, or even acknowledge, the savvy black counterframing that shaped much discourse in, and emanating out of, black communities.[50]

Mixing a Soft Racial Frame and a Counterframe: Obama's Political Strategy

In his well-received 2008 "A More Perfect Union" speech, Obama himself employed some of the counterframing common among black Americans in analyzing the character of racial oppression in the United States. He was especially candid in his analysis of the history of slavery and Jim Crow oppression. This is a very rare departure for a national politician, for most such are content to discuss racial matters through the lens of the dominant framing that is more palatable to white voters.[51] Still, rather than completely couching his remarks in the context of the black counterframe to white framing, at important junctures in his speech he resorted to a soft version of white racial framing, so as not to alienate much of his largely nonblack national audience. As such, while he used this speech to present some interpretations from the black counterframe that challenge the hard framing that many in the white-run media and the white public have used to justify ongoing racial discrimination and to oppose Obama's election, he also employed a soft racial framing that accented color-blind cooperation and minimized the reality of contemporary racial discrimination as systemic, ongoing, and endemic.

Obama began his famous speech with the acknowledgment that the founding fathers' experiment with democracy and freedom was contradicted by their concurrent operation of, and justifications for, slavery and institutionalized racial oppression. Obama then contended that this paradox necessitated ongoing social movements to provide liberty for all in the United States. In doing so, he clearly recognized that U.S. society has not worked equally well for all citizens and emphasized the importance of a "liberty and justice for all" framing to replace the dominant racist framing that has long legitimized whites' racial discrimination and racial inequality. This savvy argument is supported by social science analysis, including analysis by the second author that argues that adopting and implementing meaningfully a strong liberty-and-justice framing is one important way of eradicating the destructive messages of the old white-racist frame.[52]

Senator Obama also relied on the black counterframe when he placed African Americans' sense of anger and betrayal in the context of the historical and ongoing nature of racial inequalities and the concrete manifestations of their existence—including substandard schools, bias in the criminal justice system, and other institutional racism.[53] Rather than place the burden for racial inequalities squarely on the shoulders of African Americans, and argue that they invite or deserve such treatment because of their inferior status—the central arguments of the hard white racial framing—Obama used a black counterframing to highlight the important ways that racial oppression has historically shaped the nature of racial stratification that continues to this day.

However, at other major points in his pathbreaking speech, Obama relied heavily on a soft white racial framing that downplays the existence of structural and institutionalized racism in the present. This is ironic, given that he also argued that entrenched societal processes help to explain racial inequality and African Americans' sense of anger and frustration. But even as he pointed to the racially inegalitarian effects of these institutionalized processes, Obama appeared to categorize the inegalitarian effects as primarily relics of the past (as he did in evaluating Wright's comments) and, thus, he suggested that they are relatively transitory and not really the fault of most contemporary whites, rather than as firmly and deeply embedded in contemporary institutions controlled by whites. He also contended that African Americans' anger at the results of centuries of institutionalized oppression is "not always productive" and often "distracts attention from solving real problems," while at the same time suggesting that this black anger is somehow equivalent to whites' frustrations and bitterness in response to government remedial programs intended to alleviate some effects of this very racial oppression.[54] In this manner, Senator Obama worked within, and used the language of, a soft white framing that underemphasizes systemic white racism and the continuing impact it has on African Americans and other Americans of color. He was, clearly, trying to please his primary and intended audience of white voters, and he was substantially successful.

Conclusion

The major national controversy in spring 2008 over very short excerpts from just two of Dr. Jeremiah Wright's many sermons provides a useful opportunity to examine how both the hard racial framing and an antiracist counterframing were variously used to analyze the issues raised. Overwhelmingly, the white-controlled mainstream media outlets that discussed Wright's statements relied on a hard racial framing in order to cast the story as one of an angry, militant black preacher and to question whether Senator Barack Obama was by association an antiwhite, anti-American black man who was concealing his true unpatriotic convictions and connections. Mostly operating within a white framing, mainstream media commentators chose not to extensively analyze Senator John McCain's or Governor Sarah Palin's numerous connections to radical religious figures that made controversial public statements. The story of Dr. Wright and Obama had much more media and societal resonance because it appealed to certain central images and common-sense assumptions about black men in the four-centuries-old white racial frame.

Additionally, operating within the hard racial frame blinded many in the mainstream media to the antiracist counterframe that was also part of the increasingly heated discourse about Dr. Wright and related matters. Very few mainstream media outlets considered that Wright's words could be construed as part of an old and legitimate antiracist counterframe that helps African Americans recognize, cope with, and respond to the daily onslaughts of white hostility and discrimination. Instead, much discussion and analysis of Dr. Wright viewed their statements only through the lens of a hard racial framing and ignored the black counterframing that provided much different, and more historically grounded, interpretations of U.S. society.

Even Senator Obama, when forced by the controversies to address racial issues directly, responded with a complicated mix of black antiracist counterframing and a soft white-racist framing. His use of the black counterframe exposed some ways in which mainstream media outlets had chosen to highlight the Wright sermons using only the hard white-racist framing. The importance of this should *not* be understated, as Senator Obama is the only major party presidential candidate in U.S. history ever to publicly present and legitimize the black counterframe that runs in stark opposition to the dominant white racial framing. Unfortunately, however, he undermined his message in this regard by later relying on a soft white racial framing to explain African Americans' anger at institutionalized racism today to a largely nonblack national audience. Obama further used a soft framing when he argued that black anger at racial oppression was somehow equivalent to whites' emotional responses to modest government remedial programs that sought, for a relatively short period, to offset the effects of long centuries of antiblack oppression and inequality. Once again, we see how Senator Obama had intentionally operated within the context of soft white racial framing, even when he had for a time bravely opted to address some issues of U.S. racism directly and head-on.

During Obama's presidency, a similar pattern would emerge when Obama was faced with certain black progressive critics. In spring of 2011, professor and activist Cornel West sparked controversy when he critiqued Obama's policies, his connections to Wall Street, and commitments to poor and working-class Americans. In Chapter 9, we discuss in some detail the ways that West's statements also relied on some black counterframing to make sense of some of the problematical policy and administrative decisions Obama took during his first term. In addition, in Chapter 10 we will also see that Dr. Wright again became a symbol of black militancy and target of attack for some Republican activists in the 2012 national campaign.

The months-long controversy that emerged in response to Dr. Wright's 2008 statements threw into sharp relief the importance and significance of the black counterframe in shaping black Americans' responses to and interpretations of various contemporary racial issues. Yet, little social science research has considered whether and to what extent other groups of color employ a similar counterframing in order to cope with racial discrimination and inequalities. African Americans and whites are not the only voters in this country. How did other racial and ethnic groups respond to the hard racial framing used to define Senator Obama? How can the concept of white racial framing be used to understand their voting patterns? In the next chapter, we deal directly with these important questions.

6

THE 2008 PRIMARIES AND VOTERS OF COLOR

The 2008 presidential election was unique for the ways it forced voters, media commentators, and political candidates to talk, albeit often awkwardly and euphemistically, about issues of U.S. racism and sexism. Most of this discussion was white-framed, especially that conducted and channeled by the white-controlled mainstream media. As a result, much commentary and debate focused on racial and gender issues in rather narrow and constricted ways. The mostly white media commentators and pundits paid relatively little attention to any racial issues except those involving white and black Americans, and even then often because they were pressured to do so. In this increasingly multiracial society, such a narrow focus by the media commentators and political candidates was then, and still is, unacceptable.

During both the primary and general election campaigns, the media commentaries and other public discussions typically ignored or marginalized Latino/a and Asian-American voters, including their political perspectives and larger community issues. Media analysts frequently tracked the broad support Obama enjoyed from black Americans, and they often noted the lack of support he got from many whites. Indeed, in several opinion polls some 5–20 percent of whites stated that they would not vote for a black candidate and 40 percent, including a third of white Democrats and independents, openly admitted they negatively framed black Americans as lazier, less intelligent, less moral, or otherwise inferior to whites.[1] Operating with a lack of concern for issues facing other Americans of color, however, the media and other discussions of the role of racial matters in the 2008 campaigns mostly failed to focus on how the Republican Party's harsh emphasis on curbing undocumented immigration would impact Latino/a voting patterns, or how the nosedive in the U.S. economy during the George W. Bush years would influence the voting decisions of modest-wage and other workers concentrated in Asian-American communities in the cities. When the interrelationship of racial and gender characteristics was the subject of mainstream media discussion, the focus was usually on white women, such as those who had originally been supporters of Senator Hillary Clinton but were thought by many to be inclined to defect to the McCain/Palin ticket. Much less often was the focus on women of color, and on the ways in which narrowly framed media and campaign choices about issues of race or gender failed to capture the complexity of their experiences and the significance of their political concerns.

Although mainstream media attention focused on white and black Americans, other U.S. racial groups were obviously involved in the voting process and played an important role in both the primary and general elections. More so than in previous voting history, Latino/a and Asian American voters had a decisive role in shaping the outcome of the presidential race. These groups of color, and others such as Native Americans and Middle-Eastern Americans, are too often overlooked or marginalized in public discussions of racial discrimination and racial inequality, but they are also impacted by the racist images and stereotypes of the dominant white framing. Thus, their voting patterns and political participation can be analyzed with regard to this white racial framing. In this chapter, we focus specifically on the 2008 data that were available on several racial groups—Latino/as, African Americans, and Asian Americans—in order to assess how elements of the hard racial framing and of systemic racism generally shaped both their voting patterns and the mainstream media coverage of electoral events that related to them.

Latino/a Voting in the 2008 Democratic Primary

As the Democratic primary process became a political contest between two senatorial contenders, Hillary Clinton and Barack Obama, many factors likely to make a difference for one candidate or the other were scrutinized by the media commentators and academic researchers. One of these factors was "the Latino vote." During the Democratic primary season, Latino/as backed Senator Clinton by overwhelming majorities. On the day of the Super Tuesday primaries, Latino/a voters were 67 percent in favor of Clinton, a lead that was sustained for Clinton over the course of the long Democratic primary season.[2]

In some ways, interestingly, this pattern was not unlike that of early voting patterns among African Americans. Recall that at the onset of his presidential campaign and throughout the primary season, Senator Obama was a relatively new figure on the national political scene. Senator Hillary Clinton, by virtue of eight years as First Lady and her subsequent years in the U.S. Senate, was a familiar figure with a well-established record and a great deal of support in both Latino/a and African American communities. Consequently, during the 2008 primary season, she was much more recognizable to Latino/a voters and, initially, to black voters as well. Thus, some early Latino/a support for Clinton was likely due to the fact that she—and her political agenda, stance, and leanings—had much more of a political history with these voters than did Obama as a relative political newcomer.[3]

However, unlike African American voters, who began to shift their support to Obama after his decisive win in the January 2008 Iowa primary, a majority of Latino/a voters continued to vote for Clinton for a longer time. Predictably, these voting patterns were viewed by some commentators as evidence of interracial *tensions* between these two particular communities of color. Some media and other commentators argued that because of "long-standing" resentments, misunderstandings, and strain between these two groups, Latino/as were loath to vote for an African American candidate. In particular, observers suggested that blacks and Latino/as had become major competitors for jobs, resources, and other socioeconomic opportunities in numerous areas of the United States. In this competitive context, many alleged that supporting a black presidential candidate would have been equivalent to voting against one's own socioeconomic and political interests.[4]

This is an especially significant viewpoint considering the major demographic changes that have been taking place in the United States over the last few decades. Latino/as are now the country's largest group of color, surpassing African Americans, who previously held that distinction. U.S. Census reports have shown that Latino/as are the fastest growing group of color, now comprising about 15 percent of the country's population, compared to black Americans who are about 13 percent. Additional estimates suggest that by about the year 2042, about half of the population will be people of color, and that by about 2050, whites will be a numerical minority.[5] As these demographic changes have occurred and as Latino/as have become a more visible and influential voting population, many observers initially argued that these dynamics would adversely affect black candidates such as Barack Obama in their ability to curry significant political favor with Latino/a voters.

Yet, despite this widespread speculation that intergroup tensions would prove a long-term problem, Senator Obama generally enjoyed broad support from Latino/a voters after he clinched the Democratic Party's presidential nomination. When it came down to choosing between Senator Obama and Republican Senator McCain, Latino/as generally leaned Democratic and strongly backed Senator Obama. A July 2008 Pew Research Poll found that Latino/a voters were then breaking 66 to 23 in favor of Obama over McCain. National opinion polls in October continued to show a similarly large split.[6] The Pew Center noted that this was greater support than Senator Clinton had typically gotten from Latino/a voters during the primary season. These data unmistakably suggest that the concerns that a majority of Latino/as would turn away from Obama because of racial tensions were unfounded.

This decision to vote for the Democratic candidate was not due to a lack of effort on the part of the Republican Party, which during the previous 2000 and 2004 presidential elections had made a concerted effort to attract more Latino/a voters.[7] Indeed, Latino/as, especially in Florida, had been important to former President George W. Bush's success in the 2000 election. Before and during the 2008 general election, both Senators Obama and McCain aggressively sought the support of this important segment of the electorate. McCain's longtime support for comprehensive immigration reform helped him win backing from some Latino/a voters. However, his efforts in this regard earned the ire of many whites in the conservative Republican base, for whom curbing Latin-

American immigration was a major political goal. This conservative Republican commitment was interpreted as a show of disregard for the Latino/a community and probably affected Latino/a voters' willingness to vote for the Republican. For his part, Obama pointed to his record in energizing Latino/as and building intergroup support between Latino/as and African Americans as evidence of his ability to speak to their political–economic concerns. As many in the conservative Republican base sought to establish strict limits on immigration, then as now many Latino/a voters concluded that the Democratic Party was more aligned with their political interests.[8]

After his 2008 win, Obama gradually generated a mixed review with regard to Latino/a advancement. He built capital with this community by nominating the first woman of color, Sonia Sotomayor, to the Supreme Court. Sotomayor is Puerto Rican and represented an enormous breakthrough as the first and only woman of color, first and only Latina, and only the third woman ever to sit on the court in its long history. However, Obama elicited criticism for raising the number of deportations of "illegal" immigrants to record levels—even higher than those under the previous administration.[9] Despite this mixed record, Obama's 2012 Republican challenger Mitt Romney adversely and seriously affected his own standing with Latino/as with his opposition to the DREAM act, a piece of federal legislation supported by President Obama that would allow children who were illegally brought to the United States to remain in the country without penalty under certain circumstances.[10] Thus, by the time of the 2012 election, Obama did not have a strong record of standing up for Latino/a interests and advancement, but his record was somewhat less negative than that of his Republican rival for the presidency.

Asian Americans and the Democratic Primary

Asian-American voting patterns during the Democratic primary season—and the mainstream media response to them—were similar to those of Latino/as. Like the Latino/a population, during the 2008 primary season Asian American voters generally voted for the Democratic Party and supported Hillary Clinton in large numbers.[11] One important factor in their support for Clinton may have been the recommendation she received early on from the *80–20 Initiative*, a political action committee (PAC) that strives to achieve equal opportunity for Asian Americans by uniting their votes and support behind candidates who will best serve their political–economic goals. Again, Senator Clinton enjoyed the political benefits of being a more familiar candidate, with her years of exposure on the national political scene. Hence, during the early primaries in California and New York, states with very large numbers of Asian Americans, Senator Clinton handily won majorities of these important Democratic voters in the party primaries.[12]

As Asian-American voting patterns mirrored those of Latino/as, so too did the mainstream analyses of their political decisions. Once again, many media commentators and political pundits speculated that Asian Americans were not voting for Obama at least in part because of supposed suspicions and mistrust of black Americans. Unlike Latino/as, however, Asian Americans tend to be portrayed in the mainstream media as overrepresented in professional and other white-collar occupations, and are typically not envisioned by mainstream media and other commentators as working class and major competitors for jobs and resources with predominantly working-class African Americans. Nonetheless, intergroup tensions between black and Asian Americans do exist, such as in urban areas where Asian-American small-business owners have been viewed by black Americans as encroaching on or exploiting older neighborhoods that are predominantly black. Given these community dynamics, in some urban areas the strained relations may have contributed to some Asian Americans' mistrust of black Americans, resulting in an initial unwillingness to support a black candidate.[13]

Not surprisingly, thus, numerous media and other commentators jumped to the conclusion that Asian Americans' initial support for Clinton was likely a manifestation of their racial animosity towards blacks. One noteworthy example was a CNN segment by a reporter that aired on a February 2008 episode of "Anderson Cooper 360." The stereotyped piece, "Asian Americans to Vote for Hillary Clinton Across the Nation," featured heavily accented Asian Americans of different nationalities naming Senator Clinton as their choice for president in 2008. This important story hinted that Asian Americans' racialized fears of black Americans were a primary factor in their decision to back

Senator Clinton. Not surprisingly, this segment generated immediate outrage from Asian Americans and generated a petition that condemned the CNN feature as "a misleading portrayal behind why 75% of Asian Americans support Hillary Clinton." Furthermore, these Asian-American petitioners questioned the CNN reporter's decision to include only people with heavy Asian accents, noting that this furthered the widespread stereotype of Asian Americans as "perpetual foreigners."[14] Overall, the political concern commonly voiced by the mostly white media commentators was that Obama, in the words of a *Time* magazine article, might have "an Asian problem."[15]

As they had with the Latino/a voters, these numerous mainstream media commentators and pundits were inaccurate in their prediction of Asian-American voting patterns. Despite their early support for Senator Clinton, once she conceded the nomination to Senator Obama, Asian-Americans voters generally moved to support the Democratic nominee. A September 2008 poll showed that Asian-American voters were supporting Obama by a lopsided margin of 77 to 23, an even more dramatic split than for Latino/a voters. Moreover, the *80–20 Initiative* reported that Obama had pledged to uphold two important Asian-American goals: eliminating the glass ceiling facing Asian Americans in white-collar employment and nominating more Asian Americans to be federal judges. Senator McCain, in contrast, did not agree to support these remedial efforts to deal with anti-Asian discrimination. These political factors, coupled with the Republican Party's overt and subtle efforts to appeal primarily to white voters, may have been significant in Asian Americans' substantial support for the Democratic Party candidate.[16]

African American Voters in the Democratic Party

No voters of color were more carefully scrutinized in the 2008 election than African Americans. As discussed in Chapter 2, from the onset of his campaign Senator Barack Obama faced an onslaught of questions and speculation about whether he was really "black enough" to appeal to this important political constituency. These publicly expressed concerns were heightened given that, initially, Senator Obama did not generate a groundswell of political support from black Americans.

Furthermore, as the first black presidential candidate with a real chance for national political success, much media attention naturally focused on black voters' array of early responses to him.

Initially, as we noted previously, Obama generated a lukewarm reaction from many black voters. Although some mainstream media analysts attributed this to some sort of disjunction between the "exceptional" Obama and "regular" black Americans—a perspective informed by a hard-racist framing—African American responses to Obama were more complex. Interestingly, like other voters, many African Americans (outside Illinois) initially felt that they did not know Obama's political record, his stance on many key societal issues, or his positions on matters affecting them directly. *Washington Post* polls did not reveal many African American voters switching from Senator Clinton to Senator Obama until late February 2008.[17] This switch may have occurred, at least in part, because of black voters' increasing familiarity with Obama's positions on key socioeconomic issues. An additional factor in this change might have been increased perceptions that the Clinton campaign was using racial stereotypes to discredit Obama. Finally, and perhaps most importantly, many African American voters also doubted whether, in a racially stratified and segregated society such as the United States, Obama could gain enough support from white voters, a realistic concern that was somewhat alleviated by Obama's decisive win in the Iowa primary.

Once black voters began to support Obama in large numbers, some white media commentators contended that these voters were backing Obama solely out of racial solidarity, an argument that reflected much white popular opinion.[18] While research shows that most U.S. voters base their support for politicians on perceptions of character and personal similarities rather than issues, the fact that black voters initially strongly supported Hillary Clinton and did not mobilize around Obama until many months into his candidacy indicates that African Americans did not blindly or automatically support Obama due to nothing more than shared racial status. Commentators who assumed that black voters supported Obama merely because he was black, ignored their early support for Hillary Clinton, and they failed to acknowledge the existence of black Americans who researched Obama's position on key issues and made that the basis for their support. As such, the assumption that black Americans voted based only on racial solidarity served to reinforce racialized stereotypes of African Americans as less savvy, clear-headed, and rational than their white counterparts. Interestingly, though whites often demonstrate reluctance to vote for black candidates (evident even in the results of the November 2008 election), they are rarely perceived by the mainstream commentators to be voting just out of racial solidarity.[19]

Racial Framing of Voters of Color: A Closer Look

In mainstream media analyses of the voting patterns of different groups of color, the hard version of the white racial frame was often in play. Within the hard version of that frame, Latino/as are stereotyped as impoverished, "illegal" immigrants, and as criminals. Asian Americans are represented as perpetual foreigners, docile "model minorities," or faceless immigrants who threaten regions of the United States socially and economically.[20]

Although there are important differences in the ways each of these groups is publicly and privately represented, there are also significant similarities because powerful whites in the media and elsewhere have generated much of the important racial framing of each group, in both the past and the present. For instance, the conventional white framing has historically portrayed both Latino/as and African Americans as prone to criminal behavior and poverty. Additionally, both Asian Americans and Latino/as, including those in the United States for generations, are regularly considered or represented somehow as foreigners. Indeed, all three of these racial groups are regularly cast as fundamentally "different" from "real" (that is, white) Americans. Thus, their patriotism or American-ness is often called into question by many whites. Essentially, the dominant racial framing works to construct all people of color as rather different from and significantly inferior to whites, who are typically cast by whites themselves as the U.S. standard or ideal.

Perhaps most importantly, whites often use such racial framing to pit these groups against each other. Inasmuch as Latino/as are often depicted by white politicians, nativists, and mainstream media commentators as disproportionately "illegal" immigrants, they are also sometimes portrayed as hard-working and industrious, if mainly suitable for low-wage labor. Thus, in contrast to the stereotypes of African Americans as lazy, this dominant framing portrays hard-working Latino/as as "taking jobs" from other U.S. workers, which can mean that African Americans come to see them as a threat. Moreover, the depiction of Asian Americans as docile "model minorities," a white-bestowed term, intentionally serves to incite conflict between them and other groups of color, particularly African Americans. Legal scholar Frank Wu has argued that the model minority characterization of Asian Americans has long presented them as the "ideal" population of color to which other groups of color should aspire.[21] Viewed from the white frame, Asian Americans are constructed as the group that, unlike other groups of color, does not agitate for the "special treatment" supposedly sought by black Americans. This depiction conveniently ignores the racial hostility and discrimination Asian Americans have faced, in the past and present, and thus can generate significant tensions and conflicts between Asian Americans and other racially subordinated groups.[22] Furthermore, opportunities for upward social mobility that whites sometimes make available to certain people of color (such as lighter-skinned Latino/as and Asian Americans), coupled with the hard racial framing that creates and circulates racial stereotypes among all groups, may well inhibit cross-racial political and community solidarity among groups of color.

During the 2008 elections, numerous mainstream media analyses of voting patterns of Americans of color were driven by the hard racial framing of the (usually white) commentators, pundits, and producers who were involved. In particular, much mainstream media analysis and other mainstream commentary cast early voting patterns as examples of tensions between groups of color. For Latino/as, the primary season coincided with the release of a Census report documenting that Latino/as had surpassed African Americans as the largest group of color, and much media analysis speculated that Latino/a support for Hillary Clinton was evidence of tensions between the large and competing groups of blacks and Latino/as. One early 2008 *New York Times* article emphasized these alleged tensions and predicted that Obama would face great difficulty in gaining a significant portion of Latino/a votes.[23] Other mainstream media reports observed that Clinton had received the bulk of Latino/a votes during the Super Tuesday primaries and concluded that Senator Obama, thus, could not get the necessary political support from this important constituency. In a January 2008 *New Yorker* magazine article, a Clinton pollster stated assertively that the Hispanic voter "has not shown a lot of willingness or affinity to support black candidates."[24]

The argument that blacks and Latino/as are perennially in such conflict that Latino/as would refuse to vote for a black candidate is a clear example of hard white racial framing that highlights open conflict between these groups—a framing that likes to argue that all racial groups have tensions in order to take the focus off whites' own racist actions. Furthermore, as *Los Angeles Times* columnist Gregory Rodriguez pointed out in a January 2008 op-ed piece, this viewpoint is factually inaccurate, given that many black mayors and members of Congress represent substantially Latino/a districts and have enjoyed much support from this significant political constituency. One consequence of spreading this political misinformation was that it subtly reinforced the whitewashed notion of Obama as only "the black candidate," which in turn helped his political opponents such as Hillary Clinton to use a hard racial framing to cast him as "too different" for nonblack voters to consider.[25] Ultimately, this hard framing was evident too in attempts to interpret Latino/a voting patterns as proof of a contentious relationship between two racial groups rather than just Latino/as' well-reasoned support for a candidate whose political goals they generally shared.

A similar process occurred with Asian Americans. When Clinton won large majorities of votes from Asian Americans during the Super Tuesday primaries, the mostly white media analysts once again questioned whether this decision was indicative of some racial animosity between black Americans and Asian Americans. This was the driving point of the aforementioned segment on "Anderson Cooper 360" and was the subject of a *Time* magazine article tellingly titled, "Does Obama Have an Asian Problem?"[26] Although Asian Americans' political activity received less media scrutiny than Latino/as, a recurring conclusion among numerous mainstream commentators—that their votes for Clinton were a consequence of antiblack sentiment—remained much the same.

Once again, this argument is an example of the hard version of the old white frame, which views black Americans and Asian Americans as societal competitors and naturally at odds with one another. Asian Americans are routinely depicted by whites as a group that has "made it" just with hard work and education, and that does not face significant racial discrimination. Asian Americans are thus characterized by a great many whites as a racial population that operates in contrast to African Americans. Much white framing presents these two groups as diametrical opposites, but also elevates Asian Americans as examples of how African Americans should behave as a racial group. This omnipresent framing suggests that because of the contrasts in lifestyles, culture, and work ethic, Asian and African Americans are perpetually in conflict with each other—a "fact" supposedly played out by their support for Clinton rather than Obama.

By portraying Asian Americans as a group that has universally achieved socioeconomic "success" and that does not face discrimination, the hard racial frame draws attention away from the racial discrimination and inequality that Asian Americans experience in many institutional settings on a regular basis.[27] Furthermore, white stereotyping masks the fact that the label "Asian American" encompasses a broad variety of nationality groups, some of whom are disproportionately poor and most of whom face substantial discrimination in jobs, education, and housing. While Asian Americans of Japanese and Korean descent may be over-represented in higher education and in white-collar professional work, Asian Americans of Hmong, Cambodian, and Laotian descent are overrepresented among the country's poor and, as a group, do not have the same access to educational and other opportunities as other Asian Americans.[28] The "model minority" stereotyping that is central to the hard racial framing of Asian Americans obscures the negative experiences of Asian American groups with white discrimination and presents the white-generated fiction that Asian Americans are all doing quite well in society.

For Asian Americans, this hard racial framing was evident not only in the way their voting patterns were covered by the mainstream media, but also by what these media ignored. For example, during his earlier 2000 campaign for president, in response to a question about his captivity as a prisoner of war during the Vietnam War, John McCain had stated, "I hate the gooks . . . I will hate them for as long as I live." When pressed to apologize for his use of this white racist slur, McCain responded:

> I was referring to my prison guards, and I will continue to refer to them in language that might offend some people because of the beating and torture of my friends . . . I will call right now my interrogator who tortured me a gook . . . [I can't believe that] anybody doesn't believe these interrogators and prison guards were cruel and sadistic people who deserve the worst appellations possible. Gook is the kindest appellation I can give.

McCain's campaign advisor defended the racist terminology, saying, "If people understood the context, they wouldn't be upset."[29] Under pressure shortly before the 2000 California primary, however, McCain apologized and pledged not to use the term again.[30]

Contrary to the campaign advisor's blithe assessments, many Asian-American voters and voters in other racial groups were quite upset then and later. The term McCain used is a specific racist slur created by whites to refer to Asians and Asian Americans of all nationality backgrounds, not just to Vietnamese prison guards, and thus continues to be a profoundly offensive and disturbing term for Asians and Asian Americans.[31] Like all such white-framed epithets, this term is a way of verbally dehumanizing members of a racial group and forcibly reminding them that they are not equal citizens worthy of respect and fair treatment. Because of its racialized undertones, and the fact that the term significantly predated his use of it, McCain's use of this racist word primarily accents not his captors' cruelty, but the fact that they were Asian. His assertive statements reinforce images of Asian Americans long been present in the white racial frame—that they are unequivocally "othered" and fundamentally different from "real" Americans.[32]

Very few mainstream media sources, including those obsessed with old sermons of Dr. Jeremiah Wright, covered this important story of McCain's earlier and explosive racist commentaries. Major television networks such as CNN, Fox News, and MSNBC did not seriously address McCain's use of the term, and other than the *San Francisco*

Times, Seattle Post-Intelligencer, and *New York Times,* very few news outlets paid significant attention to this important story. Yet, as the columnists who did address this story noted, it is hard to imagine that Senator McCain would have felt comfortable recently and publicly using old racist epithets for Africans or Latino/as if he had once been taken as a prisoner of war in Nigeria or Nicaragua.[33]

This lack of media coverage may indicate white media commentators' and producers' own white framing, particularly the stereotypes of Asian Americans as essentially passive, docile, and acquiescent. One reason that most mainstream media outlets failed to report on and analyze this story may have been because of the white framing that casts Asian Americans as too submissive to raise significant objections. Another might be that inasmuch as Asian Americans are subject to white racial framing as a model minority, the ways in which they suffer from racism are frequently overlooked and given minimal media and public attention. In conjunction, McCain's white privilege seems to have protected him from the substantial media attention that went to other issues, such as Dr. Wright's old sermons. It is difficult to imagine that if Senator Obama had used and aggressively defended a common racist slur for any U.S. racial group, he would have similarly avoided a major onslaught of mainstream media coverage and discussion. McCain's repeated use of this racist epithet received little attention when it occurred in 2000, and virtually no coverage whatsoever during the 2008 election. The old white racial frame, again, seems to be complicit in shaping how mainstream media reporters and commentators cover not only Asian Americans' voting patterns, but other electoral issues that pertain to them and their communities.

Conclusion

The media analysis and commentary on the voting patterns of Asian Americans and Latino/as show that African Americans and whites are not the only groups that whites have subjected to an aggressive racial framing. All racial groups are affected by—and, in varying cases, influenced by—the still dominant racial framing that perpetuates old racial stereotypes and sincere racial fictions about different U.S. groups. Indeed, many of the media and academic efforts to understand the voting patterns of Latino/as, Asian Americans, and African Americans were made through the lens of the old white-racist frame.

Yet, the actual voting patterns of these groups in the primaries or the general election campaigns (see Chapter 7) indicated that the common-place white racial framing was not an accurate means of understanding these groups' political behaviors. Contrary to the interpretations of the hard racial frame, most Latino/as and Asian Americans likely did not vote for Senator Hillary Clinton in the primary because of nascent animosity towards African Americans. Similarly, most black voters did not blindly or unhesitatingly vote immediately for Senator Barack Obama only because of a shared racial status. The fact that upon securing the nomination, Senator Obama received the overwhelming support of African Americans, Latino/as, and Asian Americans in national opinion polls suggests that, by and large, members of these groups felt that he was a stronger political candidate and one much more attuned to their political and economic goals than Senator McCain.

In a more subtle fashion, even the character of the media and other public coverage of these diverse U.S. groups reinforced the hard version of the old white frame. The common argument by white commentators and others that racial loyalties or intergroup divisions were necessarily primary factors shaping these important voting decisions is itself indicative of a common white framing that casts people of color as somehow more contentious and less intelligent and moral than whites. Media characterizations frequently played into a hard racial framing suggesting that whites were more clear-headed, logical, and politically rational than people of color, whose votes they assumed were determined primarily by a blind racial loyalty or traditional intergroup animosity. In contrast, mainstream media sources very rarely developed a significant media analysis arguing that many whites were supporting Senator McCain only because he was white. This fact is rather ironic, given that some of the same mainstream news sources occasionally acknowledged that many whites openly stated or implied in various opinion polls that they would *not* vote for Senator Obama because he was black.[34]

One logical conclusion from these national poll data, then, was that these many whites actually were voting for McCain mainly because he was white. However, most mainstream media sources refrained from describing many white voters as substantially driven by their racial fears, prejudices, and stereotypes. Indeed, when they did touch on the related subject of some whites telling pollsters they would vote for a black candidate, yet not doing so in the voting booth, numerous media commentators tiptoed around this political reality and used euphemisms such as the "Bradley effect" or the "Wilder effect," rather than the more accurate term, the "white racism effect." Most mainstream media commentators regularly seem to have much trouble in seriously discussing the persisting reality of contemporary racism in the United States.

7
NOVEMBER 4, 2008:
A DRAMATIC DAY IN U.S. HISTORY

Senator Barack Obama's win in November 2008 was extraordinarily unlikely by U.S. historical standards. He was the first African American to have a serious chance of winning the general presidential election, and he and his team in fact pulled it off on the first try. The mainstream news media heralded it as such, as in this MSNBC report: "Barack Obama, a 47-year-old first-term senator from Illinois, shattered more than 200 years of history Tuesday night by winning election as the first African American president of the United States."

The MSNBC report further noted just how huge the celebrations were in Obama's hometown of Chicago and in many other towns and cities, including some overseas:

> A crowd of nearly a quarter-million jammed Grant Park and the surrounding area in Chicago, where Obama addressed the nation for the first time as its president-elect at midnight ET. Hundreds of thousands more . . . watched on a large television screen outside the park.[1]

How were Senator Obama and his political team able to pull off this spectacular feat in a society where racial hostility and discrimination are still systemic and often devastating in their everyday impacts on African

Americans and other Americans of color? In this chapter, we will consider this question and related questions about the reality of this very historic presidential election.

Voting for Obama

In the 2008 election, Senator Obama won 52.9 percent of the total national vote, compared to 45.7 percent for Senator McCain. This resulted in a 365–173 electoral vote victory.[2] A principal reason that Senator Obama was able to win the national vote and the electoral vote is the growing size of the population of Americans of color. U.S. Census projections indicate that by 2042 or so, half the population will be Americans of color, and soon thereafter they will significantly outnumber whites. Today, Americans of color make up a third of the population, and a large and growing proportion (about 26 percent in 2008) of voters in national elections. Significantly, if the demographic distribution of 2008 voters by racial group had been about what it was in 1988 or before, when voters of color were a more modest percentage of voters, Senator Obama would probably not have won the election. This is a central story of this election rarely told in the mainstream media or by other mainstream political observers.

Patterns of Voting: Voters of Color

Consider these striking results from the ABC News polls of voters as they exited their polling places in November 2008:[3]

	Obama (%)	McCain (%)	Other Candidates (%)
White Americans	43	55	2
Black Americans	95	4	1
Latino Americans	67	31	2
Asian Americans	62	35	3
Other Americans	66	31	3

White Americans gave Senator Obama much less than a majority of their votes, but voters of color more than made up for the deficit. While many media commentators and pundits thought Obama would have significant difficulty with voters of color, these data suggest how wrong they were. Not only did an overwhelming majority of African Americans vote for Senator Obama, but a large percentage of other Americans of color also voted for him. Nationally, Latino/a voters gave him fully two-thirds of their votes, while Asian Americans were just a little less, with other voters of color as a group also at two-thirds. In addition, some high-density Asian-American counties on the West Coast voted at even higher rates of about 70 percent for Senator Obama, while data for counties that have large Indian communities in the states of North Dakota, South Dakota, Nebraska, Montana, Nevada, New Mexico, and Colorado showed estimated percentages for Senator Obama ranging 62 to 87 percent.[4]

Turnout among voters of color was significant, especially when considered in relationship to whites. Black turnout was up, and the black share of total vote increased from 11 to 13 percent from 2004 to 2008. One important voter organization, *Project Vote*, estimated that compared to the 2004 election, the number of presidential ballots cast in 2008 increased by more than one-fifth among black Americans and by one-sixth among Latino/as, yet decreased by 1 percent for white voters.[5] The excitement over Senator Barack Obama's candidacy likely accounted for the modest increase in the overall turnout of the U.S. voting eligible population.[6]

The substantial vote by African American voters in 2008 was both centrally important and clearly expected but, as noted previously, less expected by mainstream media commentators was the large-scale voting for Obama by other citizens of color. One conspicuous feature of this pathbreaking election is the importance of the rapidly growing Latino/a population to Democratic Party candidates. Latino/as now make up approximately 15 percent of the U.S. population and, thus, are the country's largest group of color. This group is now producing ever-growing numbers of voters in numerous states. Highly energized by being able to participate in state and federal elections, since 2004 these Latino/a voters have increased their share of the Democratic Party electorate substantially.[7] As with the Democratic primaries discussed in Chapter 6, the tensions between black and Latino/a communities cited by various observers did not appear significant for voting in the 2008 election. Andres Ramirez, a legislative consultant, has pointed out that the Latino/a percentage of the electorate going for Obama was greater than his winning margin in both Florida and New Mexico.[8] Significantly, one conservative white analyst agreed on the larger impact of voters of color:

> Who would have suspected that African Americans and Hispanics would have forged a bulletproof alliance? But they did . . . 2008 might have birthed a very significant new voting bloc for the future—one that is already 30% of the population and growing.[9]

Across the political spectrum, commentators have noted the major political problems arising out of these voter patterns in this 2008 election for the future of the Republican Party.

We should note too the role of youth of color in Obama's margin of victory. In this election, young voters (those aged 18–29) were disproportionately black and Latino/a (32 percent) compared to the black and Latino/a percentage (21 percent) in the electorate as a whole.[10]

Whites For Obama in 2008: Who Were They?

A significant minority of white voters, a bit more than four in ten nationally, were clearly important to Senator Obama's 2008 victory. Some 18 of the 50 states, plus the District of Columbia, provided Obama with slight to significant white majorities. Who were these whites?

Certain white groups were especially numerous in voting for Senator Obama. One was Jewish Americans. In the first months of the general election, numerous media commentators and other political analysts argued that Senator Obama would have serious problems with many Jewish voters because of his views on the Middle East and conflicts there.[11] Republican-oriented groups targeted Jewish voters with provocative advertisements seeking to generate significant fear about Obama's policies towards Middle Eastern crises and Israel, but these efforts had little effect. Obama made efforts to address this, in part through continued statements emphasizing his support for Israel as a Jewish state. Summarizing the patterns in Jewish-American voting, the National Jewish Democratic Council prepared an important analysis with this revealing title: "2008 Jewish Vote for Obama Exceeds All Expectations." According to exit polls in states where the religion of voters was available, the Jewish-American vote for the Democratic candidate was about the same as it was for previous elections—about 78 percent.

Historically, Jewish Americans have provided the most support among whites for civil rights efforts such as the creation and sustenance of the NAACP, the 1964 Freedom Summer in the South, and the passage of major civil rights laws. One reason for this commitment among many Jewish Americans to civil rights is their own experience with long centuries of racialized oppression overseas and in the United States. As immigrants to the United States from the 1840s to the early 1900s, European Jews were not initially considered white, but were often treated as an "inferior race" by north-European whites who dominated U.S. society on their arrival. Jewish Americans still experience significant anti-Semitism, and members of white supremacist groups often still do not consider them "white" (or "white enough") and periodically engage in anti-Semitic vandalism and other violence. Thus, the old civil rights alliance held up well in the 2008 election.[12]

Young white voters were also important to the Obama victory. They helped to provide the margin for him to win difficult and surprising victories in Indiana and North Carolina. In addition, they and young voters of color provided much essential canvassing work for the campaign.[13] The increase in numbers and turnout for all young voters was particularly important because these young voters shifted significantly in the direction of the Democratic Party, from just over half for Kerry in 2004 to more than two thirds for Obama in 2008. This latter figure for a candidate sets the youth-vote record for all previous presidential candidates for which data are available. The majority of these youthful voters were white, and among these whites some 54 percent voted for Obama, a considerably larger percentage than for all other whites. At the time, some political analysts suggested these data represented a significant political shift among young voters, a generational shift that might bode well for Democratic candidates in the future.[14]

White Motivations: "An Exception to His Race"?

Clearly, some whites were pleased to vote for Senator Obama because their antiracist views coincided with their political inclinations. These whites rejected at least some significant elements of the conventional white racial framing. Indeed, researchers found that white voters who expressed low levels of racial prejudice voted in 2008 for Senator Obama in substantially larger numbers than such voters had in previous elections that offered a viable black candidate.[15]

Yet, other white voters, who still operated mostly out of a conventional racial frame, appear to have developed important rationalizations that allowed them to vote for Obama in 2008. One reason that Obama got many white voters appears to be that they came to see him as "an exception to his race," an old notion that has been part of the white frame since the 17th century. That is, they did not see him as "typically black" in the negative senses imbedded in the old white-racist frame. This exception-to-his-race approach seems to work because it makes whites more comfortable with a particular black person. Thus, one white polling commentator suggested that there is a continuum of white racist thought and that "many, or perhaps even most, white voters are a little bit racist, but for relatively few is race a complete deal-breaker. Many of them will vote for you if you're actively soliciting their votes, and they've had time to grow comfortable with you."[16] Thus, it would seem that Obama's efforts to portray himself within the soft racial frame as a more "acceptable" black candidate, which we discussed in Chapter 2, may have paid off with voters inclined to view him through this softer racial framing.

Whether "race" is a deal-breaking factor in a white voter's decision is likely related to whether the candidate is successful in making such whites comfortable with him or her. In 2008, Obama did take significant steps, as we noted, to provide a "cool" and comforting stance. Thus, one *New York Times* report stated that many white voters were glad to see Obama's detachment from traditional civil rights issues and black leaders who pressed for racial change. For example, one white volunteer in

Alabama reportedly spoke to fellow whites at a local church, and with approval, about how Senator Obama "doesn't come from the African American perspective—he's not of that tradition . . . He's not a product of any ghetto."[17]

Apparently, many whites supported Senator Obama because he did not exhibit the perspective of veteran black civil rights leaders. Indeed, Obama was careful—with the exception of his major Philadelphia speech—not to talk too openly or substantially about racial hostility and discrimination, the venerable black civil rights agenda, or the need for government to vigorously enforce civil rights laws. Thomas Edsall has noted how his 2008 campaign rhetoric was also skewed towards white views of government programs:

> Throughout 2008, the Obama campaign carefully avoided or muted discussion of such volatile issues as affirmative action and redistributive 'transfer' programs for the poor, while stressing repeatedly that the overwhelming majority of people would see their taxes cut, not raised.[18]

Generally speaking, a black candidate running in an election where whites predominate cannot talk candidly about many racialized issues of concern to Americans of color.

Another theme that came up in some media interviews with white Obama supporters was that they saw him as being "sort of white." These supporters accented to themselves and to those whites they canvassed for votes that Obama was raised mostly by whites, by a white mother from Kansas and white grandparents in Hawaii. For example, a white Obama volunteer in a western state was quoted in the *New York Times* about her encounter with a white voter who was considering a vote for Obama. The latter reportedly said:

> I don't want to sound like I'm prejudiced. I've never been around a lot of black people before. I just worry that they're nice to your face but then when they get around their own people you just have to worry about what they're going to do to you.

In this case, we see not only the societal reality that many whites have had no significant equal-status contacts with black Americans, but also the importance of conventional stereotypes from the white frame.[19] Additionally, this voter emphasizes the potential threat that blacks pose to whites. Note her concern "about what they're going to do to you." This idea of black Americans as threatening is another key aspect of the hard racial framing, as discussed in Chapter 4.

Reportedly drawing on the canvassing approach of trying not to make voters mad, the white volunteer replied to her thus: "One thing you have to remember is that Obama, he's half white and he was raised by his white mother. So his views are more white than black really." The volunteer thus assured the voter that Obama was acceptable because of his substantial white ancestry and white relatives' socialization. It is likely that this view of Senator Obama was common among many white voters, but to our knowledge no one in or outside of the mainstream media researched this motivational issue during the 2008 campaign. This white volunteer also recounted to this voter that she herself was now comfortable with Senator Obama and did not notice his skin color any more.[20] Reacting to criticism later, this volunteer also explained that she had to quickly respond to the white voter she was canvassing and could have had a better comeback if she had more time, adding that "Obama is the best candidate to run for President since I have been voting."[21]

After the election, this theme of Obama's white ancestry was given major attention in explaining the outcome. Just minutes after the result was clear, for example, a Fox News commentator put it this way: "Let's not forget that he is not only the first African American president, but the first biracial candidate. He was raised by a single white mother." On a BBC News program, journalist Christopher Hitchens asserted that "We do not have our first black president. He is not black. He is as black as he is white."[22]

Ironically, while Obama's lighter skin and "mixed race" background had made him anathema to some whites operating openly out of that hard version of the white frame, as we note below, for other whites his part-white ancestry evidently helped mitigate the fact of his blackness in order to make him a viable presidential candidate. This probably accounts for why it was somewhat easier for Obama to work out of the soft racial framing and be seen by many white voters as acceptable. His relatively light complexion probably made him an easier "sell" for some whites than would have been the case if he were very dark. Had Obama been a darker-skinned black man, he might have faced greater difficulty in escaping some "dangerous black man" characterizations that are part of the white racial frame. To this point, research on the impact of skin color and distinctive "black features" has shown that in court proceedings white judges tend to give harsher sentences to darker-skinned African Americans than lighter-skinned African Americans with similar records.[23] This is one important indicator of just how the venerable "exception to one's race" thinking probably works in everyday white practice.

However, when it comes to whites' racial framing, skin color does not exist apart from other factors. The social or political perspective of the black person being examined can play a decisive role in whether they are considered "dangerous." Thus, even though he was relatively light skinned, Malcolm X was once considered by most whites to be a dangerous black man because of his outspokenness, strong critiques of white racism, and Muslim faith. Regardless of their actual skin color, almost all black men must deal with this dangerous-man image in white minds. It appears that many white voters who went for McCain had some such image in their minds, as we will show in the next chapter. Other whites, who voted for Obama, somehow accepted a counter-image of him as an "exception to his race," an image he periodically played into, and this worked greatly to his political advantage.

Other Important Factors in the Obama Victory

Other factors contributed significantly to why Senator Obama won the 2008 election. One obvious and major reason for Obama's victory was the extraordinarily serious decline in the economy over the months leading up to the 2008 election. One survey conducted during November 1–5, 2008 asked more than a thousand registered voters across the United States about how they had been affected by this economic crisis. Among the 22 percent of the respondents who said the crisis had impacted them in a major way, some 59 percent indicated that they were voting for

Obama. Exit polls on the day of the election showed a similar pattern. It seems probable that without the especially severe economic crisis of 2007–2008, Obama's being black would have been the proverbial "deal-breaker" for many white voters, and more would probably have voted for John McCain.[24]

Yet, other factors related to the general political landscape likely helped facilitate Obama's win. Towards the end of 2008, in part because of inept actions to correct the rapidly imploding economy, President George W. Bush experienced the lowest approval numbers ever recorded for a sitting president. Indeed, mainstream media commentators, historians, and political pundits debated whether Bush would go down in history as one of the worst U.S. presidents. Candidate John McCain was tied to this Republican president and to a party that during eight years in power had not only overseen the move to a near-depression economy, but also conducted incompetent responses to Hurricane Katrina, politically motivated firings of U.S. attorneys, and a war widely thought to be unnecessary and an enormous financial drain. For his part, McCain's pick of Governor Sarah Palin as a vice presidential running mate also may have helped to mobilize support for Obama, as she proved unpopular with many independent voters.

Clearly, too, the Obama campaign was one of the best organized and most effective in outreach to voters in recent decades. It made great use of new internet technologies and organizations, such as Moveon.org and Facebook, for extensive outreach efforts, which were generally effective in broadening the base for the Democratic Party, especially among the youthful voters who are more internet-oriented. The Obama campaign and the Democratic Party generally put more effort into contacting voters in most states, and these efforts were also successful. Thus, exit poll data indicate that in this election, only 18 percent of voters reported being contacted by the McCain campaign, as compared to 24 percent for the Bush campaign in 2004. This McCain figure was also lower than the 26 percent who reported being contacted by the Obama campaign in 2008. Thus, an array of other important economic, social, and people factors played some role in Senator Obama's remarkable success in the 2008 election.[25]

Other White Voters

If it had been up to white Americans, however, Senator John McCain would have easily become the 44th president of the United States. According to exit poll data, McCain won the white vote in a substantial majority (32) of the 50 states. He garnered very large percentages of white voters in some states—more than 60 percent in 16 states. In contrast, Obama got equally high percentages of white voters in only two states, Vermont and Hawaii.[26] Any observer who paid attention to opinion polls over the months before the general election should have seen this result coming. Over this entire period, the public opinion polls consistently showed Senator McCain leading Senator Obama among white voters nationally. Thus, in early October 2008, the Research 2000 organization's polls found that Obama led Senator McCain among all registered voters, but was way behind among white voters—a 52–40 percent split in favor of McCain. At no point over the long months from Obama's announcement to his election were a majority of white voters inclined to vote for Obama.[27] To our knowledge, from the November 2008 election to the present day, no analyst in the mainstream media has yet explored in serious analytical detail this landslide white vote for Senator McCain and what it might mean for the social and political future of the United States.

Who Were These White Voters?

Who were the whites who voted against Obama? Significantly, the lowest white percentages for Obama were in states with the highest percentages of black voters. Researcher Charles Franklin did a state-by-state analysis of exit polls in regard to how the percentage of whites voting for Obama varied by the percentage of blacks voting for him. He found that in states where black voters were less than a fifth of the total voters, the percentage white for Obama was variable (30–60) and did not relate to the percent of the black vote for Obama. However, in the three states—Alabama, Louisiana, and Mississippi—where the black percentage was the highest, more than a fifth, the white percentage was remarkably low, just 10–14 percent.[28] In these Deep South states and in the states of Georgia, South Carolina, Texas, and Oklahoma, fewer than 30 percent of white voters opted for Senator Obama. In addition, the states of Arkansas, Alaska, Utah, and Wyoming had only slightly higher percentages for Obama, all under a third. Most significantly, perhaps, Obama lost the white vote in ten states whose electoral votes he actually won—the southern states of North Carolina, Virginia, and Florida; the northern states of Pennsylvania, Indiana, Ohio, Maryland, and New Jersey; and the southwestern states of Nevada and New Mexico. Senator Obama would not have won the popular and electoral votes in these states without the large percentages of voters of color who opted for him, and without some number of these states (for example, just Pennsylvania, Ohio, Florida, North Carolina, and Virginia) he would have lost the general election to Senator McCain.[29]

While a majority of whites nationally voted for Senator McCain, certain white groups were even more likely than whites as a group to give their votes to McCain. Thus, white Protestant voters, especially evangelical and "born again" voters, voted very substantially for McCain. According to a national survey at the time of the November 2008 election, white voters who said they were "born again" Christians were giving McCain nearly three-quarters of their votes, while those whites who were not "born again" were providing him just 56 percent of their votes. Those who said they were "absolutely committed to Christianity" were giving McCain some 59 percent of their votes. In contrast, black and Latino/a "born again" voters were no different from other black and Latino/a voters in voting heavily for Senator Obama. One conservative analysis of this national survey has rationalized the sharply divergent racial pattern for otherwise similar religious groups with the racially biased conclusion that these white voters for McCain were "more affected by their understanding [of] the candidates' moral positions and political experience than were other voters."[30] Note here the implication that white voters are more likely to make political decisions out of logic, sound reasoning, and judicial thinking than voters of color.

It also seems likely, given our analysis above and in previous chapters, that many white voters voted for McCain, at least in part, for racial reasons. They did not see Obama as a positive figure, even as an "exception to his race." Still, some media and other political analysts have tried to rationalize the reality of a minority of white voters going to Obama as something with no social or racial significance. For instance, numerous analysts have accented the point that in 2004, John Kerry lost somewhat more of the white vote than Barack Obama did in 2008 to argue that such data prove there was no racial factor in the 2008 white vote. Obama's racial deficit of 12 percent (43 percent of white voters versus McCain's 55 percent) was close to the 13 percent deficit for Al Gore in 2000, but less than the 17 percent deficit for John Kerry in 2004.

However, this argument shows a lack of knowledge or reflection about recent U.S. political history. For one thing, Al Gore and John Kerry ran campaigns in years (2000 and 2004) of relatively good economic conditions for most white voters. Whites did not have nearly as many good economic and other reasons to vote for the Democratic candidate in those years as they did in late 2008. Nonetheless, in the midst of the worst economic recession since the 1930s, with many of their retirement accounts down by at least 30 percent, with many losing health-care coverage, with the country involved in a very unpopular war, with the most unpopular president in living memory, with the Republican brand in poor repute, and with an extraordinarily capable Democratic candidate running one of the best-organized and most technologically savvy campaigns in history, a substantial majority of whites still gave Senator McCain their presidential votes. Thus, to compare Obama's percentage of the white vote to Kerry's, Gore's, or Clinton's is to ignore the many significant political and economic factors that favored Obama but were unavailable to any of his immediate white Democratic predecessors. That these converging issues still were not enough to compel even a bare majority of white voters to support him escaped most media commentators' critical attention and analysis.

In addition, all Democratic presidential candidates since the Voting Rights Act of 1965, which finally liberated large numbers of excluded black voters in numerous states, appear to have been seen as "too black oriented" by many whites. The reason for this lies in the growing number of black voters, party officials, and elected officials in the Democratic Party and in the Democratic Party's stated commitments to expanded civil rights and affirmative action since the late 1960s. Nonetheless, although these factors have led to the Democratic Party being identified among many whites as "too black oriented," few recent Democratic officials, especially at the national level, have openly pushed for strong and decisive legislative measures that would help aggressively eliminate racial discrimination and inequality in society.

At any rate, given these white fears and framing, no Democratic candidate has gotten a majority of white voters since the 1964 election of Lyndon Johnson. Both Al Gore and John Kerry lost majorities of the white vote because they were, in this sense, seen by many white voters as "too black oriented" or part of a "too-black party." Thus, most contemporary political analysts who argue that Senator Obama did the same as Gore, or better than Kerry, with white voters often miss the point that all three of these Democratic Party candidates were seen by many white voters as much too linked to the goals and interests of black Americans, including the civil rights agenda. All three lost the white vote in a "landslide," which suggests that all may have had a serious problem with voters operating out of a strong white frame. Note too that, compared to the Republican candidate, Senator Obama got a significantly *lower* percentage of white voters (12 percent less than his opponent) than did the other recent winning Democratic presidential candidates, Jimmy Carter (4 percent less in 1976) and Bill Clinton (2 percent less in 1992 and 1996).[31]

Whites Against Obama: Some Voters' Views and Actions

In local, state, and national political campaigns since the 1960s, the Republican Party has often aggressively represented and courted white voters, usually successfully. Thus, research on voting in presidential elections since 1992 has shown that certain of these voters, such as working-class men who once voted Democratic—have often moved to strongly supporting Republican candidates. In 2008, white working-class men in the South were especially likely to vote for Senator McCain, and a modest percentage voted for Obama. Three weeks before the 2008 election, reporter Adam Nossiter recounted how numerous white working-class voters in the South were very negative towards the thought of Senator Obama in the White House. Numerous whites seemed much more concerned with his biracial characteristics, and the "race mixing" they signaled, than with his political stands. A white pipe fitter put it this way: "He's neither-nor. He's other. It's in the Bible. Come as one. Don't create other breeds." A retired textile worker echoed the view: "I would think of him as I would of another of mixed race. God taught the children of Israel not to intermarry. You should be proud of what you are, and not intermarry." Yet, another white blue-collar worker mocked Obama with this racist-framed comment about him in the White House: "He's going to tear up the rose bushes and plant a watermelon patch. I just don't think we'll ever have a black president."[32] These views of Obama have not been limited to the southern states. Research shows that this strong support for the Republican Party among white working-class people, especially white men, can be seen in other regions as well.[33]

In addition, some working-class and middle-class whites went even further and aggressively resisted the Obama candidacy in more extremist ways that revealed a very hostile white framing. We discuss some post-election actions of this type in the next chapter, but we can note two examples that took place during the 2008 election. One very ugly dimension of this racist reality can be seen in the hostile websites—some with "nigger Obama" as a key title or theme—that spread across the internet during the primaries and the general election in 2008—and indeed also, as we will see, during his presidency and in the 2012 election. Some of these websites have had discussions touching on the possible assassination of Obama as candidate or president.

Conclusion

While the 2008 election was not as close as the previous 2000 and 2004 elections won by Republican George W. Bush, it was close enough that a shift of just 3.7 percent of the total voters from Senator Obama to Senator McCain would have given McCain a popular vote majority and, given a typical distribution across the states, a national victory. This reality makes the role of voters of color in electing Senator Barack Obama the first U.S. president of color one of the most important aspects of this historic election, yet to this day this reality has received relatively little analysis from the mainstream media. The 2008 election, as well as the 2012 election we discuss in Chapters 9 and 10, certainly signal the reality of the United States as an increasingly multiracial society and political system. These also signal the likely decline of white political dominance over the next few decades.

Why has this major political story not received the attention that it deserves? Perhaps one reason is that the mostly white-controlled, intensively white-framed mainstream media have been caught up in declaring the United States to be a "post-racial" country, an issue that we will examine in detail in the next chapter. However, as the data in this chapter on voting patterns by racial group indicate, nothing could be farther from the truth. In spite of the widespread celebrations of Obama's 2008 election as post-racial and allegedly indicative of a major increase in respect for people of diverse backgrounds and of a striking decline in racism, the country came out of this election in several ways more polarized than it was a generation ago in the 1970s. What is the evidence for this strong assertion? The 50 states are now quite politically polarized, as the "red" and "blue" political language constantly suggests. Over the years since the 1976 election, data on voting across the 50 states shows this clearly. In 1976, the average winning vote margin (percentage) across the states for either major presidential candidate was only about 10 percent. This average winning margin grew gradually to the height of 17.4 percent in the 2008 election. The number of landslide states (wins by one candidate or the other by at least 10 percent) has also increased significantly—from 19 states in 1976 to 36 states in 2008. Thus, far fewer states have been truly competitive in recent presidential elections. At a more micro-geographical level, moreover, about half of all the presidential votes in 2008 were in U.S. counties where Obama or McCain won by at least 20 percent of the total vote. Over the last few decades, the percentage of voters residing in these polarized "landslide counties" has grown substantially, from 27 percent of voters in 1976 to 48 percent of voters in 2008.[34]

Even more striking is the racial polarization of these politically polarized counties. Those where the 2008 Republican candidate John McCain won with a landslide margin of 20 percent or more were overwhelmingly white, with the black and Latino/a voting age population averaging a sixth or so of those countries' voting age populations. Where Obama won a county, in contrast, the black and Latino/a voting age population averaged about 43 percent of the voting age population. Though this country has made and continues to make some significant, important strides in terms of racial progress, the country nonetheless remains polarized, both racially and politically. One prominent analyst of these patterns, Bill Bishop, has summarized thus:

> In many ways, however, the [2008] election produced no change at all. The country is split in much the same way it was divided four and eight years ago . . . As a result, our communities (and states) are growing more like-minded.[35]

8

A "POST-RACIAL" AMERICA?

Katherine Rosman, a renowned white journalist, has recounted going to a party for a new author in Manhattan on an evening in 2003, where she noticed a black man who appeared awkward and out of place on the edge of the rather elite crowd. As he was one of a few blacks at the party, and Rosman also felt a bit uncomfortable in the crowd, she sought him out and began a conversation. Later, she was approached by a prominent white author who asked about the man to whom she had been talking. "Sheepishly he told me he . . . had asked him to fetch him a drink." The man in question was Barack Obama, then an Illinois state senator. In a bit more than five years, thus, Obama moved from being an unknown Illinois official who was stereotyped by a white man as a servant to being the 44th president of the United States.[1]

This story reveals something about the state of this country as we move farther into the 21st century. In 2009, a black man became the U.S. president, yet many if not most whites still operated substantially out of the old white racial frame. That continuing reality helps to account for the racial polarization in presidential voting across numerous U.S. states and counties documented in the last chapter. Given that polarization, dramatic differences in Americans' views of and reactions to the election of Barack Obama were to be expected. In general, people of color in the United States and across the globe mostly had positive reactions to Obama's 2008 election, while there were more mixed reactions among white people, especially white Americans. We will first examine this diversity in reactions, and then explore the implications of the 2008 election for the present and future of the United States, including its implications for the present and future of systemic racism.

Positive Reactions and Impact

President-elect Obama's Reaction

Obama himself set a very positive tone in his reaction to his own election. In comments on the 2008 election night to a large and cheering crowd in Chicago, President-elect Obama again celebrated the diversity and unity of the United States:

> If there is anyone out there who doubts that America is a place where anything is possible, who still wonders if the dream of our founders is alive in our time, who still questions the power of our democracy, tonight is your answer. Young and old, rich and poor, Democrat and Republican, black, white, Hispanic, Asian, Native American, gay, straight, disabled and not disabled, Americans have sent a message to the world that we have never been just a collection of red states and blue states. We have been and always will be the United States of America. It's the answer that led those who have been told for so long by so many to be cynical, and fearful, and doubtful of what we can achieve to put their hands on the arc of history and bend it once more toward the hope of a better day. It's been a long time coming, but tonight, because of what we did on this day, in this election, at this defining moment, change has come to America.[2]

This enthusiastic commentary brought constant cheers from a crowd estimated to be at least a quarter million people. Obama accented his year-long campaign theme of the unity in diversity and noted the hard struggle, the "long time coming" that was involved in his great achievement. His cataloguing of Americans ranged across economic, political, and social groups in a way one rarely hears from leading white politicians. Interestingly, he also began with a conventional statement about the "dream of the founders." His reference to the U.S. founders is of course typical rhetoric for politicians, yet rhetoric that ignores the great irony of such traditional appeals. A majority of the prominent U.S. founders were slaveholders, and almost all of them would have been appalled at the election of a black American as U.S. president. Obama's election, and the significant glass ceiling that it shattered, were never a part of the dream of the founders for the future of the United States.

Influential African Americans React

The Pulitzer Prize-winning author and poet, Alice Walker, wrote President-elect Obama an eloquent letter of congratulations:

> You have no idea, really, of how profound this moment is for us. Us being the black people of the Southern United States . . . [S]eeing you deliver the torch so many others before you carried, year after year, decade after decade, century after century, only to be struck down before igniting the flame of justice and of law, is almost more than the heart can bear . . . [B]ecause of all the relay runners before you, North America is a different place . . . Well done.[3]

In her black counterframed perspective, the theme deserving of most attention is that of the long human rights struggle of African Americans in the past, a struggle that provided the social and organizational foundation that enabled Senator Obama to deliver the political torch. He was, in effect, standing on the shoulders of those who came before him, and who often died before their time.

The theme of struggle was extended to the present by Ralph Everett, the head of an African American center in Washington, D.C. that does research on politics. Everett provided this optimistic commentary on the election:

> For many African Americans who have struggled against the tide for much of their lives, and who up until now may have been inclined to believe that they had little to show for it, the

promise of America shines brighter today . . . They now have in President-elect Obama an object lesson that in this country anyone can achieve their dreams if they set their minds to it and if they work hard enough. The value of this moment to future generations is immeasurable.[4]

Here we have yet another strong accent on the viability of the old American dream. The emphasis on President Obama as an object lesson or role model was a commonplace reaction to the 2008 election among black, white, and yet other commentators.

In addition, black sports figures who rarely speak on political matters did speak out because of their excitement over Senator Obama's victory. For example, the world's top-ranked golf player, Tiger Woods, who rarely makes comments beyond his sport, did so in this case:

I think it's absolutely incredible. He represents America. He's multiracial. I was hoping it would happen in my lifetime. My father was hoping it would happen in his lifetime, but he didn't get to see it. I'm lucky enough to have seen a person of color in the White House.[5]

In addition, after the election at an NFL football game, Brandon Marshall, a black Denver Broncos wide receiver who had just scored, started to pull out a black-and-white glove to celebrate the meaning of Obama's election to him. Because it would have generated a team penalty, he was restrained by teammates. Later, he made this comment in an emotional press conference:

Barack Obama's election as the 44th president of the United States is a tremendous symbol of unity. I wanted to create that symbol of unity because Obama inspires me, . . . and I know at the 1968 Olympics in Mexico Tommie Smith and John Carlos raised that black glove and that fist as a silent gesture of black power and liberation. Forty years later I wanted to make my own statement . . . In a gesture to represent the progress we made. This way, my way of honoring the progress.[6]

Significantly, Marshall's intent was to celebrate the progress that U.S. society has made on racial matters since the late 1960s, the unity that Obama himself has prominently celebrated. Ironically, however, when numerous white commentators and ordinary fans on sports blogs learned about his views on the election and his planned gesture, they were mostly hostile to this act of celebration and national unity.[7]

Influential White Americans React

A number of prominent white Americans also made important statements about Senator Obama's election, although the tone or themes were usually different. Senator John McCain gave a gracious concession speech the night of the general election in which he said, to a sometimes booing, mostly white crowd, that:

> In a contest as long and difficult as this campaign has been, his success alone commands my respect for his ability and perseverance. But that he managed to do so by inspiring the hopes of so many millions of Americans who had once wrongly believed that they had little at stake or little influence in the election of an American president is something I deeply admire and commend him for achieving. This is an historic election, and I recognize the special significance it has for African Americans and for the special pride that must be theirs tonight. I've always believed that America offers opportunities to all who have the industry and will to seize it. Senator Obama believes that, too. But we both recognize that, though we have come a long way from the old injustices that once stained our nation's reputation and denied some Americans the full blessings of American citizenship, the memory of them still had the power to wound.[8]

Unlike many of his supporters, McCain did recognize the historic reality to this election and its special significance for African Americans. Such commentary recognizing racial injustice was rather unique for Senator McCain, for he had previously ignored or downplayed civil rights issues and occasionally engaged in antiblack actions.

Even this concession speech has an odd quality to it, one clearly indicating that McCain was operating out of the soft version of the white racial frame. We observe, for example, that he pushed racial injustices into the past, accenting memories of past discrimination and thereby downplaying contemporary racial hostility and discrimination. Also striking in his and some other white comments is how seldom they have emphasized how important Obama's election is for all Americans, not just African Americans. This contrasts dramatically with Obama's broader commentary on the election. Indeed, the racial barrier broken at the presidential level is something one might expect all Americans committed to the expansion of U.S. democracy to celebrate openly.

Obama's major primary opponent, whom he later appointed as Secretary of State, Hillary Clinton, gave a rather different response to Obama's victory, one in which she did note its broader significance:

Tonight, we are celebrating an historic victory for the American people. This was a long and hard fought campaign but the result was well worth the wait. Together, under the leadership of President Barack Obama . . . we will chart a better course to build a new economy and rebuild our leadership in the world. And I look forward to doing all that I can to support President Obama and Vice President Biden in the difficult work that lies ahead . . . In quiet, solitary acts of citizenship, American voters gave voice to their hopes and their values, voted for change, and refused to be invisible any longer.[9]

Clinton's response recognized the pathbreaking character of the election for all Americans, but did not accent that important point like Obama did. Instead, she noted that voters voiced their hopes and emphasized the work the Obama team faces in dealing with U.S. economic problems and important international issues.

A few leaders in key voting groups that supported Obama strongly were quite celebratory in regard to Obama's election. Thus, Abner Mikva, a Jewish American leader who had served as President Bill Clinton's White House counsel and was an early Obama supporter, made this provocative comment:

If Clinton was our first black president, then Barack Obama is our first Jewish president. I use a Yiddish expression, *yiddishe neshuma*, to describe him. It means a Jewish soul. It's an expression my mother used. It means a sensitive, sympathetic personality, someone who understands where you are coming from.

Mikva accented Obama's awareness of the great social problems facing all Americans, a trait that doubtless helped him get elected. It is significant too that most Jewish Americans did in fact vote for Obama.[10]

Ordinary Americans React to Obama's Election

Rank-and-file Americans, especially those who were Obama supporters, signaled their enthusiasm for Obama's victory in many exuberant and revealing ways. One British journalist, Peter Hitchens, reported on his walk through the streets of Washington, D.C. on election night:

As I walked, I crossed another of Washington's secret frontiers. There had been a few white people blowing car horns and shouting, as the result became clear. But among the Mexicans, Salvadorans and the other Third World nationalities, there was something like ecstasy. They grasped the real significance of this moment. They knew it meant that America had finally switched sides in a global cultural war.[11]

This journalist was impressed by the great excitement about the Obama election in areas where voters of color predominated, but the reaction he observed was not nearly as exuberant in predominantly white neighborhoods. In his word choice, this conservative white reporter offered criticism of the United States for what he viewed as an electoral event that shifted significant political and cultural control from white hands into the hands of people of color—with major implications for a "global cultural war." This type of political and cultural shift is something most conservatives like Hitchens fear, for the United States and for Europe, but it is a shift that is exaggerated in such fearful commentaries as this. Perhaps Obama's personal ties to other countries, such as Indonesia and Kenya, as well as the perception that he is more of an ally to people in the global south than his predecessor, likely contribute to this mistaken notion that the U.S. government is now somehow on a different side of the "global culture war."

Ordinary Americans who supported Obama were indeed greatly excited by his election. This was especially true for African Americans. An African American woman in downtown Chicago was thrilled, commenting that "It seems like, it's all races, all ages, every ethnic group is screaming that Obama is their candidate. It doesn't even feel real."[12]

Black excitement often took the form of great elation over the election, coupled with a sense that an age-old dream had finally been fulfilled, and sometimes a sense that the historic event was not yet quite real. Another woman in Chicago said that Obama's election brought hope to her and her children: "Maybe people will be able to see them differently and look past the color of their skin." A black elementary school teacher in Atlanta commented that "This night will be burned into my memory and into the memory of my children." Another woman in Atlanta put it this way: "My grandfather was born a slave, so for me to see this happen means that there is hope for America."[13]

Numerous whites were also pleased with Obama's election, although many seemed to have a different set of understandings from those of African Americans and numerous other Americans of color. Reporting that she too was affected by the power of the historical moment, a woman in Chicago on election night made this distinctive comment: "He may be black in color but I think his thinking doesn't have color. I don't think he really has a color. I don't think he thinks about it." As we saw with white supporters in Chapter 7, this woman accents something a black American would be unlikely to say—that Obama is to be celebrated because he is color-less and does not think from a black perspective. A white student at the Chicago celebration portrayed Obama as "a president out of a movie," who had gotten him much more engaged in politics: "I think we're going to see people—volunteers, others—who got involved in this for the first time and who we will see engaged in politics from here on out." He stressed the media-star image that Obama developed over the course of the long campaign, an image especially common among young white Americans, as well as the idea that Obama's election will spur much more political involvement by U.S. voters.[14]

An older white man in the downtown Chicago crowd took an even broader historical view: "It's time for this city to send a new message, and this is our chance, right here." He seemed to have in mind the negative national image that Chicago had endured since the turmoil around the 1968 Democratic convention.[15] In his additional commentary, this white man demonstrated some sensitivity to the historical character of the moment for Americans, especially African Americans, who had been involved in the struggle for black advancement since the 1960s.

Even in this brief sample of black and white responses, we see some overlapping in excitement over the election and in realization of its historic character. Yet, there are differences as well. Black respondents speak much more openly of how Obama's win affected them on a personal level, likely due to the major historical significance of his presidency.

Global Reactions to Obama's Victory

Obama's victory was widely celebrated across the globe. This was an especially important reaction given the often-negative view of the U.S. government that grew globally during the difficult and often imperialistic years of the George W. Bush administration. African American publisher, Hardy Brown, described the reactions of people in other countries to Obama's presidential victory in this way:

> So on November 4th we had dancing in the street all over the world. People were swinging and swaying to Stevie Wonder's "Signed Sealed and Delivered" and in churches to "A Change is Gonna Come." It didn't matter what you wore, just as long as you were there or watching on television, they were dancing in the streets. They danced on the continents of Europe, Africa, Asia, and all over the Americas.[16]

Probably for the first time in world history, people in all time zones danced in excitement at the election of another country's political leader—indeed in this case the leader of a government that, at the time of the election, was frequently held in some disrepute by most of the same celebrators.

In Brazil, which has the largest African-origin population outside of Africa, there was much celebration of Obama's election. One official, Edson Santos, the minister of racial equality, accented the impact on many youth there: "I think it is important for young black Brazilians to know how the civil rights movement progressed in the U.S. and how it produced not just Obama, but blacks at the highest levels of American businesses."[17] A young Brazilian agreed with him about the significance and possible impact of this new U.S. reality: "We black Brazilians need him as much as the Americans do." The main reason for this is that black Brazilians, who make up at least half the Brazilian population, suffer widespread racial discrimination; and the black Brazilian civil rights movement has only recently come of age. A black organizer who works with Brazil's poor agreed that Obama symbolized the hopes of all people of African descent: "Obama represents what every black person in the world has been hoping for."[18] Racial inequalities in many countries across the globe were now highlighted.

Numerous other global leaders across Europe, Asia, Latin America, and Africa also responded very positively to the historic election of Barack Obama as U.S. president. One of the most interesting was this comment from Mwai Kibaki, the president of Kenya, the home country of Obama's father: "We the Kenyan people are immensely proud of your Kenyan roots. Your victory is not only an inspiration to millions of people all over the world, but it has special resonance with us here in Kenya."[19] It is interesting that few U.S. commentators have ever described President Obama as a Kenyan American, or even accented the *positive* significance of his African roots, which come from his Kenyan father who came to the United States to study at a university. Note too that these perceptive and poignant global reactions suggest just how truly remarkable, powerful, and significant the 2008 Obama election really was, yet such powerful global responses at the time received little attention in U.S. media commentaries and other public discussions.

Critical and Negative Reactions

Soon after the 2008 general election, CNN and the Opinion Research Corporation did a nationwide survey on the reactions of Americans to Obama's electoral victory. Survey questions revealed again how racially polarized the United States is. While 80 percent of the black respondents agreed that Obama's election was a "dream come true," only 28 percent of the white respondents said that they felt the same. Some 71 percent of the black respondents thought they would not see such a political event in their lifetime, while in contrast 59 percent of whites were more optimistic and said they thought it would happen.[20] While these survey questions were superficial, the "dream come true" question does reveal a major difference in the positive emotional reactions and interpretations of Obama's historic election across the color line. Moreover, many whites who did celebrate this election seem to have operated from a rather different perspective—given their lack of an experiential history of suffering from white racism—than did the majority of black Americans who were indeed celebrating "a dream come true."

Conservative Whites Mock Obama

Some whites went so far as to assertively mock Obama, his election, and African Americans generally. For example, in December 2008, Chip Saltsman, a Republican political operative and candidate for chair of the Republican National Committee (RNC) who was competing with Michael Steele (see Chapter 7), circulated a Christmas greeting CD to Republicans that mocked political liberals and included lyrics from a right-wing song entitled, "Barack the Magic Negro," a song first played on a right-wing talk-radio show in 2007. The song's mocking lyrics offer a negative parody of leaders such as Al Sharpton critiquing Obama as a black latecomer who came in "late and won." Some Republican conservatives defended this racialized mocking of Obama and other black leaders as inconsequential, while other Republicans, including the 2008 RNC chair, said they were appalled at Saltsman's actions and noted that actions such as this indicated the Republican Party needed more racial diversity.[21]

Prior to this event, the phrase "Magic Negro" had been used for some time by movie analysts to describe the common movie plot contrivance where a black character is a sidekick or savior for the central white protagonist. However, after Limbaugh played the song and after the Saltsman CD got much national publicity, the phrase "Magic Negro" exploded across the internet, and it has been used by many whites as a way of talking derisively about Obama and other black Americans, especially by white conservatives and white supremacists. The phrase came up some 157,000 times in connection with Obama in a recent (2012) internet search that we conducted. Moreover, on New Year's Day 2009, Fox News "accidentally" aired a text message from a viewer that said, "let's hope the magic negro does a good job."[22]

Extreme White Reactions

There is much evidence that many whites regarded the election of Barack Obama as a societal nightmare. After the general election in various northern, southern, and western cities, towns, and rural areas, a variety of hate crimes were reported. In just the first two weeks after the November election, the Southern Poverty Law Center counted more than 200 racist incidents, including more threats against President-elect Obama than have been recorded for any other presidential candidate. Indeed, the Secret Service reported that these threats represented the largest number against a President-elect they had ever verified. Such threats continued during the years of Obama's presidency.[23]

Many of these incidents involved the painting of racist graffiti on cars, houses, streets, and walls. For example, white Raleigh, North Carolina college students painted anti-Obama graffiti on their campus; these involved racist slurs and a comment on assassinating President-elect Obama. College officials refused to discipline the students because they wrote the racist commentaries on a wall in a college "free speech" area. On New York's Long Island, two dozen vehicles were inscribed with racist commentaries, including at least one "kill Obama" phrase. In Torrance, California, officials reported the painting of racist graffiti, including swastikas and the phrase "Go Back to Africa," on automobiles and a house that had Obama stickers or posters.[24]

A *Vanity Fair* article listed a broader array of racist incidents that took place after the 2008 election, including the following:

In Midland, Michigan a man paraded through an intersection in a KKK robe . . . A noose was hung from a tree at Baylor University . . . In Loxahatchee, Florida, a family home was covered in racist graffiti . . . In Stokes County, N.C., a man crossed his flag with a black X and hung it upside down . . . In Apolacon

Township, Pennsylvania, an interracial couple who supported Obama found a burned cross in their yard . . . In Mount Desert Island, Maine, black effigies were hung from nooses.[25]

This reporter concluded that there are "plenty of people out there who don't like it one bit that a black man is about to become leader of the free world." Another media report described a violent incident that took place at a house near Pittsburgh where generations of an African American family have lived. As the family was watching Obama's election night speech, presumably white arsonists threw their Obama yard sign through their window and set fire to their automobile outside.[26]

We should also note that anyone surfing the internet in weeks after the election could easily encounter much extremely racist, even violent commentary about President-elect Obama, including in comment sections of major mainstream news websites. Nonetheless, the mostly white-run mainstream media, including wire services, largely ignored these extreme anti-Obama incidents and commentaries. Obviously, aggressively and violently racist outbursts did not fit the mass media's themes of the "post-racial" society or of Obama "healing the racial divide" that had already become part of their perspective on the first black man's election to the U.S. presidency.

White Nationalists: Organizing a Second Civil War

White nationalists and others on the racist right have been rejuvenated by the election of Barack Obama to the presidency. Indeed, they may be growing in strength in the United States as a result of the election. Right after the November election, David Duke, a former Klan leader and Louisiana state representative still active in white nationalist groups, gave a press conference in Memphis where a nationalist meeting was about to be held. He reportedly asserted that:

And this is a real shock to me and it should be a shock to the community that European Americans now have to fight for our rights, in I guess Obama's "New America" . . . In Obama's America, do whites have rights? . . . I don't see him as our President. I see him as their President.[27]

Operating out of this white perspective, white nationalists have portrayed themselves as now isolated racially and strongly challenged for control of the country because of a black man's election. This is a peculiar and distorted view, given the reality that whites made up three-quarters of all voters in that election and that whites maintained the overwhelming majority of positions in both houses of Congress, as well as most important positions in President Obama's cabinet and advisory groups. In spite of this extremely high level of white political control, the white supremacist groups still have insisted, then and today, that President Obama has not been their president and have argued that his presidency somehow limits "whites' rights."

Obama's 2008 election has been seen by numerous white nationalists as an important recruiting issue. In an interview with a reporter not long before the election, David Duke said that he thought half of white Americans would be upset if Obama won and would likely move towards support of the white extremist organizations. According to Southern Poverty Law Center's "Hatewatch" website, reports emanating from leaders of white nationalist groups after the election indicated a strong increase in interest in them from other whites as a result of Obama's election. Numerous supremacist websites have used the Obama election as an issue to recruit. The head of an Arkansas-based Klan group encouraged his web viewers to join his group because Obama was the first "mulatto" president and a threat to the "future for your children." The head of the neo-Nazi group White Revolution asserted that "more and more white Americans" were awakened by the election, and that his group needed to be prepared for a new wave of interest: "People will be coming forward, shaking the cobwebs from their numbed minds, and they will need us to lead them." Although these nationalist groups may have exaggerated the interest in their groups, clearly their general reaction to the Obama election has been great enthusiasm for recruitment efforts.[28]

Among these white nationalists are members of the racist right who have been talking about a violent reaction to the Obama election and presidency. "Patriot" talk-radio hosts have called on whites to join with right-wing militias and white supremacist groups in preparing for a new "civil war," one they view as necessary because people of color are "taking over." One militia advocate, a former state trooper who broadcasts on Christian extremist and militia websites, commented thus on Obama's likely election just a few days before it happened:

> Those of you who have anointed this socialist, Muslim sympathizing, gun rights hating, Mexican illegals embracing, abortion loving charmer POTUS [President of the United States] . . . I see you as my enemy.

He added this call to arming and preparing for intergroup violence:

> American patriots, you need to decide what your battle plans are. You cannot wait any longer . . . Minuteman and militias were responsible for their own arms, ammunition and supplies. Can you muster with others and provide the essentials?[29]

Thinking from a similar framework, a female news commentator made this declaration in a November 10 column right after the November 2008 election:

> Obama is dangerous to freedom and liberty . . . Our very survival depends on the states of the Union revitalizing the constitutional militias . . . Forget states like California and New York. Real Americans in those states are outnumbered by the lazy, ignorant mobs who demand more and more from the public treasury.[30]

She then singled out the best states to work in organizing whites—some of those that went heavily for McCain.

A Post-Racial United States?

One concept that has emerged strongly among many media commentators, politicians, and academics since Obama's initial presidential victory in 2008 is that of an assertively "post-racial" United States. The terms "post-racial" and "post-raciality" have spread widely, including in the mainstream media and across the internet. Our archival research suggests that the term "post-racial" first emerged some time ago in early

1970s discussions among white southern moderates about political–economic changes that were sought, or already occurring, in the South during the 1960s and early 1970s, largely as a result of the black-led civil rights movement. These white Southerners saw in the post-segregation era new opportunities to shift the old South from a backward, substantially agricultural area to a more industrialized and commercialized area that could compete economically with the rest of the country. Thus, at a 1971 conference in Durham, North Carolina, 70 white and four black delegates discussed building a new industrialized South. Terry Sanford, president of Duke University and a leading white moderate, called on delegates to create a "truly post-racial society" that recognized the "rising participation of the black citizen" in community affairs but now moved on beyond traditional racial patterns. A *Washington Post* journalist reporting on this major conference was skeptical about its bold goals, noting that its official document did not even mention race and that at the very time of the conference there were black student protests against discrimination in Wilmington, North Carolina, only a modest drive from the conference.[31]

Subsequently, in the 1970s–1990s period, the term post-racial for the South or for the United States does not seem to have been used much, although the idea of a "decline" or "end" to racism did resurface strongly among conservative intellectuals during the 1980s conservative resurgence nationally. Since the 1980s Ronald Reagan era, the use of the concept and terminology of a post-racial society has gradually increased, accelerating greatly with the appearance of Senator Barack Obama as a viable Democratic candidate in 2007. Prior to his emergence, only a handful of scholars and commentators were using the term post-racial.[32]

By early 2008, it was increasingly clear that Senator Obama was the first viable black candidate for the U.S. presidency, and journalists increasingly began to discuss or assert the view that U.S. society was now a post-racial society. In January 2008, thus, prominent National Public Radio commentator Daniel Shorr speculated that the Obama campaign was moving the United States into a "post-racial" political era where racial barriers are unimportant, where the old black civil rights leadership is no longer relevant, and where the younger generation of Americans is more "color-blind" than earlier generations. Of course, he was mostly referring to the white younger and older generations, for Americans of color who face everyday discrimination do not have the luxury of being color-blind.[33]

The Post-Racial Theme: Still the White Racial Frame

After Obama's election in 2008, the increase in emphasis on the United States being post-racial was striking, both in the mainstream media and in an array of right-to-left political discussions in organizational and informal settings across the society. This perspective, often vehemently defended, was in many ways a relabeled version of the old white racial frame. Recall that the soft version of the white frame views the United States as a society where "race" and racism are significantly receding and are no longer important to an increasingly "color-blind" society. In this commonplace framing, overtly racist commentary is typically replaced with conceptions of African Americans and other people of color that are more subtly coded and stereotyped, particularly in public arenas and interracial exchanges. African Americans and other people of color who behave according to white norms and accept much of this white framing without overt resistance, are usually deemed more acceptable to most whites. Even so, as in the hard version of the frame, whites are viewed as culturally superior, and whiteness is still centrally, if more subtly, asserted in everyday interactions and institutional operations. In addition, as we have noted previously, the "soft" version of the white racial frame can, and does, often have serious negative effects on its targets that are similar to those of the hard white racial frame.

The post-racial perspective articulated by mainstream white commentators and academics since President Obama's 2008 election has had at least these three major elements: an emotion-laden accent on the decades-old idea of a major decline in racism; the emotion-laden idea that Obama is white-assimilated, acceptable, mixed-race, and/or less black (or not really black); and, somewhat contradictorily, the rather new view that President Obama himself has an obligation to be a racial healer who should not articulate a renewed civil rights agenda and whose election proves the fallacy of the view that white racism is still a serious barrier in the United States.

Ironically, even as the aforementioned white nationalist leaders have begun to aggressively and openly assert their old-fashioned racist framing and their view that whites must organize to "retake" a country they feel is lost, numerous mainstream commentators, especially in the mass media, have ignored this expanding supremacist activity and portrayed the 2008 election as evidence that there is no significant racism left. For example, the country's leading business newspaper, the Republican-oriented *Wall Street Journal*, asserted that Obama's 2008 election was a great tribute to how open, democratic, and non-racist the country is:

> A man of mixed race has now reached the pinnacle of U.S. power only two generations since the end of Jim Crow. This is a tribute to American opportunity, and it is something that has never happened in another Western democracy—notwithstanding European condescension about "racist" America.

After crowing about U.S. moral superiority over European countries, the white-framed editorial added this triumphant commentary:

> While Mr. Obama lost among white voters, as most modern Democrats do, his success is due in part to the fact that he also muted any politics of racial grievance. We have had in recent years two black Secretaries of State, black CEOs of our largest corporations, black Governors and Generals—and now we will have a President. One promise of his victory is that perhaps we can put to rest the myth of racism as a barrier to achievement in this splendid country. Mr. Obama has a special obligation to help do so.[34]

Here, an apparently white editorial writer explicitly noted the point we previously discussed—that Obama ran a successful campaign because he did not engage in the "politics of racial grievance." That is, Obama ran to fit within the color-blind version of the white frame, and this writer praised that effort. In addition, this writer emphasized that a few African Americans have recently served in top federal positions (yet only one of whom was elected), and this token reality should be viewed as an indication that white racism is no longer a barrier to high achievement. More than that, the writer called on Obama to lead the effort to kill the "myth of racism," an old effort that white leaders have engaged in for centuries—that is, ferreting out a few black individuals, endowing them with economic and social rewards as well as high visibility, and getting them to whitewash the reality of systemic racism by contending that it is a nonissue. Note that the irony in this argument about a "myth of racism" is lost on this writer, who earlier admitted that most whites did *not* actually vote for the first "mixed race" presidential candidate even in an era of extreme economic crisis created substantially by a Republican administration strongly supported by his electoral opponent.

Obama: Something Other than Black?

Before and after his 2008 election, many commentators focused on "who" Obama really was in terms of his racial credentials. As discussed in Chapter 4, much of the 2008 primary and general election season involved the efforts of competitors, media analysts, and voters to define Senator Obama. Often these attempts took the form of coded or overtly racialized terms and imagery. The "man of mixed race" theme that the *Wall Street Journal* writer above articulated is one that has been developed by numerous interpreters of the presidential election. Substantial debates have raged over "how black" Obama really was then, and now is. We have noted that during the election reporters, and numbers of white supporters, accented questions about whether Obama should be viewed as black, white, biracial, or some other mix. Some concerns focused on racial identity, while others were aimed at his complex cultural and family backgrounds.

This debate has continued since the 2008 election. We observe, for example, some of the post-election ruminations on these themes in a long overview article written in December 2008 by Jesse Washington, the "race and ethnicity" writer for the Associated Press (AP). Washington concluded from interviews with whites and people of other backgrounds that candidate Obama, in achieving what many thought impossible, was treated differently from previous black generations and that many white and mixed-race people now viewed Obama as something other than black.[35] He quoted analysts of various backgrounds who argued that the old racial categories were changing and that Obama and others like him now have the freedom to choose how they want to identify—as black, white, or biracial. (Recall that in Chapter 2, we discuss how this phenomenon began early in Obama's campaign, as radio personality Rush Limbaugh called him "halfrican-American" and took issue with his self-identifying as black.)

In the United States, powerful whites and their subordinates mostly control how Americans of color are racially identified, especially in public places and institutions. As a rule, Americans of color cannot independently assert a nonconforming racial identity and expect most whites —including employers, teachers, police officers, and other government officials—to easily respect and accept that personal identity choice. Not surprisingly, thus, Obama has long and regularly described himself as black. Various efforts to remake him into something he is not—that is, a white, almost-white, or not-really-black candidate—fit well into white racial framing that attributes primarily negative characteristics to black Americans or emphasizes that traits such as intelligence, decisiveness, and articulateness are qualities more readily associated with white men than black men. Blackness is so negatively viewed within that centuries-old frame that many whites seem to feel it necessary to view Obama as an "exception to his race" and to highlight his positive characteristics as ones that are really more "white" in nature, while recognizing his blackness as something limited to his physical features only.[36] By performing the visual sleight of hand that erases Obama's blackness, whites are then able to reinforce the idea that his positive characteristics are linked to—and a consequence of—his imagined "whiteness." As such, his triumphs, successes, bearing, and background become appropriated as something that whites can symbolically own, without any need to challenge the highly racist idea that these positive features are alien to blackness.

To buttress the argument that the racial world where Obama is seen as something besides black has changed, like many other journalists and analysts, this aforementioned AP writer asserts that "the world has changed since the young Obama found his place in it. Intermarriage and the decline of racism are dissolving ancient definitions."[37] Here again we see the ill-informed "decline of racism" theme, which he and the analysts he cites, typically without much evidence, buttressed by asserting that increased intermarriage is "dissolving ancient definitions" of the racial identities of Americans of color.

However, such reasoning is not supported by social science research. Many studies show persisting and high levels of racial discrimination and inequality in areas such as housing, employment, education, and politics. In addition, there is relatively little interracial marriage involving white and black Americans.[38] Neither one of these widely circulated, mostly white-generated assumptions and tropes about the racial character of contemporary U.S. society is correct.

Ultimately, the idea that Obama's intelligence, background, and behavior run counter to his blackness and are best understood as exceptional rather than typical for a black American strongly indicates fallacies in the "post-racial America" argument. As discussed in Chapter 2, questions about whether Obama was "black enough" or "too black" usually reflect issues of hard and soft racial framing. In the early days of Obama's campaign, these questions often focused on whether he was "black enough" to appeal to black voters, or whether he was "too black" for whites. Given Obama's decisive electoral victory, clearly he was black enough to gain support from the overwhelming majority of black voters—despite the hard racial framing that suggested his Ivy League education, articulateness, and charisma would be alien and off-putting to ordinary black voters. Obama's win also indicated that he was not "too black" for many whites, albeit only a minority of them.

However, as we have argued, Obama avoided being "too black" by carefully operating within the context of the color-blind racial framing and casting himself as an acceptable black person who eschewed characteristics and behaviors that might cost him white votes—for example, discussing racial inequality and personal experiences with racism or emphasizing the reality of white privilege. While Obama's decision to use soft racial framing to his political advantage was a necessary strategical move, it in no way evinces that we have now moved into a post-racial era. Indeed, the fact that so many post-2008 election discussions argued that Obama was not really black indicated just how entrenched the hard racial frame really is, and also highlighted how difficult it was, and still is, for many white Americans to accept President Obama even as someone who contrasts with much of the racist imagery and stereotyping in the old white racial frame.

Calling on President Obama to be a Racial Healer

As we have seen throughout our chapters, numerous media and other political commentators, most of whom are white, have accented that Obama's election "proves" there is a major decline in or end to racism. Oddly enough, variations on this theme of decline can often be found in analyses that also assert a rather contradictory theme of expecting President Obama to "fix" U.S. racial problems. For example, we have this commentary on the election from a white journalist and blog commentator at the *Washington Post*:

> Can he be not only the president of the United States but also the racial healer that many in the country clearly believe him to be? It's a tough task for one man. Remember that during the course of the campaign—primary and general election—Obama didn't define himself (as Jesse Jackson Jr. had) as a black man running for president. Rather, he was a candidate for president who happened to be black.[39]

The widespread calls on newly elected President Obama to "heal the racial divide" were typically asserted from within a version of the old white racial frame, since they viewed African Americans and other Americans of color as substantially or equally responsible for the "racial divide." This framing hides the reality of the still-dominant racial hierarchy headed by whites and still-widespread discrimination perpetuated by whites.

Obama's 2008 election obviously did not end white-imposed, blatant racism or the covert and subtle racism that is an everyday matter in most institutional arenas. Even as Obama was elected president, huge racial inequalities remained between black and white Americans in areas of access to health care, education, income, and wealth. Indeed, these significant racial inequalities still exist between whites and many groups of color. While many analysts who put forth the post-racial argument contend that Obama's election proves anyone who works hard can succeed, regardless of their racial characteristics, such claims conveniently overlook the systemic racism that makes it exceedingly difficult for the majority of African Americans to have equal opportunities with whites.[40]

Consequently, Obama's 2008 win may more accurately tell us this: On occasions where black Americans' hard work is coupled with a near-flawless execution of the task at hand, and when this occurs in a setting where related conditions are temporarily abysmal for their white competitors, and when said competitors make a series of major tactical and strategic errors, then white racism may not be an insurmountable obstacle. This is *in no way* a level playing field, or a world where race no longer matters as a major impediment to success. Were the United States truly post-racial, it would not be necessary for Obama to studiously avoid discussions of racial inequality in order to make himself more palatable to white voters. Further, a truly post-racial country would not have these systemic racial barriers in place for its millions of citizens of color. Only aggressive civil rights law enforcement by top U.S. officials, which would be new for this country, and continuing antiracist organization at the grass-roots level against the various forms of continuing racial discrimination have a chance of changing the still systemically racist character of the United States. President Obama certainly does not have the power to do national racial "healing" alone.[41]

After the 2008 general election, the *Christian Science Monitor*, one of the country's national newspapers, published a strong editorial by its board that revealed much about the white elite's thinking about Obama's lack of racial agenda.[42] It began thus: "The great paradox in the election of America's first black president is that Barack Obama broke a historic racial barrier without campaigning on a black agenda." In this opening, this editorial board is looking at the election from a white point of view, as there is no "paradox" here for African Americans, who understood well that the only way for Obama to have won was not to offend whites by bringing up racial issues in a recurring way. Nonetheless, like many other whites, this editorial board clearly feared that Obama might revert to a civil rights agenda and "promote government programs specifically for African Americans" because of pressures from outside the White House:

> Many blacks may expect Obama to focus on their communities in addressing social and economic ills. They will count how many African Americans he names to his cabinet and expect him to take up a "black agenda"—the high incarceration rate of young black men, for instance.[43]

Once again we have a white framing, which sees something wrong with African Americans expecting attention to economic and other societal ills, many of which have been caused or exacerbated by white racism in the past and present. Moreover, since very few African Americans have ever served in presidential cabinets, it is reasonable for African Americans to examine Obama's cabinet closely for racial skew and bias. Indeed, his new 2009 presidential cabinet had only one African American in a major cabinet position, that of attorney general.

Then the editorial board accented yet more of a soft version of the white racial frame:

> The reality of our time is that racism still lives . . . But the much bigger reality is that racism wasn't vibrant enough to stop Obama's election. Our times include a new generation that's more neutral toward race . . . In his campaign, Obama did not run from race, but he did not run on it. His more universal approach seems the right one for this time.[44]

As with the previously cited *Wall Street Journal*, we have here elite editorial writers lecturing Obama about the "bigger reality" of a supposed decline in racism and a new generation that is "neutral to race." The intensity of this denial of racism's continuing impact in these various commentaries suggests that something racially significant is going on beneath the surface of this argument, in the mostly white minds of those who own and control major media outlets such as the *Wall Street Journal*, the *Christian Science Monitor*, and the *Washington Post*. There is apparently a concern here that during the Obama administration there may be a renewed discussion of the seriousness of white racism and a vigorous enforcement of the now weakly enforced civil rights laws.

We should note, however, that some media analysts have not bought into this clever media narrative of post-raciality. This is especially true of Americans of color. For example, in January 2008, Uzodinma Iweala, the Nigerian-American author of the novel *Beasts of No Nation*, wrote an opinion article for the *Los Angeles Times*, in which he argued that:

> Many in the media seem to think that race would not be or should not be mentioned. It is as if we think that not speaking about race is the equivalent of making progress on race issues. The only thing more amusing than the use of a new term, "post-racial," to describe the positive response to Barack Obama's campaign is the lamentation at the loss of "post-raciality." This entire narrative is a media-concocted fiction. America is decidedly not "post-racial."[45]

A media-created and white-created fiction, it is indeed.

Debating the Obama Administration: Initial Progressive Perspectives

After the 2008 election, numerous progressive activists and social scientists raised questions about how much the Obama administration would operate within the significant constraints imposed by a still white-controlled social and political system. For example, at a fall 2008 sociology conference, the respected Duke University scholar of U.S. racial matters, Eduardo Bonilla-Silva, gave a provocative address raising questions that most Obama supporters had been unwilling to face about Obama's past political actions and likely presidential policies. Bonilla-Silva examined problems with Obama's relatively conservative approach to foreign policy. He presciently questioned whether Obama would appoint true progressives in important government positions. As it turned out, not one of Obama's major cabinet posts went to a progressive. Centrist and center-right Democrats, and a Republican, got the top cabinet and White House staff positions. Only one person of color, Eric

Holder, was appointed to a top cabinet position (Attorney General), although a few other people of color were appointed to lesser positions.[46]

Bonilla-Silva further asked what the Obama administration would do about racial issues: Obama "took an accomodationist post-racial stance on the matter. And because he took such a post-racial posture during his campaign, I do not believe he can take a strong stance on race matters now." As we have demonstrated, Senator Obama played into the color-blind version of the white frame by running a de-racialized campaign, with no mention of programs to eradicate racial discrimination except occasionally when his hand was forced, as in his Philadelphia speech. In this still systemically racist country, he had to do that to be elected.

In contrast, other progressive activists and social scientists took a different view of Obama's likely future policy actions. For example, the savvy African American social scientist, Bob Newby, countered Bonilla-Silva's critiques with an optimistic perspective:

> When the question was asked about his appointments and that they did not look like much change, [Obama's] response was "The change comes from me!" While it would be great to have . . . for Secretary of Human Services Jesse Jackson or Al Sharpton, such appointments would marginalize him from the [get-go] . . . Barack as an African American is controversial by definition, when it comes to white America. His first mission is to assure the American people that he is on their side. To do that he has surrounded himself with people who are hard to criticize, whose credentials are stellar in the eyes of everyday Americans.[47]

In Newby's view, the appointment of centrist government officials well known for their abilities would be essential for Obama to operate in a white-dominated country. Obama's actions have indeed represented a long-term and pragmatic political strategy, one that has had major effects in not reproducing arch-conservative officials as in the Bush administration. In his commentary Newby then added that:

> Electoral politics and revolutionary, or movement politics, are a different breed of cat. A revolutionary (or someone the American

people thought was a revolutionary) could not get elected President . . . Surely, we are not expecting the revolution from electoral politics? If not the revolution, it is time to struggle for decency. A decency as free as we can make it from the maintenance of racism, sexism, homophobia and most of all class inequality.

Newby compared the reality of the Obama administration with the Bush administration. He accented Obama's departure from the reactionary policies and overt racism, classism, sexism, and homophobia that periodically appeared during the Bush years. Newby as a black pragmatist was less concerned with Obama moving to a full progressive agenda than with the abandonment of the destructive conservative policies of the recent past. If the George W. Bush administration is used as the standard, the Obama administration did move the country once again in a more democratic and progressive direction.

Public Discussions of Racial Matters

How did Obama's remarkable 2008 election impact the ways and the extent to which scholars, policymakers, academics, and ordinary citizens are able to discuss or research racial issues? As we have seen, several media analysts and social scientists have suggested that the United States is moving into a post-racial social system where a dominant white ideology of color-blindness reigns—yet, a society that in reality still enables the structural processes of racial inequality to continue unabated, if substantially concealed. In Chapter 1, we argued that this accent on the dominance of a color-blind ideology fails to take into consideration the ways in which contemporary white actors move freely from this color-blind ideology with its professed unawareness of "race" and racism to engage in many statements, actions, and behaviors that are clearly racially motivated and still linked to the harsher version of the old white racial frame.[48] Our view of the hard and soft versions of this still-dominant racial frame explains this apparent paradox, and we have focused in this book on the ways in which both variations of the dominant white racial frame have been used by whites and others to shape, understand, and react to the 2008 Obama election and subsequent political developments. As we predicted in the first edition of this book, the hard and the soft versions of the old white racial frame have continued to greatly shape public and private discussions of race and racism in the United States.

How can it be that the election of the country's first African American president has arguably led to fewer significant public and policy discussions of U.S. racism? As we have shown in detail, a key part of Obama's 2008 campaign strategy involved operating out of a soft color-blind framing that downplayed the existence of continuing racial inequality and intentional discrimination. Given that one result of the remarkable 2008 election year was a strenuous, often insistent attempt by many in the mainstream media and other public arenas to argue that Obama's election represented a U.S. triumph over its racist past, we have correctly expected that those analysts who draw attention to the myriad ways racial inequalities and discriminatory behaviors remain present in society have often been publicly doubted or dismissed. Obama's 2008 electoral win led to more emphasis on a soft racial framing in both public and private discussions as people, especially whites, became increasingly attached to the often sincere, color-blind fiction that his pathbreaking election proved racial discrimination and inequality are no longer serious societal issues.

Indeed, when in the first year of the administration Attorney General Eric Holder memorably contended that the U.S. was comprised of "a nation of cowards" when it came to talking openly about racial matters, even President Obama acknowledged that he would have used different wording to make this point, stating:

> I'm not somebody who believes that constantly talking about race somehow solves racial tensions . . . I think what solves racial tensions is fixing the economy, putting people to work, making sure that people have health care, ensuring that every kid is learning out there. I think if we do that, then we'll probably have more fruitful conversations.[49]

Over his first years as president, Obama mostly continued to express this type of lukewarm support for calls to eradicate racial inequality, racist framing, and related racial problems. Obama himself has been complicit in stifling important racial dialogue and change. For example, the administration's early decision to boycott the United Nations' World Conference on Racism—due in part to organizers' inclusion of language calling for reparations for slavery—certainly did not send an encouraging message about the need to engage in difficult dialogue or action related to racial issues.[50] Those who have highlighted the continuing manifestations of racial discrimination and racial inequality—police shootings of unarmed black men, the racial wealth gap, underrepresentation of people of color at the uppermost levels of most institutional arenas—have found that their arguments frequently have fallen on unsympathetic White House ears. Indeed, this large-scale racial inequality remains obvious today in the political system where, in spite of Obama's service as president, people of color are still usually significantly underrepresented at the highest levels of the federal government.

Important societal issues such as these were periodically alluded to during the course of Obama's first presidential campaign. For example, in a July 2008 CNN article entitled "Could an Obama Presidency Hurt Black Americans?" the writer John Blake pointed out that, should Obama win, his success could be used to "dismiss legitimate black grievances," "signal the decline of individual racism but not systemic racism," and solve the "race problem" without white Americans addressing the fact of their own racial privilege.[51]

Centuries of Action for Societal Change: The Continuing Role of African Americans

Since the 2008 election, numerous progressive analysts have called for increased grass-roots movements and assertive progressive organization to constantly pressure President Obama and the Democrats in Congress to move in much more progressive directions on important policy matters, including those dealing with persisting white racism and overseas U.S. colonialism. No one is more aware of the need for constant progressive organization than African Americans. Indeed, Obama's success in the 2008 election and the extremely high level of support and political organization he got from black voters signaled, among other things, that black Americans are among the most consistently progressive large political groups. Judging from past history, they often provide the *most reliable base* for seeking democratic social change in the United States, past or present. African Americans have provided numerous antiracist and truly democratic thinkers, leaders, and activists since at least the slave rebellions of the 18th century and the abolitionist movement of the mid-19th century. Most strikingly perhaps, during the U.S. Civil War in the mid-19th century, half a million African Americans, a majority of them formerly enslaved, volunteered and helped mightily as Union soldiers and support troops to ensure that the United States would abolish slavery and become more democratic. More recently, we have seen the reality of the black impact on expanding U.S. democracy in the black-led civil rights movements moving the country in a more democratic direction in the 1960s, in court cases such as the NAACP-generated 1950s *Brown* decisions breaking with legal segregation, and in numerous civil rights leaders and freedom thinkers such as W. E. B. Du Bois, Diane Nash, Dr. Martin Luther King, Jr., Fannie Lou Hamer, and Jesse Jackson.

Historically, black civil rights leaders and organizations have mostly taken progressive, indeed mostly social democratic, positions on important racial and political–economic issues. Groups as diverse as the Brotherhood of Sleeping Car Porters, the NAACP, the Congress of Racial Equality, the Southern Christian Leadership Conference, the Student Nonviolent Coordinating Committee, and the Black Panther Party have consistently been willing to work in significant alliances with white Americans and other Americans of color for major societal changes in the direction of greater democracy and equality.[52] Activists in predominantly black organizations, including those who worked hard for the election of the first African American president, are quite aware that they need to keep outside pressure on President Obama, as well as subsequent presidents over the 21st century, to bring progressive changes badly needed in this society.

Conclusion

Sadly enough, systemic racism is still very much alive in the United States, as we have demonstrated many times in this book. Even with the election of an African American, the deep realities of systemic racism throughout this society have not changed very much. While most white

Americans have more or less resigned themselves to Obama's presidency, and many are indeed enthusiastic about it, this does not mean that the aggressively racist framing in most white minds has disappeared. Research studies we have cited throughout this book make this continuing systemic reality quite clear.[53] While many whites today know not to project, especially in public, numerous elements of the hard-racist framing of President Obama and other Americans of color, a great many of these and other whites still buy into, and act out of, traditional racist stereotypes, images, and interpretations of the hard-racist framing, especially in private settings with their friends and relatives. Some have abandoned certain of the harsher elements of the hard white racial frame and operate out of what we have termed the soft version of the white frame. These whites have sometimes openly embraced Obama and/or voted for him, and have continued to support him as president, because of his appeal to this soft racial framing. Many of these whites have tended to view President Obama as "not like most" black Americans—that is, as somehow an "exception to his race."

This is not to say that every white person who voted for Obama thinks aggressively out of the soft version of the white frame. Obviously, a modest minority of whites have done the necessary and ongoing work of developing a strong antiracist framing, and they demonstrated this effort during the long 2008 campaign, as they have for the long 2012 campaign. Voting for Obama in 2008 or 2012 was not an automatic marker of being free of racism, nor has it done much to free the country of its deep structures of racism. In this book, we have offered sound social science interpretations of Obama's political efforts and for why they do not signal an end to systemic racism, even though this is the way that the 2008 election has long been portrayed by media and other analysts and the way that many white Americans seem desperate to conceptualize it as well.

In contrast to this common white view, the social science and other research evidence shows well the continued existence of extensive white racial hostility and racial discrimination in numerous sectors of this society, and Obama himself discussed a little of this research in his famous March 2008 Philadelphia speech. There, and very occasionally elsewhere, Obama has himself indicated that it is naive to think that this country's racist history can be erased through a few election cycles. Like all African Americans who deal with the omnipresent white-dominated world that is the United States, Obama has found himself caught between a clear personal understanding of the racial hostility and discrimination faced by African Americans (and other Americans of color) and his need to please most white Americans to be elected. Thus, he carefully and briefly indicated his understanding of systemic racism issues in an *Essence* interview conducted in fall 2007, well before the Democratic Party primaries and before he was considered a leading presidential candidate:

> I don't believe it is possible to transcend race in this country . . . Race is a factor in this society. The legacy of Jim Crow and slavery has not gone away. It is not an accident that African Americans experience high crime rates, are poor, and have less wealth. It is a direct result of our racial history . . . When you [talk about negative patterns or issues within the black community] you have a corollary responsibility to take on [racial] issues that White candidates might not speak to, that it is now incumbent upon you to do.[54]

Even though during the presidential campaign Obama regularly played into the soft racial frame, at the same time he carefully engaged in specific outreach efforts to black voters in which he signaled that he was savvy about racism. He was very tactical in communicating to black audiences that he "gets it," while being sure not to scare off white voters by talking directly about racial oppression. It appears from their overwhelming vote for Obama in 2008 (and 2012) that most African Americans understood his necessary tactics, perhaps in part because they themselves have to play this game as well. For blacks who operate often in predominantly white environments, this sort of duality may be second nature; and those blacks who do not spend much time in these predominantly white settings may also understand, as members of a subordinated racial group, that this dissembling is often necessary for dealing with whites who will get angry or worse if they have to face up to the reality of white racism. The reality of the everyday black experience—and recognizing the commonality of that experience in Obama's efforts to win the Presidency—explains some of Obama's huge support among black Americans—to the present day. It may have also bought him some leeway from black Americans when he has deployed a soft racial frame to do such things as criticize absent black fathers, so long as some of his other actions—such as appointing a talented black lawyer as attorney general and improving civil rights enforcement—speak directly to alleviating some effects of systemic racism on black Americans. Though his words to this effect are infrequently quoted, perhaps Obama's own observation that his candidacy and 2008 election have not brought about an end to U.S. racism should carry the most weight in rebutting the now commonplace statements to the contrary.

The systemically racist reality Obama has occasionally acknowledged remains very much with us. In one report on racial inequality, *Forty Years Later: The Unrealized American Dream*, researcher-activist Dedrick Muhammad has provided strong challenges to the end-of-racism theme that various white commentators have periodically pressed on the U.S. public. In his research analysis, he has accented societal trends between 1968, the year Dr. Martin Luther King, Jr., was assassinated, and the present day:

1 The black high school graduation rate has increased fast enough that, if continued at this pace, black youth will equal the white rate in less than a decade, by the year 2018.
2 However, the income gap between black and white Americans is closing far more slowly—so slowly that, at the current rate, black Americans will gain income equality with white Americans only in about 537 years.
3 Most strikingly of all, the wealth gap between black and white Americans is closing even more slowly—so slowly that, if the current rate continues like it has since 1983, black Americans will equal white Americans in wealth only in about 634 years.[55]

These facts about long-term racial inequalities, and additional facts about their being caused by systemic racism are well known to many researchers and civil rights activists, and to President Obama. However, since the late 1960s, they have not had much impact on public policy at the state or national level, especially in recent years. We are still a country where doing something major to reduce these huge racial inequalities, which reflect the effects of past and present white racial hostility and white racial discrimination, not surprisingly, remains on the public policy back-burner for white political officials and their minions. Long after Dr. King's death, this society's white top policymakers have not come close to implementing the kinds of enforcement and redress programs necessary to realize Dr. King's famous "dream" of racial equality for all in the United States. Obama's pathbreaking election has not altered this sad societal reality.

According to a nationwide U.S. survey in the year of Obama's pathbreaking 2008 election, whites clearly revealed that they have a long way to go even in understanding these data on racial inequalities and their individual and structural causes. In this survey, six in ten black respondents thought that U.S. racial relations were still generally bad, nearly twice the figure for white respondents. The opinion poll found that four in ten black respondents saw no progress over the last few years in getting rid of discrimination, again more than twice the figure for white respondents. Moreover, compared to a similar 2000 survey done by the same organization, the current racial reality has gotten some-what worse as reported by the black respondents. Relatively few of the black respondents said that their residential areas were significantly integrated, and there were some increases in reports of racial discrimin-ation. Nearly 70 percent of the black respondents reported that they had faced significant racial discrimination, which was up from 62 percent in the earlier survey. Four in ten black respondents reported that they had been stopped by police officers because they were black, while very few of the white respondents reported a similar experience. Moreover, on a question about who had the better chance of getting ahead in society, two-thirds of the black respondents said that whites did, again a percentage up from 2000.[56]

The black respondents in the recent survey were at least as likely as black respondents in earlier 1990 and 2000 surveys to see U.S. racial conditions as still bad, while white respondents were much more likely to rate U.S. racial relations as good over the period since 1990. These survey results are not surprising, given the data on political polarization we discussed in Chapter 7. While we acknowledge that there has been important racial progress in the United States, in some significant ways this country is more polarized and segregated today than it was a generation ago. Recall that the U.S. counties that Obama won in 2008 had black and Latino/a populations that averaged 43 percent of their voting age populations, a significant contrast with the counties that voted with a significant majority for McCain and that averaged white population percentages above 83 percent. Half of all presidential votes were cast in counties that Obama or McCain took by at least a fifth of the votes, "landslide counties" that in recent decades have seen ever more voters residing in them. Reviewing these data, Bill Bishop has put this even more pointedly, suggesting that after an

> election of a man who billed himself as a post-partisan candidate of a unified America, this country is more divided than it was four or eight years ago. Or, less abstractly, while some danced in the streets over Barack Obama's victory, others bought guns.[57]

This political polarization is much in line with other types of racial segregation in U.S. rural and urban areas. A Pew Research Center study found that a majority of Americans say they prefer communities that are diverse in racial, religious, economic, and political terms, with black Americans being overwhelmingly in favor of such community conditions. Yet, Census and other government data indicate that, in spite of these professed preferences, U.S. communities have in recent years often become more homogenous in political and economic terms.[58]

Nonetheless, we do not downplay the significance of Obama's presidential victory. We recognize the unprecedented historic nature of this great electoral event. We are well aware that had President Obama been born a mere generation or two earlier, the prospect of being president would have been simply unthinkable, as he would have faced the threat of death for even attempting to register to vote in many areas of the country. Obama's election as president undoubtedly brings the United States a bit closer to its often-stated ideals of equality and liberty. But we also feel it is incumbent upon us as researchers to put this incredible achievement in its proper and accurate historical context. One of Obama's most widely recognized 2008 campaign slogans was the statement "Yes we can," which was intended to indicate to disaffected voters that change was in fact possible. We agree that, yes, we can create major racial changes in this society, but this will continue to be very difficult. In bringing significant racial and political–economic changes, the challenge for the Obama administration, and indeed for all people in the United States, remains great and indeed daunting.

9

PRESIDENT OBAMA'S 2009–2013 TERM AND THE 2011–2012 PRIMARIES

Obama's Pragmatism and Policy Achievements

During his first years in office, President Obama governed as he had made clear he would to those who listened closely to his campaign speeches—as a pragmatic progressive. Over time, the public came to see that he had a clear recognition of the limits of presidential action within our strongly capitalistic, elite-dominated economic and political system. As numerous actions soon demonstrated, Obama played a long-term strategy, one in which he mostly kept long-term political goals in mind even if that meant a significant period of appearing to lose to conservative political enemies. In the long run, however, he often won his important stated goals, to the consternation of many ideological purists on the right and the left of the political spectrum.

If one only listened to the U.S. right-wing commentators, one would think President Obama had a radical "socialistic" agenda way out of line from the mainstream political traditions of the past. If one only listened to the most intense critics of the left, one would think that Obama had not achieved very much during his time in office. Many on the left portrayed him as not really a "populist" who cared about needs of ordinary Americans. Yet, every few months after he got into the presidential race in 2007, he indicated in populist speeches his great sensitivity to everyday needs of ordinary Americans. This was not surprising given his back-ground as an urban community organizer.[1]

The list of Obama's actual achievements over his presidential years is substantial and very much in the liberal political tradition. Indeed, his achievements looked quite impressive given the economic circumstances he faced. In 2009, Obama came into office with a much worse national economic situation than he or most economic and political analysts had ever expected. He confronted the most serious economic decline—the economy losing 750,000 jobs a month, for example—since the 1930s Great Depression. However, he met this huge challenge with numerous decisive actions, including continuing the Bush bailouts of troubled Wall Street banks and insurance firms, bailing out the auto industry, and implementing a large economic stimulus package. Most serious economic analysts give these actions credit for keeping the U.S. economy from entering a new Depression. Still, many political analysts and activists faulted him for the economic policy decisions bailing out these corpora-tions with relatively lax requirements for their future operations and with no major prosecutions (as of 2012) for likely economic crimes.[2]

Working with his Democratic allies in Congress, Obama succeeded in his first years in passing a major health care reform law, the most important in several decades. Among other important features, it allowed parents to keep children in their twenties on their insurance, abolished pre-existing condition exemptions, expanded Medicaid, and added a requirement for insurance companies to use more of their premiums for health-care payments. In addition, working with his Department of Justice, Obama implemented the Fair Sentencing Act retroactively, imposed fuel efficiency standards for many vehicles, provided major help for New Orleans storm protection, and worked on expanding funding for national transport and services infrastructures. Working with his foreign policy team, Obama implemented a successful attack on Osama bin Laden and other terrorist leaders, greatly improved the U.S. image abroad by presenting a less combative demeanor towards the Arab world than his predecessor (even as he was criticized for ramping up an aggressive foreign policy towards Pakistan that included more civilian casualties), ended the Iraq War, and began major efforts to end the unpopular Afghanistan War. He ended anti-gay policies in the military, spoke out for gay marriage rights, and worked to significantly reduce unnecessary defense expenditures.[3]

In the area of civil rights, where as we will see below he has often been criticized, Obama and key cabinet officials made significant efforts, and they abandoned previous Republican attempts to end much civil rights enforcement. For example, impressive Obama Justice Department appointees were added by Attorney General Eric Holder, the first black attorney general. Holder moved his department towards much more aggressive civil rights enforcement and hired more than 100 career lawyers, most with significant real-world experience in civil rights enforcement. He also responded much more forthrightly to international and United Nations requests for reports on the U.S. civil rights situation.[4]

Although receiving little public or media recognition, numerous major progressive government policy changes were made by Obama and his administration, including much more aggressive enforcement of civil rights laws and a dramatic improvement in the federal relationship with and fair treatment of Native Americans—including, after many years of delays by previous administrations, billions of dollars in compensation to Native American groups for federal mismanagement of Indian land trusts. Native American activists described these changes as the most significant since the 1960s. Yet, most of these actions got little significant mainstream media coverage and little serious public discussion. Such actions provided major contrasts to the weak or nonexistent enforcement of civil rights and other human-protective laws under the previous George W. Bush administration. Actually, no U.S. president, including Democrats Jimmy Carter and Bill Clinton, had accomplished more progressive policy goals since the 1960s presidency of President Lyndon Johnson. Even with the frequent lack of good media coverage, moreover, a majority of Americans by 2011 were cataloging Obama as "liberal" in his presidential efforts.[5]

Obama's Decision-Making Context: Barriers and Attacks

President Obama's policy successes stand as all the more impressive because of the array of political attacks and barriers he regularly faced. Obama accomplished much while many arch-conservative Republican political leaders routinely fought him, periodically declaring their main goal was to make him a one-term president. Most of these politicians rarely supported Obama in most of his efforts to better fund the necessary programs of government, even as he was reducing the number of federal employees and trimming some federal programs such as Medicare supported by his own political base. Such government program reductions were anything but "socialistic," which was a major accusation against him by many conservatives. Most Republicans also aggressively opposed efforts to increase taxation, most especially on rich Americans, to buttress the federal government during the major economic crises.

As we have seen previously, many conservatives attacked Obama during his first presidential campaign for being insufficiently patriotic. This line of attack continued throughout his first years as president and during his second presidential campaign. Consider the example of the common nationalistic perspective often called "American exceptionalism." In a 2010 Gallup poll, the overwhelming majority of those polled agreed that the United States has "a unique character because of its history and Constitution that sets it apart from other nations as the greatest in the world"—that is, they agreed with contemporary American exceptionalism. A significant majority (58 percent) of all respondents thought President Obama felt the same way, but a significant majority (61 percent) of self-identified Republicans thought Obama did not see the U.S. as exceptional.[6] One likely reason for this Republican reaction was the fact that conservative leaders and activists had long proclaimed their view that Obama did not value the United States and think it exceptional. During his first presidential campaign and years in office, this was commonly asserted, and in the 2012 Republican primary campaigns major Republican candidates articulated this view. As the main Republican candidate and ultimately Republican nominee, Mitt Romney, put it, "We have a president right now who thinks America's just another nation. [But] America is an exceptional nation."[7]

Once again, however, specific data on U.S. presidents and their relevant views did *not* support this undocumented assertion. One study found that President Obama spoke more often about America's exceptionalism than any of the four Republican and Democratic presidents before him. In addition, research in presidential archives revealed that over the last eight decades Obama was the only U.S. president to have explicitly used the term "American exceptionalism" and specifically embraced it as such.[8]

President Obama faced many personal and general racist attacks from white conservatives during his first years as president, just as he did in his two electoral campaigns. Numerous political attacks on Obama were overtly racist and often out of a harsh version of the white anti-black frame. One common and vicious racist stereotype is that black Americans such as Obama and family are animalistic and ape-like. Many examples of this simianizing of Obama and family exploded across the mainstream media, as well as the white supremacist internet websites, over the Obama years. A Los Angeles newspaper reported a 2011 account of a California Republican official who emailed to a number of associates a picture of Barack Obama's face on the body of a chimpanzee. The picture was captioned with "Now you know why—No birth certificate!"[9] Another Republican official called on her to resign, noting that the message attacking Obama was "dripping with racism." Like many whites, her defense was the typical one: "I am not a racist. It was a joke. I have friends who are black." She claimed she did not know the message was racist. Lack of awareness that such common imagery is racist is implausible because she had to know that imagery for the simianizing message to be seen as a "joke." When influential whites make such racist attacks on President Obama and other African Americans— because they substantially control the society's dominant racial framing —they often get to decide what is "racist" activity, and what is not. One Republican Committee member defended this racist message as only "light-hearted," and indicated that local committee members often sent out such "fun" and "motivational" stuff. Clearly, racist messages in the white backstage are permissible. Yet another serious aspect of this incident was that numerous Republican officials seemed to be at least as concerned about who had released this backstage racist "joke" to the mainstream media as with its racist messaging.

This particular "chimp joke" was not an isolated incident. The use of such hostile racist imagery was also commonplace in comments on various internet websites, including some of the mainstream media. For example, on the Fox website in January 2011, there was a light-hearted news story on videos that portrayed a gorilla moving upright like human beings. The comments of some conservative Fox site viewers after the news story targeted Obama and other black political leaders. Some spoke of the gorilla as having "evolved from Obama's family," as reminding them of black activists, as looking like black member of Congress, and as having gotten a Hawaiian birth certificate over the internet.[10] The Fox site was not unusual. At other news websites, there were often comments by whites mocking President Obama and other black leaders using the simianizing and other blatantly antiblack imagery.

In addition, some important government officials have periodically come up with racist attacks using yet other antiblack imagery or attacks on Obama's personal history. There were many attacks on Obama's ancestry during his first electoral efforts, and these continued during his presidency and the 2012 electoral campaign. For example, in February 2012 a federal judge sent friends an email in which he communicated a racist "joke" about a young Obama talking with his white mother, who in the joke suggests Obama's mixed ancestry might have resulted from drunken party sex, jokingly alluding to potential sex with a dog. A "mongrelizing" of people who have diverse racial heritages is an old target in white-racist framing. This white judge admitted he was anti-Obama and that the joke was racist, yet like most whites who get called on racist actions still insisted that he was not "a racist" and only intended for this email to stay private among his (white) friends. A few days later, he sent a letter of apology to President Obama.[11]

Such racialized attacks were not limited to politicians and officials during the 2012 campaign. A *New York Times* story in May 2012 cited white residents of a small Ohio town who still maintained misgivings about the president due to his race and employed negative stereotypes of black Americans in order to explain his victory. One person quoted in the story posited that Obama won because of "black ignorance," while another speculated that "blacks came out to vote for the first time because he was black."[12] While such stereotypical representations and beliefs are not as virulent as the uptick in ape imagery, they still reflect a belief that Obama is overly beholden to, and maintains his position due to, black communities that blindly vote for another black person. And, yet again, they set a tone that may help shape Obama's continuing embrace of soft racial framing that avoids open, critical discussions of ongoing racial inequality and racial misperceptions.

Progressive White Critics: Avoiding the "Angry Black Man" Stereotype

During Obama's term, a significant group of white liberals and progressives began to attack him, often stridently, for his alleged failure to achieve major progressive goals. Liberal political sites such as dailykos.com and salon.com regularly provided settings for such political attacks. One example of such critique came from the prominent white analyst Glenn Greenwald:

> [Obama] doesn't try, doesn't use the weapons at his disposal: the ones he wields when he actually cares about something (such as the ones he uses to ensure ongoing war funding) . . . [This] leads to the rational conclusion that he is not actually committed to (or, worse, outright opposes) many of the outcomes which progressive pundits assume he desires.[13]

Looking at these difficult political decisions, however, the African American commentator Ishmael Reed early on suggested that Obama's apparent moderation in regard to some progressive goals was shaped significantly by his being a black man operating in white-controlled political institutions. Reed criticized white progressives who harshly asserted that Obama is "weak" and "spineless," or urged Obama to "man up" in dealing with Republicans. These liberal critics forgot the age-old racist framing: black intellectuals "have been called 'paranoid,' 'bitter,' 'rowdy,' 'angry,' 'bullies,' and accused of tirades and diatribes for more than 100 years."[14]

Thus, if Obama ever appeared too aggressive, such as the 1940s President Harry Truman did in numerous presidential actions, he would have been dismissed by many whites as an out of control "angry black man," a negative image that has been in traditional antiblack framing for generations. Such widespread dismissal would have made most of Obama's policy goals very difficult to achieve, and Obama not surprisingly maintained his "cool" political stance discussed previously throughout his years as president. White liberals commonly miss this aspect of an African American politician's political life. Ishmael Reed also pointed out that Obama's black and Latino/a voter base had not slipped much in support because, unlike those carping white progressives, those in this base "are not used to getting it all."[15]

In addition, political scientist Melissa Harris-Perry strongly criticized this tendency of numerous white progressives to see Obama as a "weak," "incompetent," or a non-progressive president, because these progressives failed to contrast Obama's actual, and major, achievements with those of recent Democratic presidents who had weaker progressive records. In her view, a certain "liberal electoral racism" could be glimpsed in the inclination of these progressive white critics "to hold African American leaders to a higher standard than their white counterparts." In numerous areas, as we noted previously, Obama's progressive achievements have often been greater than those of previous Democratic presidents such as Bill Clinton—for example, securing the first important health care insurance reform legislation, eliminating official anti-gay discrimination in military branches, and speaking out in support of gay marriage.[16] Harris-Perry's analysis of liberal racism was on target, although too cautious because most whites still view this society out of some version of a white racial framing and do not try to look at it as most people of color do.

The political implications of these white progressive attacks on Obama were significant. It was clear that as the 2012 political season began, if some white and other progressives stayed home and/or did not work actively for Obama, then his path to election might be seriously hampered. Over his first years, Obama faced not only negative racialized framing from many conservative whites, but also this electoral racism on the part of numerous white progressives.

Progressive Black Critics: A Somewhat Different Tack

Over Obama's first years, a few prominent black progressives also openly criticized Obama for errors and problems they saw in his presidential record. Their criticisms bore some resemblance to those of the white progressives, but there were significant differences in contextualization and emphasis. Perhaps the most famous black critic has been former

Princeton professor Cornel West, a leading intellectual who campaigned aggressively for Obama in 2008. In a 2011 interview, West accented criticisms in regard to certain Obama economic policies, like the white progressives, but he also insisted on the importance of the president acting to reduce racial barriers for the black community, something rarely suggested by white critics. West harshly assessed Obama as a "puppet of corporate plutocrats." He expected Obama to be constrained by capitalism, but also expected "some voices concerned about working people, dealing with issues of jobs and downsizing and banks, some semblance of democratic accountability for Wall Street oligarchs and corporate plutocrats who are just running amuck."[17] At *The Nation*, the aforementioned political scientist, Melissa Harris-Perry, was critical of West for what she viewed as a too harsh attack, and one apparently motivated as much by personal grievances as by strictly political differences.[18]

However, like numerous others critical of West, she neglected his mostly on-target structural critique of Obama's recurring orientation to corporate interests. Working-class Americans, especially forthright black Americans, have had very few voices in the upper ranks of the Obama administration. With few exceptions, Obama did appoint members of the moderate wing of the established white elite to top positions and sought economic goals supported by more centrist, well-off Democratic politicians. In his critique, West was emphasizing how individual black success in politics often does not mean significant advances for black Americans as a group.

Speaking out again in early 2012, West insisted he represented the "black prophetic tradition" in his renewed criticisms of President Obama's decisions, this time not only criticisms of Obama's continuing support of numerous interests of the "plutocratic" elite but also for his neglecting issues of racial inequality and racialized poverty. West noted that President Obama was "much better" than Republican alternatives, but he insisted that if Obama "continues to hang out with [Treasury Secretary] Tim Geithner and company, I am going to tell the truth about him and remain a serious critic." He did make the point that contrary to the assertions of the conservative media and politicians, Obama was *not* a socialist. "This man believes in capitalism to its core."

In this case, another progressive black leader, Reverend Al Sharpton, criticized West for political naïveté, noting that during the 2008 election West travelled across the country and campaigned with access to Obama, during which time "Obama never said he was going to do all this stuff that Cornel wants him to do."[19]

Most African American leaders did not speak out against President Obama, but seemed to agree with Sharpton. Many were aware of Obama's quiet progressive achievements in areas such as civil rights enforcement, and most recognized well the numerous political and structural, especially racial, barriers that Obama had long faced as the first black president.

Still Publicly Avoiding Racism Issues

Although he seemed to miss the importance of the numerous and very important policy actions that President Obama had taken, more or less quietly, on behalf of communities of color, Cornel West was correct in his assessment of Obama's unwillingness to publicly accent or discuss racial inequality and racial discrimination. For example, in March 2011, President Obama made an important trip to racially diverse Brazil, a country with the largest African-origin population outside Africa. Brazilian officials have frequently pointed to similarities in the racial realities of Brazil and the United States. This has included Brazilian president Dilma Rousseff, the first woman to hold that position and a former socialist guerilla. During Obama's 2011 trip, she noted the voters of each country had:

> dared to take at the highest level someone of African descent and a woman, demonstrating that the basis of democracy allows [us] to overcome the largest barriers to build societies that will be more generous and live more in harmony.

She also pointed up the fact that both countries had significant African-origin populations and thus had "a long track record of the struggle of the minorities."[20] In contrast, during his visit President Obama did not once note these racial similarities or discuss the racial breakthroughs or persisting high levels of racial discrimination in both countries— something even the usually color-blind *New York Times* noted. Once again, the pathbreaking black U.S. president did not publicly accent or assess contemporary white racism, but responded with timidity as he had in the Dr. Jeremiah Wright case—apparently again out of fear of alienating white voters.

We should note that this avoidance of discussing the dimensions of racial inequality and other racism was not unique to President Obama or other Democratic officials. As the primary season politicking was heating up in fall and spring 2011–2012, a few commentators in the mainstream media began to notice the lack of such serious discussions. In a *New York Times* op-ed piece, Desmond King, an Oxford political scientist, and Rogers Smith, a Penn State political scientist, jointly discussed the failure of both major parties to openly discuss U.S. racial matters seriously, especially issues such as the high unemployment rates for many other Americans of color:

> The economic crisis in the United States is also a racial crisis. White Americans are hurting, but nonwhite Americans are hurting even more. Yet leaders in both political parties ... act as though race were anachronistic and irrelevant in a country where an African American is the president.[21]

They briefly presented important data on these inequalities—summer 2011 unemployment rates of 16.8 percent for black workers and 11.3 percent for Latino/a workers, versus 8.2 percent for white workers—yet at no point did they discuss why there was such systemic racial inequality and exactly who the important decision makers on policy issues dealing with inequality were. Not only were whites not called out as agents of discrimination, but the elite white men whose racial and class actions have mostly generated the political parties' neglect of racial issues were not critically discussed as the most important agents shaping persisting structures of inequality.

Interestingly, President Obama did courageously if belatedly speak out on expanding marriage rights for gay and lesbian Americans. In late spring 2012, pressured by open support of some in his cabinet for gay marriage rights, Obama became the first sitting president to support such civil rights. The first national polls showed great variability in support for his position across the United States, significantly with more women supporting his position than men. Initial online (nonrandom) polls suggested that more voters were likely to change their votes away from Obama than to him because of his new gay rights position. Moreover, prior to Obama's statement in support of equal marriage rights, there had been a decline in gay/lesbian groups contributing to the Democratic Party and the 2012 Obama campaign, but after his statement there was a dramatic increase in such contributing and fundraising.[22] There was significant discussion in the mainstream media about Obama's statement hurting his support from African American voters, who had often opposed gay marriage in opinion polls, but polling after his statement revealed little negative impact on his political support from black voters and leaders.[23]

A Measured Liberal Critique: Some Governing Weaknesses

In an early 2012 *Atlantic* magazine article, the usually insightful white political analyst James Fallows argued that Obama had demonstrated an array of political and policy strengths and weaknesses. Fallows praised Obama for demonstrated ability to grow and become an effective decision maker, as noted in Obama's aforementioned strategic successes. Fallows pointed out effective political speeches that moved public opinion, including Obama's speech on racial matters in connection with the 2008 attacks on Dr. Wright. Weaknesses that Fallows underscored were (1) Obama's initial lack of political experience and dependence on more experienced Democratic appointees (many from the Clinton administration); (2) Obama's often "cold" and "distancing" style in private political relationships; (3) Obama's appointment of a mostly mediocre staff; and (4) the major mismatch between Obama's dramatic election rhetoric of progressive change and his much more limited policy goals. For example, Fallows suggested that many early economic errors that Obama made, such as in regard to Wall Street bailouts, resulted from relying on appointees with experience in the Clinton years.[24] In our view, Fallows was mostly correct about the operational weaknesses of a relatively inexperienced Obama's first years in presidential office. Reviewing the record to that date, moreover, Fallows then concluded that Obama had not yet completed his progressive goals and that a re-election loss for Obama in 2012 would likely mean that in the history books Obama would "forever seem a disappointment: a symbolically important but accidental figure who raised hopes he could not fulfill and met difficulties he did not know how to surmount."[25]

Even in this more measured liberal analysis, however, Fallows left out the critical white-racial context in which Obama has had to work throughout his entire political career. For example, Fallows made critical comments in passing about Obama being too close to his (only) major black political advisor and friend, Valerie Jarrett, but revealed no understanding of why the racially and politically savvy Jarrett has been important to Obama's political understandings and successes. Fallows showed no understanding as to why Obama had a particularly hard political time with the almost all-white Republican party leadership and that party's often whitewashed framing of society. There is a major tendency for white political analysts of various political orientations to miss the subtle and overtly racist contexts in which Obama had to operate on a daily basis. In order to make sense of many racialized barriers and events during Obama's presidential years, one must understand the extensive empirical evidence that serious black candidates for state and national political offices in the United States cannot openly adopt, even occasionally, a strong black counterframed perspective on the government action necessary to remedy or end the extensive discrimination and severe socioeconomic problems faced by black communities and other communities of color across the country, and still expect to win most political offices.[26]

In contrast, white political candidates and officials often tell their white constituencies what they will do for them in overt, or thinly disguised, racial terms. When they do, almost no one publicly accuses them of "playing the race card" when they take such a political tack. If black candidates even touch publicly on issues of developing *major* anti-discrimination programs for Americans of color, they are usually called out as racially biased or extremist. Even if a black candidate's associates call out the continuing white-racist system—as we saw Dr. Jeremiah Wright do during the 2008 elections—they must disassociate themselves from these associates and openly honest racial evaluations. Still, as we have seen, Obama by no means ignored the needs of communities of color during his first years as president, although for the most part he had to engage in generalized, unheralded, or behind-the-scenes actions in order to take actions to significantly benefit communities of color. Even as president, he was not able to talk openly about the massive and systemic racism of U.S. society—such as, to take one major example, the "new Jim Crow" system that is the oppressive U.S. prison-industrial complex.

The Undemocratic Political Context

James Fallows, like almost all other such U.S. analysts of any political stripe, assumes that Obama and other U.S. politicians are operating within a truly democratic political environment, when in fact the U.S. has a Constitutional foundation and current political reality that are in many ways undemocratic—even, in some instances, antidemocratic. Good examples of this political reality are an undemocratic electoral college that sometimes elects presidents receiving a minority of the popular vote, a very undemocratic U.S. Senate (for example, its represen-tation of states not population and its minority filibuster rule), and an unelected Supreme Court that can trump decisions made by elected officials. This often undemocratic and plutocratic reality is nothing new, but has been the U.S. political structure for centuries. Given these and other undemocratic and anti-democratic institutions, there are major limitations on any U.S. president that are set by a small, plutocratic, mostly white male ruling elite—and most especially on a president of color not from their elite political–economic circles.[27]

Not even the progressive black intellectual Cornel West or the progressive white journalist Fallows dared to do a fully honest evaluation of these obvious white-male-elite limits to Obama's political power. Putting all the progressive streams of criticism of President Obama into the context of U.S. political and structural history, we should note well that Obama's acceptance of numerous economic goals and interests of the white political–economic elite is by no means distinctive. This acceptance is not a character flaw, but rather about the foundational reality and continuing strength of the white-racist and classist system that is the United States. Indeed, all U.S. presidents, past and present, have had to "sell out" to the major corporate and other elite interests of their particular time in history—because these interests have controlled much that goes on in most major institutions. Thus, a more thorough political analysis of the issues raised by the aforementioned progressive critics of Obama must necessarily involve a much deeper critique and analysis of our undemocratic U.S. political and economic institutions.[28]

The Republican Party: Racialized Realities of Political Opposition

In this socio-political environment of Obama's first years as president, as we have seen, the Republican Party largely doubled down on racialized rhetoric, language, and imagery in opposing and working against President Obama. This is a strategy that the Republican Party has effectively utilized for many years. Let us go back some decades and look at the history of U.S. society and the organization of mainstream political parties, especially the Republican Party since the 1960s, in regard to racial issues.

One key to making sense out of racism and contemporary U.S. politics is the fact that since the early 1950s, because of President Harry Truman's move to desegregate the U.S. army and the Democratic Party's increasing support for civil rights, the Republican Party has gradually become the white-oriented political party of the United States, indeed in some important ways a "white nationalist" political party. This became conspicuous in the 1960s when many leaders in the party (including Ronald Reagan and George H. W. Bush, both of whom would become president), and the party generally, were opposed to the 1964 Civil Rights Act, the 1965 Voting Rights Act, the 1968 Fair Housing Act, and, more generally, the civil rights movement. What was once called the "party of Lincoln" because of its role in bringing down slavery in the 1860s had by the mid-1960s begun to replace the Democratic Party as the party of antiblack or anti-civil rights sentiment and, thus, the regular home for a majority of white voters. The civil rights movement, urban riots, and civil rights laws of the 1960s all contributed to a shift in white opinion that correlated closely with societal events that sought to end racism.[29]

White-Oriented Political Strategies

From the late 1960s to the present, Republican leaders have brought about their party's political resurgence by explicitly using a racialized politics that works substantially because the racist legacies of slavery and segregation have persisted into our contemporary society. Since the 1960s era, an explicit Republican political strategy has put much emphasis on the political–economic interests of whites, with a special effort to recruit whites residing in suburbia, rural states, and southern states. One dimension of this white-oriented approach can be seen in the Republicans' "southern strategy," which has operated since the 1960s to court white southern voters. It is important to understand that this widely used term, "southern strategy," is itself a racism-denying euphemism used by Republican operatives, mainstream media analysts, and academic researchers. Thus, the phrase "southern strategy" actually means a "white southern strategy" or "white racist strategy." These latter phrases are accurate because some 15–30 percent of Southerners are, depending on the particular southern area, not white and are thus not being courted by this biased political strategy.[30]

This white-southern strategy helped Republican Richard Nixon become president in 1968 and 1972. In presidential campaigns of the 1980s, it was again used effectively by Ronald Reagan and George H. W. Bush. Indeed, Reagan began his presidential campaign asserting strongly a states' rights doctrine, and he picked Philadelphia, Mississippi —where civil rights workers had been lynched—to make his symbolic appeal to white voters. Once in office, Reagan and associates sought to dismantle numerous civil rights enforcement efforts. Early in the 1980s Reagan administration, Lee Atwater, a Republican political operative, explained in an interview how the Republican Party had used language since the 1950s to appeal to southern whites. Atwater explained thus: "You start out in 1954 by saying, 'Nigger, nigger, nigger.' By 1968 you can't say 'nigger'—that hurts you. Backfires. So you say stuff like *forced busing, states' rights* and all that stuff."[31] At least since the 1980s, for many white leaders and rank-and-file members of the Republican Party, the phrases of "less government," "balancing budgets," and "cutting taxes" have often been coded ways of talking about U.S. racial issues. They frequently refer to reducing or eliminating social programs that are thought to oppose the interests of white Americans as a group—programs thought to be (at least from this white point of view) significantly tilted towards African Americans and other Americans of color.

Running for president in 1988, Republican George H. W. Bush and his political associates conducted a racist campaign that used visual images of a disheveled black rapist (but none from the majority of rapists, who are white males) from his Democratic opponent's home state, to intentionally scare or entice white voters into voting Republican. Once in office, Bush and his appointed officials continued the weakening or rollback of government antidiscrimination and related policy efforts. The "southern strategy" and related pro-white strategies have often been successful. Researchers have shown that an important reason for the shift to the Republican Party by many white voters was their view that it was more in tune with their interests and needs than the Democratic Party with its increasing connections to black Americans and important civil rights issues.[32]

In the late 1990s, another leading political activist, Ralph Reed, assessed the present and future of the Republican Party: "You're going to see a new Republican party that is still primarily white and that is fiscally and morally conservative, but that also is attempting to project an image of racial tolerance and moderation."[33] Reed's wording acknowledges that this message of racial harmony is simply an image, rather than a major political effort substantiated by important policy or legislative goals. To the contrary, Republican complicity in efforts to challenge the voting rights of numerous communities of color through voter purges, voter identification laws, and similar restrictive techniques —in the past and very recently—reveal that the "image" of racial inclusion often does not extend to political practice. Following this pro-white perspective and image-making, most Republican leaders have since continued to maintain a Republican Party that is overwhelmingly white, but one that occasionally foregrounds a few token Republican officials of color, such as Clarence Thomas and Condoleezza Rice.

Protecting White Interests

Yet, more recently, after losing presidential elections in the 1990s to the moderate Democrat William Clinton, the Republican Party succeeded in electing George W. Bush in presidential elections in 2000 and 2004. The GOP again focused heavily on soliciting white voters, often with implicit racial appeals; and some Republican officials sought, again often successfully, to restrict voting by voters of color in key states. A significant proportion of the white vote for the Republican Party in presidential elections since the 1960s seems to have been, at least in part, racially motivated.

We should note too that there is much more to the Republican Party's racial strategies since the 1960s than just the white-southern strategy. Various other strategies and actions taken by Party leaders and members have also been directed, often more covertly, at enhancing or protecting white interests. One of these is the Party's official and often expressed hostility to government action and intervention. Yet, this anti-government hostility is not typically directed at military development or any of the other many government actions that benefit corporate America and well-off Americans. Most of the Republican Party's hostility to government action has focused on social support programs, especially those that have emerged since the reformist era of the 1960s when many of these social programs were spurred by the civil rights and anti-poverty movements. Thus, the 2008 Barack Obama election appeared significant for a future United States possibly not so beholden to the Republican Party and not so caught up in conservative anti-government rhetoric. In the coming years, thus, there may conceivably be more voter support for new or renewed government action on important health care, environmental, labor, and employment security issues. The Republican and other conservative attacks on "big government" may gradually become no longer effective for a country that faces serious and chronic economic and political crises.

Many moderate Republicans have appeared worried about the fact that in 2008 John McCain got the smallest percentage of the black vote ever recorded for a Republican and also got low percentages for most other groups of color. Obama's moderate stance on issues such as Middle East policy and his middle-of-the-road approach on other policy matters have brought him support from moderate groups such as the one called Republicans for Obama. In 2008, they worked for Obama because the country required a "new kind of leader" who would work to improve

U.S. economic prosperity and standing in the world, and they continued this work for what some called Eisenhower or moderate Republicanism throughout the 2012 campaigns as well.[34] Clearly, the national political problem for the Republican Party had become much broader than just the fact that John McCain lost the 2008 presidential election.

Today, the Republican Party remains an omnipresent and vigilant political guardian of the interests of white Americans. In November 2008, the Party yet again got a large majority of white voters, including a majority in more than 60 percent of the states. This continued in the midterm elections of 2010. Some media and expert commentary on the 2008 election argued that the Republican southern strategy was shown by the Obama victory in three of the southern states (and elsewhere) to no longer be viable. However, in 2008 Obama *lost* most southern states and all border states except Maryland. He barely won in North Carolina, Virginia, and Florida, which then suggested that Republicans might have good chances to win back these southern states. Still, ongoing demographic changes, including the growing numbers of Latino/a and Asian voters in areas of the South and Southwest, may eventually help the Democratic Party to consistently win more states there. The GOP today remains very influential with white voters and for some time to come is likely to garner large percentages of white voters not only in historically white suburban areas around big cities in all states, but also in most southern, border, and mountain states.

Alienating Americans of Color

In contrast, few black Americans now vote for the Republican Party in any state, even though prior to the 1930s the black vote was heavily for the "party of Lincoln." In presidential elections between 1992 and 2008, the Republican Party got a remarkably small percentage of black voters. In addition, majorities of other large groups of color (except for Cuban Americans) did not vote Republican in November 2008, and they mostly have not voted in the majority for the Republican Party in other recent national elections.[35]

Despite sweeping gains in the House of Representatives during the midterm elections of 2010, the Republican Party in 2012 only boasts two African American members. The other Americans of color serving there are mostly Democrats. For example, in 2012 there were just eight Republicans among the 26 Latinos in the U.S. Congress. The Republican congressional delegation remains overwhelmingly white and male. In late 2012 the Republican Party has no African American governors in the states, and in recent years the GOP has had very few black appointed officials in high political offices in the states or federal government. Moreover, those people of color who do represent the Republican Party often echo the rhetoric and incendiary language and framing emblematic of the Republican Party at large—railing against immigrants and social programs designed to alleviate poverty, and in a few cases using hard racial framing to denigrate President Obama.

In addition, recent national Republican conventions have had a tiny percentage of black delegates. The 2008 Republican National Convention in St. Paul, Minnesota was no exception. Among the Republican delegates, there were only 36 African Americans, less than 1.5 percent of the total, and a declining percentage compared to the convention of 2004. There were also few other delegates of color. In 2008, the Republican National Committee had no black members from the mainland United States, and only one black member (from the U.S. Virgin Islands). Moreover, at the 2012 Republican National Convention there were a few more African American delegates (47), but their percentage among the overwhelmingly white delegates was again quite small (2.1 percent). In contrast, the Democratic Party had much higher African American percentages (more than 20 percent) of the delegates at their 2008 and 2012 conventions.[36]

Ironically, while the Republican Party has in effect become the "white party" in the United States because of its tacit and overt outreach to white voters at the expense of voters of color, the Democratic Party has not provided a consistently antiracist alternative. For example, in spite of his popularity with black Americans, during the 1990s President Bill Clinton implemented three-strikes sentencing laws and social welfare reform policies that have disproportionately harmed many black Americans and some other Americans of color. While the Democratic party is much more diverse in racial terms than the Republican party, especially at the level of national elective offices, its governing policies have not been designed to ameliorate racial discrimination and racial inequality on a large scale. Additionally, important issues such as the police shootings of unarmed black men such as Trayvon Martin, Oscar Grant, Sean Bell, and Amadou Diallo, or the racially motivated Algiers Point police murders in the aftermath of Hurricane Katrina, have not prompted national Democratic politicians to propose major legislation intended to address the root causes of these persisting racial discrimination issues. Indeed, numerous Democratic candidates for national or statewide office periodically make statements or comments intended to distance themselves from the concerns of black Americans and to reassure white voters that their political concerns will not be ignored or neglected.

Hence, while many in the Republican Party have for some decades made clear their willingness to use coded racialized language and open racist appeals to white voters' prejudices as a strategy for electoral success, both parties have long been complicit in perpetuating government policies that reproduce and perpetuate systemic racial inequality. The Republican Party often does so more overtly and with greater national visibility than the Democratic Party. We can now briefly turn to a recent example of this—the turbulent 2011–2012 Republican primary season that led up to the 2012 national election we discuss in the next chapter.

The 2011–2012 Republican Primary Season: Cain, Gingrich, Paul, Santorum, and Romney

Barely three years into his term as president, the Republican political machine aggressively emerged and revealed its strong white orientation yet again, this time in the 2011–2012 primary season. Even during the first months of this primary season, much racist imagery and argument was generated by Republican primary candidates. Negative imagery about black Americans was periodically utilized by Republican candidates and activists as they campaigned against each other and against President Obama. Some of this racialized discourse stated or implied that many Americans were making undeserved use of various government welfare and "entitlement" programs, with such terms frequently signalling opposition to government aid for the poor and people of color (and much less so for older whites on Social Security).

Let us consider a few examples of this discourse from various major Republican candidates in these primaries. During this primary campaign former House Speaker Newt Gingrich, once the second most powerful top federal official in the 1990s, prominently called Obama the "best food stamp president in history," a term with clear links to conventional white-framed images of poor people of color as undeserving recipients of such federal aid.[37] Gingrich criticized the Obama administration for supporting such "entitlement" programs. At one point, he also made a strongly worded suggestion that poor children (who are disproportionately children of color) should work as janitors in their schools. He explicitly argued they had a need to learn a community commitment and a work ethic, again signalling negatively stereotyped images long central to the old white framing of black Americans.[38]

Another Republican presidential candidate, former Senator Rick Santorum, made similarly stereotyped comments to a mostly white campaign audience: "I don't want to make black people's lives better by giving them somebody else's money. I want to give them the opportunity to go out and earn the money and provide for themselves and their families."[39] Santorum later defended himself by stating that he actually said "blah people," though this defense was widely disparaged. Both these leading white Republicans periodically linked President Obama to programs seen as unfairly expanding or providing "entitlement" programs for the country's poor, especially the poor of color. Many white conservatives heard these Republican candidates speak on these and similar racial issues at various meetings, often cheering their openly racialized statements.

In addition, Ron Paul, a libertarian Republican candidate also running in numerous primaries, had long been famous for a racist conservative newsletter published under his name, a publication he argued during his campaign that he had not read carefully when it was published. Mitt Romney, the leading candidate for much of the Republican primary season, also sent out explicit messages about vetoing pro-immigrant legislation such as the "Dream Act" if he were president. He too explicitly sought to reduce the scope of what he termed the "entitlement society." Indeed, Romney made campaign comments suggesting that President Obama was trying to move the United States away from a meritocracy and make it into even more of an "entitlement society," going so far as to say that Obama "hates free enterprise." These Republican candidates sometimes suggested President Obama was not proud of his country, even though as we have seen Obama actually had given more speeches accenting the United States as a world model than any previous president.[40]

These types of statements were not limited to white candidates for the Republican nomination. Before suspending his campaign, Herman Cain, the sole Republican candidate of color in the initial group of nine candidates, drew attention when he argued that black Americans were "brainwashed into not being open minded, not even considering a conservative point of view." Cain contended that this brainwashing helped explain blacks' broad support for President Obama and the Democratic Party generally. He also stated that he did not "believe racism in this country holds anybody back in a big way," and criticized Obama specifically for, among other things, not being a "strong black man." Ironically, when Cain faced increasing pressure to drop out of the race after repeated allegations of sexual harassment surfaced, he attributed this pressure to "racial politics"—though he had previously denied that race remains a salient factor in shaping aspects of social life.[41] More so than any of his white counterparts, Cain was explicit in denying the reality of structural and interpersonal racism (which, in reality, is supported by voluminous data and empirical evidence), and simultaneously—albeit in a contradictory fashion—using racial imagery and language to bolster his campaign.

Significantly, as Lee Siegel, a *New York Times* columnist, put it early in the 2012 primary season, Mitt Romney, who eventually became the Republican nominee, was the perfect Republican candidate because he implicitly and explicitly exuded views and values often associated with the large conservative sector of white America:

> [In] . . . countless subtle and not-so-subtle ways he telegraphs . . . he is the cultural alternative to America's first black president. It is a whiteness grounded in a retro vision of the country, one of white picket fences and stay-at-home moms and fathers unashamed of working hard for corporate America.

That is, Romney provided these conservatives with "the white solution to the problem of a black president."[42]

We should note too that the racialization of the primary season went well beyond these Republican candidates. For example, in the midst of the Republican primaries in April 2012, the very white and Republican-oriented Fox cable network tried to raise anew the issue of a "controversial" Dr. Jeremiah Wright, clearly to try to tarnish the public image of President Obama as he ran for re-election. Commenting on recent sermons Wright had given at a Baptist church revival in West Virginia, several Fox network commentators argued aggressively that Wright's sharp (and accurate) sermon comments on issues of Thomas Jefferson's enslaved teenaged "mistress," on white supremacy in U.S. foreign policy, and on powerful white politicians making decisions over black lives were actually "hate-filled," an inaccurate term various Fox commentators kept repeating as apparently a contrived conservative mantra. Yet, these mostly white conservative commentators missed the real point of much of what Wright was actually arguing to a mostly black audience in the quotes they selected out of context. Wright had said:

> There are [white] politicians who are making decisions about you, about your life, about your future, about your family, about your children. And the real tragedy is they live in a different world from your world altogether. [There are] people in power right now who have opinions about you based on their privilege of skin color.

He also said: "The ignorance and arrogance of white supremacy have the shapers and movers of world policy living in a different world from people of color altogether." Both views about the conceptual and social segregation of powerful white decision makers from African Americans were indeed correct, as much social science data has demonstrated.[43]

Conclusion

In this chapter, we have first provided a nuanced overview and context of the challenges and accomplishments that President Barack Obama faced during his first years as president. Then, in the last two sections, we have offered a brief assessment of the strongly white character of the contemporary Republican Party that has emerged in recent decades, and come to a sharp focus in the Party's dealings with the first black president. We have concluded this chapter by examining the numerous racialized challenges and commentaries coming from Republican primary candidates in the last year of Obama's first term, as a prelude to considering events during the main national election later in 2012.

We substantially agree with some progressive critiques of President Obama's governing weaknesses, especially in his first years. These included his initial lack of political experience, heavy dependence on previous Democratic appointees, corporate economic advisors, and often-mediocre staff. We also agree to some extent that there has been a major mismatch between Obama's election rhetoric about progressive change and his more limited policy goals, especially in regard to economic inequality and economic change.

However, we have also examined the numerous ways in which the racialized social and political realities, including those created by an often-racialized Republican Party, have dramatically curtailed Obama's ability to govern effectively. These realities clearly shaped why and how he chose to continue operating within soft racial framing of U.S. politics and society. Obama's aggressive white critics have mostly missed the depth and scope of this racialized reality and have generally assumed that he could govern like a white Democratic president. Yet, as we have seen, this is not the case. Most white critics of Obama, including white liberals, do not see their own white racial framing and have been unable to understand how systemically racist U.S. society remains, as well as how that reality adds many distinctive and racialized political barriers for our first black president.

Many political analyses may disagree with our view of this contemporary systemic-racism reality, even though the social science evidence is extensive.[44] They might assert, too, that a few of Obama's outspoken black critics, such as Cornel West, have also been critical of Obama's policies and underplayed the racism we emphasize. They are correct, but only to a point. Thus, there are no black progressive critics who have not realized this racist reality faced by Obama, and either nuanced at least some of their criticisms of Obama's performance with that reality in mind or remained publicly supportive of his actions while being critical in private. Indeed, even Cornel West has focused a significant part of his critique of Obama's policies on the president's failure to take overt action to dramatically improve the racial inequalities faced by African Americans and other Americans of color—issues of racial oppression much less often addressed by any of Obama's white critics.

Moreover, unlike almost all other analysts of the Obama presidency, we have touched briefly on the barriers created for a progressive president by the undemocratic character of much of the U.S. political system. Our political system was originally created to protect foundational and systemic classism and racism, which began as slavery. We still live under a Constitution made undemocratically, and to a substantial degree by major slaveholders. We have an undemocratic U.S. Senate, in that it represents acreage not people, and we operate under an unelected Supreme Court that has mostly been operated historically by elite white men. In addition, most members of both houses of the U.S. Congress have come, in the past and present, from the white elite or the class of well-off Americans immediately below that group in privilege and power. Today, both houses of Congress have relatively few women of any background, and people of color are underrepresented, most glaringly in the U.S. Senate. President Obama has had to govern within this rather undemocratic political setting, which has regularly set serious limits on his desires and ability to deal with the socioeconomic problems faced by lower- and middle-income Americans, including Americans of color.

One conspicuous example of political barriers can be seen in the actions of the Republican Party and its representatives in Congress. As we have shown in this chapter, the Republican Party's decades-long identification with and cynical use of white racial framing for political purposes inside and outside of Congress has been an ongoing strategy that shows no signs of abating. In effect, the Republican Party has become the white party of the United States, with its overwhelmingly white national committee, conventions, and members of Congress. Only rarely have these national committees and congressional delegations included more than one or two African Americans. And the often whitewashed goals sought by Republican representatives, senators, and other leading officials have generally ignored or downplayed the serious issues of U.S. racial inequalities, racial discrimination, and civil rights enforcement. This neglect and opposition are key reasons why Americans of color, and especially African Americans, have in recent years voted overwhelmingly for the Democratic Party in most state elections and in national elections.

In the next chapter, we will conclude by addressing the explicit ways that these political issues played out over the course of the 2012 national presidential campaign.

10

THE 2012 NATIONAL ELECTION

The final months of the 2012 election campaign for the U.S. presidency were dramatic and revealing in regard to the continuing realities of white racial framing and other aspects of systemic racism and to the persisting weaknesses and strengths of the political system.

Republican and Democratic Political Advantages: The 2012 Election

From the beginning of the 2012 campaign, many media analysts and other political analysts thought Republican candidate Mitt Romney had certain major advantages. The Republican Party had made decisive political gains in the 2010 midterm elections. Many expected this to continue in 2012. Early in Obama's presidency, white approval of his performance stood at 61 percent, but by early 2012 his favorability rating was just 37 percent for whites (versus 85 percent for blacks and 55 percent for Latino/as).[1] For months before the November election, analysts speculated that Obama's low level of white support might cost him the election.[2] In addition, Associated Press (AP) surveys indicated that in 2012 Americans as a group were *more* likely to express antiblack views than in 2008, a shift suggesting problems for Obama's re-election. In the 2012 survey, about 60 percent of whites openly (and also implicitly) expressed antiblack views, the highest percentage for any reported racial group.[3]

However, in a spring 2012 analysis, Joan Walsh suggested white working-class voters in Midwestern states might be showing regret for previous support of Republicans. Working-class opposition had emerged because of Republican governors trying to reduce labor union rights in states such as Wisconsin and Ohio.[4] By fall 2012, especially in auto-industry states such as Ohio and Michigan, Obama's successful rescue of the auto industry had become a major issue, with Romney's opposition to that bailout apparently hurting his chances with some white voters in Midwestern states. In addition, some statistical models of major political analysts suggested that a slowly improving U.S. economy would have a positive effect on Obama's prospects.[5]

Moreover, African American, Latino/a, Asian American, and Native American voters had given candidate Obama a very large majority of their votes in 2008, and spring 2012 data suggested this would be repeated. In February 2012, one national poll revealed that Obama was holding onto similar percentages of support among registered voter groups that he won in 2008, but was losing among whites, at least at the level of 2008.[6] Significantly, little of substance was said publicly by either candidate or top campaign officials about this racial divide all through the long 2012 campaign.

2012 Republican Electoral Strategies

One important change in U.S. politics over recent decades involves extensive Republican efforts to restrict voting, particularly of those likely to vote Democratic. Restriction efforts have sought to reduce voter registration drives, early voting, same-day registration, and voting privileges for former felons, as well as to require identification documents that can be difficult for some voters to secure. After the resurgence of the Democratic Party in 2006–2008, numerous white-conservative-controlled state legislatures passed legislation with such provisions. Such requirements were often intended to screen out voters of color, and studies showed they did disproportionately affect those voters. However, in the 2012 election, these restriction attempts backfired in numerous areas, as they reportedly stimulated many voters of color to be certain to vote.[7]

In early 2012, in a Democratic-oriented memo, Andrew Levison suggested that conservative Republican attacks on President Obama would involve Romney mostly taking the "high road" by attacking Obama on weaknesses in economic and related policy issues. Other attacks would involve well-funded Super PACs (Super Political-Action Committees, well-funded groups not officially part of campaigns) and involve "culture war" attacks such as Republicans used in 2008. For example, Sarah Palin had insisted the 2008 Republican ticket was the one representing "real Americans," a phrase often targeting white voters. In 2012, thus, conservatives would again try to link Obama to foreigners, "illegal" immigrants, and Muslims. A third level of attack might involve "vastly expanded dissemination of a third, flagrantly dishonest and utterly propagandistic 'low road' attack . . . above and below the radar."[8] Levison was correct in these predictions. Moreover, in 2012, these Republican attacks, and Democratic countering, involved extensive use of cyber media, such as the web's newer social media, as well as the older "robo" phone calling.[9]

There was a major weakness in Levison's and other political commentators' predictions in spring and early summer 2012, as they suggested there would be no conservative political efforts explicitly using "racial prejudices." Yet, as we predicted, there was a long and continuing series of serious racist incidents reported in Internet and traditional media, most of it involving conservative whites. Whites at various levels engaged in a recurring, racialized demonization of Obama, with much commentary making him into a racist caricature. Why had the likely increase in, and significance of, this overtly racial dimension of the 2012 election been missed or downplayed by numerous mainstream commentators? One reason was that a substantial majority of 2012 mainstream media reporters and analysts were whites, many of whom apparently accepted the view of a "post-racial" America. One news survey revealed that *93 percent* of front-page newspaper stories on major issues—including 95 percent on immigration—during the 2012 campaign were by white journalists.[10]

Racist commentary and incidents relentlessly followed Obama up to his re-election. For example, important consultants for one Republican

Super PAC offered a political attack plan to bring up Obama's ties to Dr. Jeremiah Wright, and thus to stigmatize and racialize Obama again during the summer Democratic convention. When significant protest arose over this plan, including in online social media, Republican officials rejected it. This incident revealed the hard racial framing of major white conservative activists, a strong framing that persisted in various political sectors over the campaign.[11]

One campaign effort that not so subtly racialized Obama periodically made the misleading argument in major political ads that Obama had erased work requirements for "welfare recipients," a charge that was factually inaccurate and implicitly evoked stereotypes about Americans of color as welfare cheats who take undue advantage of government largesse.[12] This ad disappeared for a time after former president Bill Clinton offered an analysis of its inaccuracies at the Democratic National Convention. But, in spite of the refutations of its misrepresentations, it appeared again just before the November election.

The issue of Obama's "American-ness" arose constantly. For example, late in the 2012 campaign, the major pollster James Zogby reported receiving an official fund-raising letter from the Romney campaign not so subtly othering Obama. In just 15 lines, the pro-Romney letter mentioned "America" and "American" 10 times: "I believe in America . . . I believe in the American Dream . . . This election is a battle for the soul of America . . . [This campaign is] to reclaim America for the people." As Zogby noted, the Romney campaign was aggressively saying that Romney was the "real American" and implying Obama was less American or foreign, a culture-war theme reiterated from the 2008 campaign.[13]

When former general Colin Powell endorsed Obama, Romney's campaign co-chair John Sununu said Powell's reason was that Obama was of his "own race." Earlier, Sununu had said he wished Obama "would learn how to be an American," and after the first presidential debate he asserted the president was "lazy" and "disengaged." In these instances, Sununu used language and imagery from the hard racial frame, yet he was only one of many whites who did so all through the primary and final campaigns.

2012 Democratic Electoral Strategies

In the early stages of politicking during the election campaigns of 2011–2012, federal deficit debates put Democrats on the defensive. Republicans argued that it was "spendthrift" Democratic politicians who, among other policy errors, had given their tax monies to undeserving Americans—signalling implicitly or explicitly that the poor and Americans of color were at the front of their (usually white) minds. Given this difficult political situation, policy analyst Thomas Edsall argued that the Democratic strategy had to be "to shift the attention of the electorate to issues like inequality, the declining fortunes of the middle class, corporate greed and diminishing social and economic mobility."[14] Significantly, numerous speeches made by Obama long before 2012, as well as during this campaign, did emphasize important inequality, fairness, and rich people's greed issues—those with significant appeal to much of the electorate.

By late spring, President Obama was attacking a central feature of the Republican campaign—that Romney's leadership of an equity (Bain Capital) firm qualified him to lead the country out of economic troubles. Obama's speeches and Democratic Party ads pointed out that heading Bain did not make Romney a "job creator" (the campaign catchword) because such firms are primarily interested in creating profits for investors and often lay off workers to make troubled firms profitable. Democratic activists and commentators referred to this as "vulture" capitalism, but a majority of Americans polled viewed Romney's business experience as qualifying him to deal well with the economy. While the Romney campaign constantly focused on major economic issues, to Obama's good fortune, the economy did slowly improve over the presidential campaign.[15]

In a post-election PBS discussion, reporter Judy Woodruff summed up one consensus view of how Obama had won: he "secured a second term thanks in part to building a massive ground game, coupled with an early investment in negative television ads defining Mitt Romney." Analyst Sasha Issenberg added that the Obama campaign had done scientific experiments on how to better target its base, including "parts of the electorate that traditionally voted at a low rate," and that the campaign had to "reengage them and mobilize them again."[16] The Obama campaign was more technologically sophisticated than the Romney campaign and made extensive use of cloud computing and online outreach (social media), and especially of new data collection, analysis, phone calling, and donation software.[17] This sophistication greatly helped Obama's team to turn out much of their primary political constituency—younger voters, voters of color, unmarried white female voters, GLBT voters, and well-educated professionals.

Moreover, Obama's recurring electoral speeches about the importance of government in helping ordinary Americans succeed in troubling situations were strongly reinforced by Mother Nature. Hurricane Sandy, hitting the east coast a few days before election day, offered President Obama the chance to display support for ordinary Americans in difficulty, which he did well—to the point of getting praise from both Republican and Democratic state officials.

Throughout his presidency and the re-election campaign, Obama continued to operate out of the soft version of the white racial frame that accents a color-blind perspective, such as by accenting the supposed societal reality of equal opportunity for all. Obama and his aides were also cautious about the black officials invited to the White House and about references to racial issues in Obama's speeches and interviews. Not surprisingly, Obama continued to get substantial criticism from some in the black community. For example, during the fall campaign, Tavis Smiley, a prominent black television host, noted that:

> Tragically, it seems the president feels boxed in by his blackness. It has, at times, been painful to watch this particular president's calibrated, cautious and sometimes callous treatment of his most loyal constituency. African Americans will have lost ground in the Obama era.[18]

Interestingly, Obama did occasionally signal publicly, if briefly, that he recognized the importance of certain voters of color. In one interview with an Iowa newspaper just before the election, he pointed out that, if he should win, "a big reason I will win a second term is because the Republican nominee and the Republican Party have so alienated the fastest-growing demographic group in the country, the Latino community."[19] While he did not make equally strong statements about other voters of color who were in fact critical to his re-election—African, Asian, and Native American voters—his campaign staff understood well, and early on, that a winning strategy would involve a "ground game" appealing to these voters, and they constructed their successful voter efforts accordingly.[20]

The Dramatic Election Results

In the 2012 election, Obama won about 51 percent of the popular vote, as compared to 52.9 percent in 2008. This resulted in a 332–206 electoral vote victory, substantial but lower than the 365–173 figure for 2008. As they had in 2008, media and academic commentators of various political persuasions insisted this electoral victory meant "race no longer matters" in U.S. politics. Meanwhile, top conservative Republican leaders —reportedly including Romney himself—and right-wing commentators were "shocked" at the result. Some, such as the Fox network's Bill O'Reilly, moaned that the re-election meant "the white establishment is now the minority."[21]

Nothing could be farther from the truth. Whites made up 72 percent of voters in the 2012 election, down 2 percent from 2008. Exit polls indicated that white voters gave Obama a lower percentage of their votes (39 percent) in 2012 than in 2008 (43 percent). Romney got a majority nationally and in most states. His biggest white majorities were in southern, Appalachian, and Rocky Mountain states where Republicans captured many local political positions. About 89 percent of those voting for Romney were white. Exit polls indicate Obama lost all white age and gender groups by substantial margins. Media and academic discussions of Obama winning the "youth and female vote" were misleading because it was youth and women of color who provided such majorities for him. He only got 44 percent of whites under age 30 and just 42 percent of white women. He also secured just 35 percent of white men.[22] Significantly, however, one survey indicated Obama got 70 percent of the Jewish American vote, perhaps the only large-majority percentage for a major white subgroup. (He also got about 86 percent of the racially diverse Muslim vote.)[23]

In the 2008 and 2012 elections, Obama was the first *winning* presidential candidate to lose this white vote by double digits. Why did he lose such a large share? We have noted the 2012 survey indicating the antiblack views of about 60 percent of whites. This negative framing likely affected significant numbers of white voters in both direct and indirect ways. For example, some social scientists have suggested that Obama was held by many whites to a higher level of competence and performance (and qualifications) than an otherwise comparable white president might have been—much like the situation for many black professional sports coaches.[24] Many whites could thus justify not voting for him in terms of his presidential performance—especially as that was negatively presented in the conservative mass media.

As in 2008, voters of color often provided the state margins of victory for President Obama, and their percentage of the electorate increased from 26 percent in 2008 to 28 percent in 2012. Black voters gave him 93 percent of their votes; Native Americans, more than 90 percent; Latino/as, 71 percent; and Asian Americans, 73 percent. The percentages for Latino/a and Asian voters increased significantly from their 2008 percentages.[25] Black voters turned out in larger numbers than 2008 in key areas of states such as Virginia and Ohio, likely providing his margin of victory in several areas. Moreover, Romney and his party's hard-right positions on immigration were cited by Latino/a analysts as a major reason for his huge loss of Latino/a voters. Indeed, after winning the Republican candidacy in 2012, Romney admitted to a fundraising gathering that Obama's percentage among Latino/as in polls likely "spells doom for us" and suggested Republicans offer moderate legislation on immigration to secure Latino/a voters.[26]

A significant sector of the Democratic base is now Latino/a. In national polls, 70 percent of Latino/a voters say they are Democrats or lean that way, compared to 16 percent for the Republican Party.[27] One report on congressional reapportionment after the 2010 census revealed that states getting new congressional seats had an eligible voter population 15.2 percent Latino/a, much more than for those losing seats.[28] As Latino/a voters increase, Latino/as are playing a much more important role in state and national politics. Even if conservative politicians get the restrictions on Latino/a immigrants they often seek, major changes will result from ongoing demographic realities—including new congressional seats and electoral college votes in numerous key states.[29] This does not bode well for the future of a Republican Party whose white-conservative base is still strongly supportive of relatively extreme legal restrictions on Latino/a and other immigrants.

The Future of a White-Centered Republican Party

After the 2012 election, there was much debate in the Republican Party over why they lost the election. Most of the conservative contingents that control the party seemed shocked and confused by the result and/or argued that Romney and Republican officials were not conservative enough. Some downplayed the significance of changing voter demographics, while others such as Republican consultant Dick Morris asserted after the election that "This isn't your father's America." Representing many conservatives, talk show host Rush Limbaugh lamented that "I went to bed last night thinking we've lost the country" and insisted *conservatives* did not really lose because it was difficult to beat Obama when many degenerate voters wanted government handouts.[30]

A few Republican moderates spoke out about the need for a more centrist Republican Party or about the importance of the demographic trends. Rod Dreher, editor of *The American Conservative,* insisted "The Republican Party is becoming a perversely rigid sect, more concerned with being militantly correct than being pragmatic and successful," and called for more Republican compromise. Senator Lindsay Graham insisted there were not enough "angry white guys" to win national elections anymore. *New York Times* columnist Ross Douthat admitted most conservatives were too confident—in viewing Obama's presidency as "not only embattled but self-evidently disastrous" and seeking "to raise the ideological stakes at every opportunity," thinking this would win. Douthat suggested the Obama win represented a major political alignment—a new political coalition of an "emerging Democratic majority." He and other influential Republicans suggested the need for somewhat more moderate Republican positions on key policy issues, especially immigration.[31]

However, one key figure in the 1990s centrist shift of the Democratic Party argued that centrist reorganization would be very difficult for the

Republicans, given that most Republican office-holders were not prag-matists, but dogmatic conservatives whose perspective embraced "smaller government, laissez-faire economics, and cultural conservatism" and *"no compromises* with Democrats."[32]

Conclusion

As with the 2008 election, the response around the globe was generally favorable to Obama's 2012 re-election. There was also much celebration in U.S. communities of color and among white progressives. Simul-taneously, however, segments of the population still expressed strong elements of the hard racial frame in response to Obama's win. There were riotous anti-Obama protests by white conservatives at the University of Mississippi and Virginia's Hampden-Sydney College. News accounts circulated stories of many racist tweets from young whites and others calling for the president's assassination and using racist epithets from the hard racial frame to describe him.[33] The fact that these outbursts often came from young whites is significant, as many point to younger white generations as being immune to the hard racist framing thought to characterize older generations. However, the open, public use of racist framing and violent threats against Obama on social media and campuses suggests that young whites may not be as non-racist as many mainstream analysts might like to believe.

Significantly, in his victory speech to supporters after his re-election was clear, President Obama assessed his re-election from the idealistic, hopeful, and still color-blind perspective on the present and future United States he had long used:

> Tonight, more than 200 years after a former colony won the right to determine its own destiny, the task of perfecting our union moves forward . . . We believe in a generous America; in a compassionate America; in a tolerant America, open to the dreams of an immigrant's daughter who studies in our schools and pledges to our flag. To the young boy on the South Side of Chicago who sees a life beyond the nearest street corner. To the furniture worker's child in North Carolina who wants to become a doctor or a scientist, an engineer or entrepreneur,

a diplomat or even a President. That's the future we hope for
... I believe we can keep the promise of our founding—the idea
that if you're willing to work hard, it doesn't matter who you
are, or where you come from, or what you look like, or where
you love—it doesn't matter whether you're black or white, or
Hispanic or Asian, or Native American, or young or old, or rich
or poor, abled, disabled, gay or straight—you can make it here
in America if you're willing to try.[34]

NOTES

1 White Racial Framing and Barack Obama's First Campaign

1 Steve Scully, "Interview with Secretary of State Condoleezza Rice," C-Spanish, November 10, 2008, www.state.gov/secretary/rm/2008/11/111756.htm (accessed November 24, 2008).

2 "Text of Forwarded Email," *Tampa Bay Online*, www2.tbo.com/content/2008/oct/30/text-forwarded-e-mail/ (accessed November 16, 2008).

3 See the articles in Michael Brown et al., *Whitewashing Race: The Myth of a Color Blind Society* (Berkeley, CA: University of California Press, 2003).

4 For a more detailed discussion, see Joe R. Feagin, *The White Racial Frame* (New York: Routledge, 2009).

5 Michael Omi and Howard Winant, *Racial Formation in the United States* (New York: Routledge, 1994).

6 Joe R. Feagin, *Systemic Racism: A Theory of Oppression* (New York: Routledge, 2006).

7 Eduardo Bonilla-Silva, "Rethinking Racism: Toward a Structural Interpretation," *American Sociological Review* 62 (1997): 465–480; Eduardo Bonilla-Silva, *White Supremacy and Racism in the Post-Civil Rights Era* (Boulder, CO: Lynne Reimer, 2001); Eduardo Bonilla-Silva, *Racism Without Racists* (Lanham, MD: Rowman and Littlefield, 2003).

8 See Leslie Carr, *Color-Blind Racism* (Thousand Oaks, CA: Sage, 1997); Leslie Houts Picca and Joe R. Feagin, *Two Faced Racism* (New York: Routledge, 2007).

9 W. E. B. DuBois, *The Philadelphia Negro* (Philadelphia, PA: University of Pennsylvania Press, 1996).

10 Adia Harvey Wingfield, *Doing Business with Beauty* (Lanham, MD: Rowman and Littlefield 2008).

11 Joe R. Feagin, *Systemic Racism*.

12 Dee Brown, *Bury My Heart at Wounded Knee* (New York: Henry Holt, 2001).

13 The Supreme Court made this decision in the 1857 Dred Scott case, in which the court established that black Americans had no rights to citizenship or its benefits.

14 Joe R. Feagin, *Systemic Racism*.

15 W. E. B. DuBois, *The Philadelphia Negro*.

16 Michael Brown et al., *Whitewashing Race*.

17 Eduardo Bonilla-Silva, *White Supremacy and Racism in the Post-Civil Rights Era*.

18 Michael Brown et al., *Whitewashing Race*; Melvin Oliver and Thomas Shapiro, *Black Wealth/White Wealth* (New York: Routledge, 1995); Joe R. Feagin and Eileen O'Brien, *White Men on Race* (Boston, MA: Beacon Press, 2003).

19 Thomas Shapiro, *The Hidden Costs of Being African American* (New York: Routledge, 2004).

20 Joe R. Feagin and Eileen O'Brien, *White Men on Race*.

21 Ibid., pp. 160–161.

22 Joe R. Feagin, *Systemic Racism*; Wendy Leo Moore, *Reproducing Racism* (Lanham, MD: Rowman and Littlefield, 2008).

23 Charles Gallagher, "Racial Redistricting: Expanding the Boundaries of Whiteness," in *The Politics of Multiculturalism: Challenging Racial Thinking*, Ed. Heather Dalmadge (New York: SUNY Press, 2004), pp. 59–76; Eduardo Bonilla-Silva, *Racism Without Racists*.

24 Yen Le Espiritu, *Asian American Women and Men* (Thousand Oaks, CA: Sage Publications, 1997); Rosalind Chou and Joe R. Feagin, *The Myth of the Model Minority* (Boulder, CO: Paradigm, 2008); Joe R. Feagin and Clairece Y. Feagin, *Racial and Ethnic Relations* (Upper Saddle River, NJ: Prentice Hall, 2008), pp. 159–322.

25 Kim Lersch and Joe R. Feagin, "Violent Police–Citizen Encounters: An Analysis of Major Newspaper Accounts," *Critical Sociology* 22 (1996): 29–49; Yen Le Espiritu, *Asian American Women and Men: Labor, Laws, and Love* (Lanham, MD: Rowman and Littlefield, 2000); Patricia Hill Collins, *Black Sexual Politics* (New York: Routledge, 2004).

26 Ivy Kennelly, "'That Single Mother Element': How White Employers Typify Black Women," *Gender & Society* 13 (1997): 168–192.

27 Wendy Leo Moore, *Reproducing Racism*.

28 Angie Beeman, "Emotional Segregation: A Content Analysis of Institutional Racism in U.S. Films," *Ethnic & Racial Studies* 30 (2007): 687–712.

29 Ann Arnett Ferguson, *Bad Boys: Public Schools and the Making of Black Masculinity* (Ann Arbor, MI: University of Michigan Press, 2003).

30 Joleen Kirschenman and Kathryn Neckerman, "'We'd Love to Hire Them, But . . .': The Meaning of Race for White Employers," in *Rethinking Race*, Ed. Charles Gallagher (New York: McGraw-Hill, 2000); Dee Royster, *Race and the Invisible Hand* (Berkeley, CA: University of California Press, 2000).

31 Judith Lorber, *Breaking the Bowls* (New York: W. W. Norton, 2006); Ella Bell and Stella Nkomo, *Our Separate Ways* (Boston, MA: Harvard Business School 2001).

32 Michael Brown et al., *Whitewashing Race*; quote is from Joe R. Feagin and Eileen O'Brien, *White Men on Race*, p. 173.

33 Adia Harvey Wingfield, *Doing Business with Beauty* (Lanham, MD: Rowman and Littlefield, 2008).

34 Rosalind Chou and Joe R. Feagin, *The Myth of the Model Minority*.

35   Patricia Hill Collins, *Black Feminist Thought*; and Meg Lovejoy, "Disturbances in the Social Body," *Gender & Society* 15 (2001): 239–261.

36   See Joe R. Feagin, *Systemic Racism*.

37   Quoted in Joe R. Feagin, *Racist America: Roots, Current Realities, and Future Reparations* (New York: Routledge, 2000), p. 122. No name was given. The spelling and punctuation are as in the original letter. It was signed in capitals.

38   Buchanan is quoted describing Adolf Hitler as "an individual of great courage, a soldier's soldier in the great war," a man of "extraordinary gifts," whose "genius" was due to his "intuitive sense of the mushiness, the character flaws, the weakness masquerading as morality that was in the hearts of the statesmen who stood in his path." Tim Wise, "Farrakhan is Not the Problem," *Racism Review*, May 26, 2008, www.racismreview.com/blog/2008/05/26/farrakhan-is-not-the-problem/ (accessed October 19, 2008).

39   Quoted in John Dillin, "Immigration Joins List of '92 Issues," *Christian Science Monitor* (December 17, 1991): 6.

40   Joe R. Feagin and Eileen O'Brien, *White Men on Race*, p. 119.

41   See Thomas Shapiro, *The Hidden Costs of Being African American*, and Joe R. Feagin and Eileen O'Brien, *White Men on Race*, for examples of these viewpoints.

42   Joe R. Feagin, "MSNBC's Chris Matthews and the Racial Frame: 'Not a Sociologist?'," June 11, 2008, www.racismreview.com/blog/2008/06/11/ msnbcs-chris-matthews-the-racial-frame-%E2%80%9Cnot-asociologist%E2%80%9D/ (accessed October 19, 2008).

43   Sut Jhally and Justin Lewis, *Enlightened Racism: The Cosby Show, Audiences, and the Myth of the American Dream* (Boulder, CO: Westview Press, 1983).

44   Ibid., p. 97.

45   Ibid., p. 47.

46   Eduardo Bonilla-Silva, *White Supremacy and Racism in the Post-Civil Rights Era*.

47   Ibid.

48   Leslie Houts Picca and Joe R. Feagin, *Two Faced Racism*.

2   "Too Black?" or "Not Black Enough?"

1   Lynne Olsen, *Freedom's Daughters* (New York: Scribner, 2001).

2   Joe R. Feagin and Clairece B. Feagin, *Racial And Ethnic Relations*, 8th edition (Upper Saddle River, NJ: Prentice Hall, 2008), pp. 166–196.

3   "Address before the Democratic National Convention," July 18, 1984, www.pbs. org/wgbh/pages/frontline/jesse/speeches/jesse84speech.html (accessed January 17, 2009).

4   Former Senator Carol Mosely Braun (D-IL), former U.S. Ambassador Alan Keyes, and Reverend Al Sharpton are three well-known examples.

5   Matt Bai, "Is Obama the End of Black Politics?" *New York Times*, August 6, 2008, www.nytimes.com/2008/08/10/magazine/10politics-t.html (accessed January 17, 2009).

6   Transcript of McNeil-Lehrer News Hour, August 1, 2000, www.pbs.org/news hour/bb/election/july-dec00/powell_8-1.html (accessed January 17, 2009).

7   Andrea Billups and David R. Sands, "Obama Term Expected to be Post-racial Agenda Heavy with Economy, Foreign Policy," *Washington Times*, November 9, 2008, www.washingtontimes.com/news/2008/nov/09/obama-presidency-expected-to-be-post-racial (accessed November 21, 2008).

8   Ibid.

9   Lola Adesioye, "Ralph Nader's Guilt Complex," *Guardian*, June 27, 2008, www.guardian.co.uk/commentisfree/2008/jun/27/barackobama.ralphnader (accessed October 18, 2008).

10 Jennifer Steinhauer, "Door to Door: Volunteers for Obama Face a Complex Issue," *New York Times*, October 14, 2008, www.nytimes.com/2008/10/15/us/politics/15nevada.html?_r=1 (accessed October 15, 2008).

11 This address was Obama's first introduction to national audiences and was the beginning of his meteoric rise. The speech was extremely well received and brought Obama unprecedented attention.

12 Ta-Nehisi Paul Coates, "Is Obama Black Enough?" *Time*, February 1, 2007, www.time.com/time/nation/article/0,8599,1584736,00.html (accessed October 18, 2008).

13 Hazel Trice Edney, "Obama v. McCain: NAACP Questionnaire Reveals Contrasting Agendas on Issues Important to Blacks," *Chicago Defender*, October 29, 2008, www.chicagodefender.com/article-2298-obama-v-mccain-naacp-questionnaire-reveals-contrasting-agendas-on-issues-important-to-blacks.html (accessed November 25, 2008).

14 "The Long Siege," *Newsweek*, www.newsweek.com/id/167755/page/4 (accessed November 25, 2008).

15 See AP Report, "Many Blacks Worry about Obama's Safety," February 22, 2008, www.editorandpublisher.com/eandp/news/article_display.jsp?vnu_content_id=1003714423 (accessed October 18, 2008).

16 Joe R. Feagin and Clairece Y. Feagin, *Racial and Ethnic Relations*, pp. 186–193.

17 Xuan Thai and Ted Barrett. "Biden's Description of Obama Draws Scrutiny," CNN, February 9, 2007, www.cnn.com/2007/POLITICS/01/31/biden.obama/ (accessed July 22, 2008).

18 Eric Boehlert and Jamison Foser, "Limbaugh on Obama: Halfrican American," *Media Matters*, January 24, 2007, http://mediamatters.org/items/200701240010 (accessed October 18, 2008). Conservative commentator Brian Sussman has also used the same term to describe Obama.

19 Joe R. Feagin, *Racist America* (New York: Routledge, 2000), pp. 20 and passim.

20 Kerry Ann Rockquemore and David L. Brunsma, *Beyond Black* (Lanham, MD: Rowman & Littlefield, 2007). We draw here on the foreword by Joe R. Feagin.

21 Barack Obama, *Dreams from My Father* (New York: Three Rivers Press, 2004); Barack Obama, *The Audacity of Hope* (New York: Vintage, 2008).

22 Ta-Nehisi Paul Coates, "Is Obama Black Enough?" *Time*, February 1, 2007, www.time.com/time/nation/article/0,8599,1584736,00.html (accessed November 24, 2008).

23 Eugene Robinson, "An Inarticulate Kickoff," *Washington Post*, February 2, 2007, www.washingtonpost.com/wp-dyn/content/article/2007/02/01/ AR2007020101495. html (accessed December 3, 2008).

24 Adam Nagourney, Jim Rutenberg, and Jeff Zeleny, "Near-Flawless Run Is Credited in Victory," *New York Times*, November 5, 2008, www.nytimes.com/2008/11/05/ us/politics/05recon.html?_r=3&hp=&oref=slogin&pagewanted=all (accessed November 25, 2008) (emphasis added).

25 Krissah Thompson, "A Year Later, Sherrod Won't Go Away," *Washington Post*, June 15, 2011, www.washingtonpost.com/politics/a-year-later-sherrod-wont-go-away/2011/06/07/AGjHEVWH_story.html (accessed March 27, 2012).

26 Andrew Breitbart, "Video Proof: The NAACP Awards Racism,"*Big Government*, July 19, 2010, www.webcitation.org/5rbhsjhzR (accessed March 27, 2012).

27 Krissah Thompson, "A Year Later, Sherrod Won't Go Away," *Washington Post*, June 15, 2011, www.washingtonpost.com/politics/a-year-later-sherrod-wont-go-away/2011/06/07/AGjHEVWH_story.html (accessed March 27, 2012).

3 From Susan B. Anthony to Hillary Clinton

1 Both candidates referred to each other in this manner in a January 31, 2008 debate in Los Angeles, CA. See "Clinton, Obama Debate with Less Finger-Pointing," *CNN*, February 1, 2008, www.cnn.com/2008/POLITICS/01/31/ debate.main/index. html (accessed October 18, 2008).

2 Lynne Olsen, *Freedom's Daughters* (New York: Scribners, 2001).

3 Angela Davis, *Women, Race, and Class* (New York: Random House, 1981).

4 Ibid.

5 In many cases, only propertied or wealthy white men could consider voting an inalienable right.

6 Frederick Douglass, *Narrative in the Life of Frederick Douglass* (Boston, MA: Bedford Press, 1995); Lynne Olsen, *Freedom's Daughters*.

7 Paula Giddings, *A Sword Among Lions* (New York: Amistad Press 2008); John Hope Franklin, *From Slavery to Freedom* (New York: Knopf, 2000).

8 Lynne Olsen, *Freedom's Daughters*.

9 Paula Giddings, *A Sword Among Lions*.

10 Lynne Olsen, *Freedom's Daughters*, p. 31.

11 Ibid., p. 31.

12 Ibid., p. 32.

13 Jessie Daniels, "Beyond Separate Silos," *Gender & Society* 22 (2008): 83–87.

14 Fifteenth Amendment, www.loc.gov/rr/program/bib/ourdocs/15thamendment. html (accessed October 18, 2008).

15 Title VII of the Civil Rights Act of 1964, www.eeoc.gov/policy/vii.html (accessed October 18, 2008).

16 Maria Charles and David Grusky, *Occupational Ghettos: The Worldwide Segregation of Women and Men* (Palo Alto, CA: Stanford University Press, 2004); Nijole Benokraitis and Joe R. Feagin, *Modern Sexism* (Upper Saddle River, NJ: Prentice

Hall, 1992); "Statistics. Rape, Abuse, and Incest National Network (RAINN)," www.rainn.org/statistics (accessed October 18, 2008).

17 Irene Browne and Joya Misra, "The Intersection of Race and Gender in the Labor Market," *Annual Review of Sociology* 29 (2003): 487–513; Yen Le Espiritu, *Asian American Women and Men: Labor, Laws, and Love* (Thousand Oaks, CA: Sage, 2003); Jennifer Lee, "From Civil Relations to Racial Conflict: Merchant-Customer Interactions in Urban America," *American Sociological Review* 67 (1998): 77–98.

18 "Women of Color in Congress," *Women in Congress*, http://womenincongress.house. gov/data/women-of-color.html (accessed March 13, 2009).

19 Jennifer Nelson, *Women of Color and the Reproductive Rights Movement* (New York: NYU Press, 2003).

20 Patricia Hill Collins, *Black Feminist Thought* (New York: Routledge, 1990); bell hooks, *Ain't I a Woman?* (Boston, MA: South End Press, 1984).

21 This is not unique to the political arena. In her study of litigators in a law firm, Jennifer Pierce finds that women litigators face a similar bind. Litigators are expected to be aggressive, domineering, and argumentative. Yet, when women attorneys attempt to display these traits, they are labeled "shrill." If they do not display these characteristics, they are viewed as ineffective. Pierce concludes that the occupation is intrinsically masculinized in ways that create gender-specific challenges for women. Jennifer Pierce, *Gender Trials* (Berkeley, CA: University of California Press, 1995).

22 Nijole Benokraitis and Joe R. Feagin, *Modern Sexism*.

23 Patrick Healy, "The Clinton Conundrum: What's Behind the Laugh?" *New York Times*, September 30, 2007, www.nytimes.com/2007/09/30/us/politics/30clinton. html?_r=1&oref=slogin (accessed July 31, 2008); Robin Givhan, "Hillary Clinton's Tentative Dip into New Neckline Territory," *Washington Post*, July 20, 2007, www.washingtonpost.com/wp-dyn/content/article/2007/07/19/ AR2007071902668. html (accessed July 31, 2008).

24 David Nason, "Are We Ready to See Hillary Age?" *News*, December 19, 2007, www.news.com.au/story/0,23599,22946872-2,00.html (accessed July 31, 2008).

25 Gloria Steinem, "Women are Never Front Runners," *New York Times*, January 8, 2008, www.nytimes.com/2008/01/08/opinion/08steinem.html (accessed July 31, 2008).

26 Katharine Q. Seelye and Julie Bosman, "Ferarro's Obama Remarks Become Talk of Campaign," *New York Times*, March 12, 2008, www.nytimes.com/2008/03/12/ us/politics/12campaign.html (accessed July 31, 2008).

27 Ibid.

28 In early March 2008, Ferraro resigned her post as an advisor to the Clinton campaign.

29 Michael McAuliff, "Hillary Clinton's Speech to Supporters Marks End of Historic Run," *New York Daily News*, June 7, 2008, www.nydailynews.com/news/ politics/ 2008/06/07/2008–06–07_hillary_clintons_speech_to_supporters_ma.html (accessed November 26, 2008); Catherine Morgan, "Yes Hillary, We are So Proud. Thank You," *Political Voices of Women*, June 10, 2008, http://politicsanew.com/2008/06/ 10/yes-hillary-we-are-so-proud-thank-you (accessed July 31, 2008).

30   Lois Romano, "Clinton Puts Up a New Fight," *Washington Post*, May 20, 2008, www.washingtonpost.com/wp-dyn/content/article/2008/05/19/ AR2008051902729. html (accessed October 19, 2008).

31   Anne E. Kornblut, "For Bill Clinton, Echoes of Jackson in Obama Win," *Washington Post*, January 26, 2008, http://blog.washingtonpost.com/the-trail/2008/01/ 26/ for_bill_clinton_echoes_of_jac.html (accessed August 1, 2008).

32   Anne E. Kornblut, "For Bill Clinton, Echoes of Jackson in Obama Win," Washington Post.com, January 26, 2008, http://blog.washingtonpost.com/the-trail/2008/ 01/26/ for_bill_clinton_echoes_of_jac.html (accessed August 1, 2008); Jake Tapper, "False Pushback from Clinton Allies," *Political Punch*, January 28, 2008, http://blogs. abcnews.com/politicalpunch/2008/01/false-pushback.html (accessed December 2, 2008).

33   Perry Bacon, Jr., "Clinton Campaign Volunteer out Over False Obama Rumors," *Washington Post*, December 5, 2007, http://blog.washingtonpost.com/the-trail/ 2007/12/05/clinton_campaign_volunteer_out.html (accessed August 1, 2008).

34   Evan Thomas, "The Long Siege," *Newsweek*, November 6, 2008, www.newsweek. com/id/167755/page/3 (accessed November 6, 2008).

35   David Kurtz, "Obama Is a Native Somali?" *Talking Points Memo*, February 26, 2008, www.talkingpointsmemo.com/archives/180147.php (accessed November 6, 2008).

36   Ewen MacAskill, "Clinton Aides Claim Obama Photo Wasn't Intended as Smear," *Guardian*, February 25, 2008, www.guardian.co.uk/world/2008/feb/25/ barack obama.hillaryclinton?gusrc=rss&feed=networkfront (accessed August 1, 2008).

37   Kathy Kiely and Jill Lawrence, "Clinton Makes Case for Wide Appeal," *USA Today*, May 27, 2008, www.usatoday.com/news/politics/election2008/2008–05–07-clinton interview_N.htm (accessed August 14, 2008).

38   Joe Conason, "Was Hillary Channeling George Wallace?" *Salon*, May 9, 2008, www.salon.com/opinion/conason/2008/05/09/clinton_remarks/ (accessed August 14, 2008).

39   "Memo Could Keep Clinton-Obama Rift Open," *CNN*, August 12, 2008, www. cnn.com/2008/POLITICS/08/12/atlantic.clinton.staff/index.html (accessed August 14, 2008) (emphasis added); the full memo is at Joshua Green, "The Front-Runner's Fall," *Atlantic Monthly*, September 2008, www.theatlantic.com/a/green-penn- 3–19–07.mhtml (accessed December 5, 2008) (emphasis added).

40   Charles Blow, "Racism and the Race," *New York Times*, August 9, 2008, www. nytimes.com/2008/08/09/opinion/09blow.html?_r=1&emBlack Voters Can't Put Obama in the White House (accessed November 30, 2008); see also Earl Ofari Hutchinson, "Black Voters Can't Put Obama in the White House," *New America Media*, March 11, 2008, http://news.newamericamedia.org/news/ view_article. html?article_id=7cad57d478821ffac3db0efd9c9ef6f8 (accessed November 30, 2008).

41   Eugene Robinson, "No Longer Unimaginable," *Washington Post*, January 8, 2008, www.washingtonpost.com/wp-dyn/content/article/2008/01/04/ AR2008010403567. html (accessed March 11, 2009).

42 Patricia Hill Collins, *Black Feminist Thought*; Deborah K. King, "Multiple Jeopardies, Multiple Consciousness," *Signs* 14 (1988): 42–72.

43 Kimberle Williams Crenshaw and Eve Ensler," Feminist Ultimatums: Not in Our Name," *Huffington Post*, February 5, 2008, www.huffingtonpost.com/kimberle crenshaw-and-eve-ensler/feminist-ultimatums-not-_b_85165.html (accessed August 17, 2008).

44 Kathy Kiely and Jill Lawrence, "Clinton Makes Case for Wide Appeal," *USA Today*, May 27, 2008, www.usatoday.com/news/politics/election2008/2008–05–07-clinton interview_N.htm (accessed August 17, 2008).

45 Lynn Vavreck, "Where have all the Clinton Voters Gone and what does Race have to do with it?" October 27, 2008, http://blogs.princeton.edu/election2008/2008/ 10/ where-have-all-the-clinton-voters-gone-and-what-does-race-have-to-do-with-it.html (accessed November 30, 2008).

46 Ben Smith, "Muslims Banned From Photo at Obama Event," *USA Today*, June 18, 2008, www.usatoday.com/news/politics/election2008/2008–06–18-detroit event_N.htm (accessed August 18, 2008).

47 Ron Suskind, *Confidence Men* (New York: Harper Collins, 2011).

48 Rosabeth Moss Kanter, *Men and Women of the Corporation* (New York: Basic Books, 1977); Ella Bell and Stella Nkomo, *Our Separate Ways* (Cambridge, MA: Harvard Business School Press, 2001).

4 The Cool Black Man vs. The Fist-Bumping Socialist

1 "Transcript: Illinois Senate Candidate Barack Obama," *Washington Post*, July 27, 2004, www.washingtonpost.com/wp-dyn/articles/A19751–2004Jul27.html (accessed August 23, 2008).

2 Jeff Zeleny and Jim Rutenberg, "DNC Plans All-American Image for Obama," *MSNBC*, August 17, 2008, www.msnbc.msn.com/id/26258253 (accessed August 23, 2008).

3 Julie Bosman, "Obama Sharply Assails Absent Black Fathers," *New York Times*, June 16, 2008, www.nytimes.com/2008/06/16/us/politics/15cndobama.html?emc= rss&partner=rssnyt (accessed November 10, 2008).

4 Robert Lerman and Elaine Sorensen, "Father Involvement with their Nonmarital Children: Patterns, Determinants, and Effects on their Earnings," *Marriage and Family Review* 29 (2000): 137–158.

5 "Jesse Jackson Apologizes After Saying He Wanted to 'Cut Barack Obama's Nuts Out'," *Times Online*, July 10, 2008, www.timesonline.co.uk/tol/news/world/ us_ and_americas/us_elections/article4306177.ece (accessed November 10, 2008).

6 Ibid.

7 Jonathan D. Salant, "Jackson's 'Crude' Remarks May Give Boost to Obama (Update2)," *Bloomberg*, www.bloomberg.com/apps/news?pid=20601087&sid= aat OueE_l3MI&refer=home%7D%7D (accessed November 8, 2008).

8 Michael Omi and Howard Winant, *Racial Formation in the United States* (Philadelphia, PA: Temple University Press, 1994).

9   Oliver Knox, "Karl Rove-Linked Group Crossroads Slams 'Cool' Obama," *Yahoo News*, http://news.yahoo.com/blogs/ticket/karl-rove-linked-group-crossroads-slams-cool-obama-141833323.html (accessed April 26, 2012).

10 For a discussion of how terrorist acts spark a rise in "hot" nationalism, as opposed to the "banal nationalism" that typically characterizes the collective consciousness, see Michael Billig, *Banal Nationalism* (Thousand Oaks, CA: Sage, 1995).

11 See Mike Glover, "Obama Stops Wearing Flag Pin," *Associated Press*, www.breitbart.com/article.php?id=D8S2K3UO0&show_article=1 (accessed December 2, 2008).

12 David Wright and Sunlen Miller, "Obama Dropped Flag Pin in War Statement," *ABC News*, October 4, 2007, http://abcnews.go.com/politics/ Story?id=3690000& page=1 (accessed August 24, 2008).

13 "Was Barack Obama Shunning the American Flag?" *Fox News*, October 5, 2007, www.foxnews.com/story/0,2933,299580,00.html (accessed October 19, 2008); David Wright and Sunlen Miller, "Obama Dropped Flag Pin in War Statement," *ABC News*, October 4, 2007, http://abcnews.go.com/politics/ Story?id=3690000& page=1 (accessed August 24, 2008).

14 David Wright and Sunlen Miller, "Obama Dropped Flag Pin in War Statement," *ABC News*, October 4, 2007, http://abcnews.go.com/politics/Story?id=3690000 &page=1 (accessed August 24, 2008); Jay Newton-Small, "Obama's Flag Pin Flip Flop?" *Time*, May 14, 2008, www.time.com/time/politics/article/0,8599,1779544,00. html (accessed August 24, 2008).

15 Jay Newton-Small, "Obama's Flag Pin Flip Flop?" *Time*, May 14, 2008, www.time.com/time/politics/article/0,8599,1779544,00.html (accessed August 24, 2008).

16 "Michelle Obama Takes Heat for Saying She's 'Proud of My Country' for the First Time," *FOX News*, February 19, 2008, www.foxnews.com/politics/ elections/2008/ 02/19/michelle-obama-takes-heat-for-saying-shes-proud-of-mycountry-for-the-first-time/ (accessed December 2, 2008).

17 Ibid.

18 Steven Benen, "Lieberman Drops the Pretense, Attacks Obama's Patriotism," *The Carpetbagger Report*, August 13, 2008, www.thecarpetbaggerreport.com/archives/ 16535.html (accessed August 25, 2008); "Obama Tells McCain to Lay Off Character," *MSNBC*, August 19, 2008, www.msnbc.msn.com/id/26288983/ (accessed August 25, 2008).

19 Sarah Baxter, "Desperate McCain Gets Tough with Attack on Obama's Character," *Times Online*, October 5, 2008, www.timesonline.co.uk/tol/news/world/ us_and_ americas/us_elections/article4882402.ece (accessed October 19, 2008).

20 "Palin Accuses Obama of 'Palling Around with Terrorists'," *Fox News*, October 4, 2008, http://elections.foxnews.com/2008/10/04/palin-accuses-obama-pallingterrorists/ (accessed October 19, 2008).

21 Rachel Weiner, "Obama Hatred at McCain-Palin Rallies: 'Terrorist!' 'Kill Him!'" *Huffington Post*, October 6, 2008, www.huffingtonpost.com/2008/10/06/ mccain-does-nothing-as-cr_n_132366.html (accessed October 19, 2008).

22   See Drew Westen, *The Political Brain: The Role of Emotion in Deciding the Fate of the Nation* (New York: Public Affairs Press, 2007).

23   "The Politics of Satire," *New Yorker*, July 21, 2008, www.newyorker.com/online/covers/slideshow_blittcovers (accessed December 2, 2008).

24   "Editor defends New Yorker," *CNN*, www.cnn.com/video/#/video/politics/2008/07/14/tsr.remnick.newyorker.cnn?iref=videosearch (accessed December 2, 2008).

25   Sam Wang, "The Brain Who Mistook a Joke for Fact," *American Academy of Political and Social Science Blog*, July 23, 2008, http://blog.aapss.org/index.cfm?comment ID=66 (accessed August 25, 2008); see also Brent Jones, "Obama Cartoon Riles Democrats," *Baltimore Sun*, July 15, 2008, www.baltimoresun.com/news/nation/politics/bal-te.magazine15jul15,0,4906395.story (accessed August 25, 2008).

26   Russ Mitchell, "King Announced Bid for Fourth Term," *Daily Reporter*, March 8, 2008, www.spencerdailyreporter.com/story/1316727.html (accessed August 25, 2008).

27   "Karl Rove on Obama's Tie to Terrorist," *Fox News*, April 10, 2008, www.foxnews.com/story/0,2933,349408,00.html (accessed August 25, 2008); see, for example, this far-right website, which long had these stories up: www.freedomsenemies.com.

28   Denita Smith, "No Regrets for a Love of Explosives; in a Memoir of Sorts, a War Protestor Talks of Life with the Weathermen," *New York Times*, September 11, 2001, http://query.nytimes.com/gst/ fullpage.html?res=9F02E1DE1438F932A257 5AC0A9679C8B63&scp=10&sq=Bill+ Ayers&st=nyt (accessed August 25, 2008).

29   Bill Ayers, "Episodic Notoriety: Fact and Fiction," http://billayers.wordpress.com/2008/04/06/episodic-notoriety-fact-and-fantasy/ (accessed August 25, 2008).

30   Michael Dobbs, "Obama's 'Weatherman' Connection," *Washington Post*, February 19, 2008, http://blog.washingtonpost.com/fact-checker/2008/02/obamas_weatherman_connection.html (accessed August 25, 2008).

31   Lynn Sweet, "Obama's Ayers Connection Never Bugged Anyone," *Chicago Sun Times*, April 18, 2008, www.suntimes.com/news/sweet/901879,CST-NWSsweet 18.article (accessed August 25, 2008).

32   Scott Shane, "Obama and '60s Bomber: A Look into Crossed Paths," *New York Times*, October 3, 2008, www.nytimes.com/2008/10/04/us/politics/04ayers.html (accessed October 19, 2008).

33   Robert Barnes and Mary Pat Flaherty, "'60s Radical Ayers Among Subjects of McCain Robocalls," *Washington Post*, October 18, 2008, www.washingtonpost.com/wp-dyn/content/story/2008/10/17/ ST2008101702930.html (accessed October 19, 2008).

34   Shushannah Walshe, "Palin: 'No Time to Experiment with Socialism.'" *Fox News*, October 19, 2008, http://embeds.blogs.foxnews.com/2008/10/19/palin-uses-the-sword-socialism/ (accessed October 20, 2008).

35   "'Socialist,' 'Muslim,'—Ugly Reception for Obama," *Politico*, October 19, 2008, www.politico.com/news/stories/1008/14728.html (accessed October 20, 2008).

36   Bret Hovel, "McCain: Obama Has No Experience in National Security, Warfare," *ABC News Blogs*, March 31, 2008, http://blogs.abcnews.com/politicalradar/2008/03/mccain-obama-ha.html (accessed August 25, 2008); Tim Shipman, "Clinton:

Barack Obama's Not Ready to Lead," *Telegraph*, October 1, 2007, www.telegraph.
co.uk/news/worldnews/1564690/Clinton-Barack-Obama's-not-ready-to-lead.html
(accessed August 25, 2008).

37 "Clinton: Obama 'Irresponsible and Naive'," *CBS News*, July 24, 2007, www.cbs
news.com/stories/2007/07/24/politics/main3094391.html (accessed August 25,
2008).

38 Larry Rohter, "Obama Says Real-Life Experience Trumps Rivals' Foreign Policy
Credits," *New York Times*, April 10, 2008, www.nytimes.com/2008/04/10/us/
politics/10obama.html (accessed August 25, 2008).

39 In 1987, former President Ronald Reagan gave his historic speech here where he
uttered the famous line "Mr. Gorbechev, tear down this wall," as an exhortation
to end the Cold War.

40 Jason Carroll, "Rove, Critics Try to Pin 'Arrogant' Label on Obama," *CNN*, June
26, 2008, www.cnn.com/2008/POLITICS/06/26/obama.rove/ (accessed August
25, 2008).

41 Dana Milbank, "President Obama Continues Hectic Victory Tour," *Washington
Post*, July 30, 2008, www.washingtonpost.com/wp-dyn/content/article/2008/07/29/
AR2008072902068.html (accessed August 25, 2008).

42 Mike Soraghan, "Westmoreland calls Obama 'Uppity'," *The Hill*, September 4,
2008, http://thehill.com/leading-the-news/westmoreland-calls-obama-uppity-2008–
09–04.html (accessed October 20, 2008).

43 Jim Galloway, "Barack and Michelle Obama are 'Uppity,' Says Lynn Westmoreland," *AJC*, September 4, 2008, www.ajc.com/metro/content/shared-blogs/ajc/
politicalinsider/entries/2008/09/04/barack_and_michelle_obama_are.html (accessed
October 20, 2008).

44 Brent Staples, "Barack Obama, John McCain, and the Language of Race," *New
York Times*, September 21, 2008, www.nytimes.com/2008/09/22/opinion/22observer.
html?_r=4&em&oref=slogin&oref=slogin&oref=slogin&oref=slogin (accessed October
20, 2008).

45 Stephanie Condon, "Poll: One in Four Americans Think Obama Was Not Born
in US," *CBS Political Hotsheet*, April 21, 2011, www.cbsnews.com/8301-503544_
162-20056061-503544.html (accessed March 22, 2012).

46 Brian Montopoli, "Sherriff Joe Arpaio Suggests Obama's Birth Certificate is a
Forgery," *CBS Political Hotsheet*, March 1, 2012, www.cbsnews.com/8301-503544_
162-57388911-503544/sheriff-joe-arpaio-suggests-obamas-birth-certificate-is-a-forgery/
(accessed March 22, 2012).

47 Brian Montopoli, "Congressman Regrets Knocking Michelle Obama's 'Large
Posterior'," *CBS Political Hotsheet*, December 22, 2011, www.cbsnews.com/8301-
503544_162-57347417-503544/congressman-regrets-knocking-michelle-obamas-
large-posterior/ (accessed March 22, 2012).

48 "Rush Limbaugh Criticizes First Lady Michelle Obama's Weight, Nutritional
Campaign," *Daily Dish*, February 22, 2011, http://latimesblogs.latimes.com/
dailydish/2011/02/rush-limbaugh-crtiticizes-first-lady-michelle-obamas-weight-
nutritional-campaign.html (accessed March 22, 2012).

49 "'Hottentot Venus' Goes Home," *BBC News*, April 29, 2002 http://news.bbc. co.uk/2/hi/europe/1957240.stm (accessed April 26, 2012).

50 See, for example, "The Obama File," www.theobamafile.com (accessed December 5, 2008).

51 Joe R. Feagin, *Systemic Racism: A Theory of Oppression* (New York: Routledge, 2006).

52 Betsy Reed, "How Hillary Clinton Played the Race Card and Drove a Wedge into the Feminist Movement," *The Nation*, May 19, 2008, www.thenation.com/doc/ 20080519/betsyreed (accessed August 31, 2008).

53 Wendy Leo Moore, *Reproducing Racism* (Lanham, MD: Rowman & Littlefield, 2008).

54 Ibid., p. 75.

55 Ibid., p. 78.

56 Joe R. Feagin, *The White Racial Frame* (New York: Routledge, 2010).

57 We refer here to major white supremacist websites, whose URLs we do not include here.

58 See Dinesh D'Souza, *The End of Racism: Principles for a Multiracial Society* (New York: Free Press, 1995). Here, a man of color articulates this white supremacist view.

59 Joe R. Feagin, *The White Racial Frame*.

60 Journalist Ida B. Wells documented that the oft-given rationale for lynching was a distortion of fact or, in many cases, based on outright lies. Through careful research, Wells learned that black men were often lynched because they became more economically successful than neighboring whites, or because they failed to show the appropriately subordinate demeanor in their interactions with whites. For in-depth descriptions of Wells' work, see Lynne Olsen, *Freedom's Daughters* (New York: Scribner, 2001); and Paula Giddings, *Ida: A Sword Among Lions* (New York: Amistad Press, 2008). On lynchings, see Joe R. Feagin, *Racist America*, pp. 23–176.

61 Patricia Hill Collins, *Black Sexual Politics* (New York: Routledge, 2004); Leslie Houts Picca and Joe R. Feagin, *Two Faced Racism* (New York: Routledge, 2007).

62 Joe R. Feagin and Melvin Sikes, *Living with Racism* (Boston, MA: Beacon Press, 1994); Charisse Jones and Kumea Shorter-Gooden, *Shifting* (New York: Harper Perennial, 2000); Jennifer Pierce, "'Racing for Innocence': Whiteness, Corporate Culture, and the Backlash Against Affirmative Action," in *White Out*, Eds. Ashley Doane and Eduardo Bonilla-Silva (New York: Routledge, 2002), pp. 199–214.

63 Jennifer Pierce, "'Racing for Innocence': Whiteness, Corporate Culture, and the Backlash Against Affirmative Action," in *White Out*, Eds. Ashley Doane and Eduardo Bonilla-Silva (New York: Routledge, 2002), pp. 199–214.

64 See Joe R. Feagin and Melvin Sikes, *Living with Racism*.

65 Joe R. Feagin and Eileen O'Brien, *White Men on Race* (Boston, MA: Beacon Press, 2003), p. 158.

66 Among others, Rudy Giuliani, Karl Rove, Joe Biden, John McCain, and both Hillary and Bill Clinton have argued that Senator Obama was too inexperienced for the presidency.

67 For documented examples, see Paula Giddings, *Ida: A Sword Among Lions*.

68   Paul Jenkins makes this point as well in a commentary in the *Huffington Post*. See Paul Jenkins, "Obama Still Does Not Know His Place," *Huffington Post*, July 28, 2008, www.huffingtonpost.com/paul-jenkins/obama-still-does-notknow_b_115671.html (accessed September 2, 2008).

69   Doug Feaver, "Angry McCain, Cool Obama," *Washington Post*, October 16, 2008, http://voices.washingtonpost.com/dot.comments/2008/10/angry_mccain_cool_obama.html (accessed October 20, 2008); Jed Lewison, "McCain's Angry Debate Disappoints Morning Joe Panel," *Huffington Post*, September 27, 2008, www.huffingtonpost.com/2008/09/27/mccains-angry-debatedisa_n_129915.html (accessed October 20, 2008).

70   "Colin Powell Endorses Obama," *CNN*, October 20, 2008, www.cnn.com/2008/POLITICS/10/19/colin.powell/ (accessed October 20, 2008).

71   David Brooks, "Thinking About Obama," *New York Times*, October 16, 2008, www.nytimes.com/2008/10/17/opinion/17brooks.html?_r=1&oref=slogin (accessed October 20, 2008).

72   Adia Harvey Wingfield, *Doing Business with Beauty* (Lanham, MD: Rowman & Littlefield, 2007).

73   Alter made this comment on Hardball with Chris Matthews on October 16, 2008.

74   Jennifer Steinhauer, "Volunteers for Obama Face a Complex Issue," *New York Times*, October 14, 2008, www.nytimes.com/2008/10/15/us/politics/15nevada.html (accessed October 20, 2008).

75   Ben Smith, "How Obama Quietly Targets Blacks," *Politico*, October 6, 2008, www.politico.com/news/stories/1008/14347.html (accessed October 20, 2008).

5   The Dr. Jeremiah Wright Controversy

1   See Jeremiah A. Wright, Jr., *What Makes You So Strong? Sermons of Joy and Strength*, Ed. Jini Kilgore Ross (Valley Forge, PA: Judson Press, 1993); Jeremiah A. Wright, Jr., *Good News! Sermons of Hope for Today's Families*, Ed. Jini Kilgore Ross (Valley Forge, PA: Judson Press, 1995).

2   "Trinity United Church," www.trinitychicago.org/index.php?option=com_content&task=view&id=12&Itemid=27 (accessed September 8, 2008).

3   Ibid.

4   Johnnetta Cole and Beverly Guy-Sheftall, *Gender Talk* (New York: Ballantine Books, 2003).

5   Aldon Morris, *The Origins of the Civil Rights Movement* (New York: Free Press, 1984).

6   Bernice McNair Barnett, "Invisible Black Women Leaders in the Civil Rights Movement: The Triple Constraints of Gender, Race, and Class," *Signs* 7 (1993): 162–182; Bernice McNair Barnett, "Black Women's Leadership in Movement Organizations: Their Struggles During the Doldrums," in *Women's Organizations*, Ed. Myra Marx Ferree and Patricia Yancey Martin (Philadelphia, PA: Temple University Press, 1995), pp. 199–219; Belinda Robnett, *How Long? How Long?* (New York: Oxford University Press, 1997); Lynne Olsen, *Freedom's Daughters* (New York: Scribner, 2001).

7   Stokely Carmichael and Charles Hamilton, *Black Power: The Politics of Liberation in America* (New York: Vintage Books, 1967).

8   James Cone, *Black Theology and Black Power* (New York: Seabury Press, 1969).

9   Ibid.; Joe R. Feagin, *Systemic Racism: A Theory of Oppression* (New York: Routledge, 2000).

10 Liberation theology is present among other cultures as well. In some Latin American countries, priests rely on liberation theology as a means of mobilizing parishioners to rebel against oppressive dictatorships and regimes. See Mark Danner, *The Massacre at El Mozote* (New York: Vintage Books, 2005) for a discussion of the murder of some of these priests during the 1981 massacre orchestrated by U.S.-trained forces in El Salvador.

11 Margaret Taley, "Obama's Church Pushes Controversial Doctrines," McClatchy *Report*, March 20, 2008, www.mcclatchydc.com/227/story/31079.html (accessed September 10, 2008).

12 "Black Liberation Theology, in its Founder's Words," March 31, 2008, www.npr.org/templates/story/story.php?storyId=89236116 (accessed September 10, 2008).

13 See website at www.trinitychicago.org/index.php?option=com_content&task=view&id=13&Itemid=28 (accessed September 10, 2008).

14 "Transcript of Wright's Full Sermon, City Hall Election 2008," March 21, 2008, http://community.comcast.net/comcastportal/board/message?board.id=cityhall&thread.id=430506 (accessed September 10, 2008).

15 Sam Stein, "Meet the (White) Man Who Inspired Wright's Controversial Sermons," *Huffington Post*, March 21, 2008, www.huffingtonpost.com/2008/03/21/meetthe-white-man-who-_n_92793.html (accessed September 10, 2008).

16 Joe R. Feagin, "Dr. Wright is Still Right on Racism: Check the Research Data," *Racism Review*, April 28, 2008, www.racismreview.com. The sermon is quoted from www.pbs.org/moyers/journal/04252008/transcript1.html (accessed September 10, 2008).

17 See, for example, this website, copyrighted in 2007: www.freedomsenemies.com/_more/obama.htm (accessed December 8, 2007).

18 Alex Mooney and Peter Hamby, "Clinton: Wright Would Not Have Been My Pastor," *CNN*, March 25, 2008, www.cnn.com/2008/POLITICS/03/25/clinton.wright/ (accessed September 10, 2008).

19 "CBS News Transcripts, 60 Minutes," November 9, 2008, *Lexis/Nexis*, http://74.125.113.132/search?q=cache:VaU0U0PjvgIJ:www6.lexisnexis.com/publisher/EndUser%3FAction%3DUserDisplayFullDocument%26orgId%3D574%26topicId%3D100007217%26docId%3Dl:881651019%26start%3D1+cbs+transcript+%2260+minutes%22+%22inner+circle%22+Obama+staff+wright+speech&hl=en&ct=clnk&cd=6&gl=us (accessed November 21, 2008).

20 Adam Nagourney, Jim Rutenberg, and Jeff Zeleny, "Near-Flawless Run Is Credited in Victory," *New York Times*, November 5, 2008, www.nytimes.com/2008/11/05/us/politics/05recon.html?_r=3&hp=&oref=slogin&pagewanted=all (accessed November 25, 2008).

21 "The Long Siege," *Newsweek*, www.newsweek.com/id/167755/page/4 (accessed November 25, 2008).

22 Ibid.

23 "CBS News Transcripts, 60 Minutes," *Lexis/Nexis*, November 9, 2008, http://74.125.113.132/search?q=cache:VaU0U0PjvgIJ:www6.lexisnexis.com/publisher/EndUser%3FAction%3DUserDisplayFullDocument%26orgId%3D574%26topicId%3D100007217%26docId%3Dl:881651019%26start%3D1+cbs+transcript+%2260+minutes%22+%22inner+circle%22+Obama+staff+wright+speech&hl=en&ct=clnk&cd=6&gl=us (accessed November 21, 2008).

24 Brian Ross and Rehab El-Buri, "Obama's Pastor: God Damn America, US to Blame for 9/11," *ABC News*, March 13, 2008, http://abcnews.go.com/Blotter/Story?id=4443788 (accessed September 10, 2008).

25 "CBS News Transcripts, 60 Minutes," *Lexis/Nexis*, November 9, 2008, http://74.125.113.132/search?q=cache:VaU0U0PjvgIJ:www6.lexisnexis.com/publisher/EndUser%3FAction%3DUserDisplayFullDocument%26orgId%3D574%26topicId%3D100007217%26docId%3Dl:881651019%26start%3D1+cbs+transcript+%2260+minutes%22+%22inner+circle%22+Obama+staff+wright+speech&hl=en&ct=clnk&cd=6&gl=us (accessed November 21, 2008).

26 Barack Obama, "A More Perfect Union," www.npr.org/templates/story/story.php?storyId=88478467 (accessed September 10, 2008). See also "The Long Siege," *Newsweek*, www.newsweek.com/id/167755/page/4 (accessed November 25, 2008).

27 See Joe R. Feagin, *Systemic Racism*.

28 Cited in Joe R. Feagin, "Speaking about Racism," *Racism Review*, www.racismreview.com/blog/2008/03/18/speaking-about-racism-a-critical-speech-by-senator-obama/#more-203 (accessed February 6, 2009).

29 "The Long Siege," *Newsweek*, www.newsweek.com/id/167755/page/4 (accessed November 25, 2008).

30 Ibid.

31 Jake Tapper, "Huckabee Defends Obama and the Dr. Wright," *ABC News Blogs*, March 19, 2008, http://blogs.abcnews.com/politicalpunch/2008/03/huckabeedefend.html (accessed September 10, 2008).

32 Ibid.

33 "Dr. Wright at the National Press Club," *New York Times*, April 28, 2008, www.nytimes.com/2008/04/28/us/politics/28text-wright.html?pagewanted=7 (accessed September 10, 2008).

34 Ibid.

35 "Obama Quits Church, Citing Controversies," *CNN*, May 31, 2008, www.cnn.com/2008/POLITICS/05/31/obama.church/ (accessed September 10, 2008).

36 Dan Balz, "McCain Reconnects with Liberty University," *Washington Post*, May 13, 2006, www.washingtonpost.com/wp-dyn/content/article/2006/05/13/ AR2006051300647.html (accessed September 10, 2008).

37 John F. Harris, "God Gave U.S. 'What We Deserve,' Falwell Says," *Washington Post*, September 14, 2008, www.washingtonpost.com/ac2/wp-dyn/A28620–2001Sep14 (accessed September 15, 2008).

38   Dan Balz, "McCain Reconnects with Liberty University."

39   Mosheh Oinounou, "McCain Defends Hagee Endorsement Despite Differences,"
     Fox News Blogs, February 29, 2008, http://embeds.blogs.foxnews.com/2008/02/29/
     mccain-defends-hagee-endorsement-despite-differences/ (accessed September 10,
     2008).

40   John Hagee, *Jerusalem Countdown: A Prelude to War* (New York: Charisma House,
     2006); see also Bruce Wilson, "'Pro Israel' Christian Leader Blames Jews for the
     Holocaust," *Talk to Action*, March 5, 2007, www.talk2action.org/story/2007/
     3/5/105015/2167/ (accessed September 10, 2008); and Glenn Greenwald, "The
     McCain/Hagee Story Picks Up Steam," *Salon*, February 29, 2008, www.salon.com/
     opinion/greenwald/2008/02/29/hagee/ (accessed September 10, 2008).

41   Mosheh Oinounou, "McCain Defends Hagee Endorsement Despite Differences,"
     Fox News Blogs, February 29, 2008, http://embeds.blogs.foxnews.com/2008/02/29/
     mccain-defends-hagee-endorsement-despite-differences/ (accessed September 10,
     2008). We got this figure of mass media coverage from a Google search in late
     summer 2008.

42   Randi Kaye, "Pastor: GOP May Be Downplaying Palin's Religious Beliefs," *CNN*,
     September 9, 2008, www.cnn.com/2008/POLITICS/09/08/palin.pastor/ (accessed
     September 10, 2008); "Today on the Presidential Campaign Trail," September 25
     2008, http://ap.google.com/article/ALeqM5iNxTApa2sQRu0Xx99P3jt2bEXw7
     gD93DK3980 (accessed September 25, 2008).

43   Bill O'Reilly, "Honesty in the Public Arena," *Fox News*, May 2, 2008, www.
     foxnews.com/story/0,2933,353981,00.html (accessed September 18, 2008); Thomas
     Sowell, "Wright Bound," *National Review*, March 19, 2008, http://article.national
     review.com/?q=MDMyZTU1M2YyZDBlZDczMjY2Y2QyZWYwZjFiYWU4Y
     WE= (accessed September 18, 2008).

44   See Leslie Houts Picca and Joe R. Feagin, *Two Faced Racism* (New York: Routledge,
     2007); Joe R. Feagin and Eileen O'Brien, *White Men on Race* (Boston, MA: Beacon
     Press, 2005); Charles Gallagher, "Racial Redistricting: Expanding the Boundaries
     of Whiteness," in *The Politics of Multiculturalism: Challenging Racial Thinking*, Ed.
     Heather Dalmadge (New York: SUNY Press, 2004), pp. 59–76.

45   Meg Lovejoy, "Disturbances in the Social Body," *Gender & Society* 15 (2001):
     239–261; Melissa Milkie, "Social Comparisons, Reflected Appraisals, and Mass
     Media: The Impact of Pervasive Beauty Images on Black and White Girls' Self
     Concepts," *Social Psychology Quarterly* 62 (1999): 190–210; Kushal Patel and James
     Gray, "Judgment Accuracy in Body Preferences Among African Americans," *Sex
     Roles* 44 (2001): 227–235; Adia Harvey Wingfield, *Doing Business with Beauty*
     (Lanham, MD: Rowman and Littlefield, 2008).

46   See Kenneth Bolton and Joe R. Feagin, *Black in Blue: Black Police Officers in White
     Departments* (New York: Routledge, 2004).

47   "Reverend Wright at the National Press Club," *New York Times*, April 28, 2008,
     www.nytimes.com/2008/04/28/us/politics/28text-wright.html?pagewanted=3
     (accessed October 25, 2008).

48 See Joe R. Feagin, *Systemic Racism*.

49 Peggy McIntosh, "White Privilege: Unpacking the Invisible Knapsack," *Peace and Freedom* (July/August, 1989): 10–12.

50 This is unsurprising considering much of mainstream media is owned by white elites. Gonzales and Delgado document how white owners of many media outlets are staunch Republicans who fail to provide balanced media coverage. Manuel Gonzales and Richard Delgado, *The Politics of Fear* (Boulder, CO: Paradigm Press, 2006).

51 Bill Clinton's vocal castigation of activist Sister Soulja is one example. Clinton derided Sister Soulja for "racist statements" about whites, even though her remarks were grossly taken out of context. Many considered Clinton's denouncement to be a political signal that he would remain sympathetic to whites. See Michael Omi and Howard Winant, *Racial Formation in the United States* (Philadelphia, PA: Temple University Press, 1994).

52 See Leslie Houts Picca and Joe R. Feagin, *Two Faced Racism*.

53 Transcript of Obama's speech, http://my.barackobama.com/page/content/hisown words (accessed September 21, 2008).

54 Ibid.

6 The 2008 Primaries and Voters of Color

1 Charles M. Blow, "Racism and the Race," *New York Times*, August 8, 2008, www.nytimes.com/2008/08/09/opinion/09blow.html?em (accessed December 10, 2008); Ron Fournier and Trevor Tompson, "AP Poll: Racial Misgivings of Whites Loom Over Election," *Huffington Post*, September 20, 2008, www.huffington post.com/2008/09/20/ap-poll-racialmisgivings_n_127996.html (accessed September 20, 2008).

2 Alex Johnson, "For Clinton, Latino Vote Could Seal the Deal," *MSNBC*, February 8, 2008, www.msnbc.msn.com/id/23058132/ (accessed October 4, 2008).

3 Ibid.

4 Jamie Reno, "Black-Brown Divide," *Newsweek*, January 26, 2008, www.news week.com/id/104725/page/1 (accessed October 4, 2008); Mandalit del Barco, "Uneasy Black-Latino Ties a Factor in California Primary," *NPR*, January 24, 2008, www.npr.org/templates/story/story.php?storyId=18375165 (accessed October 4, 2008).

5 Robert Bernstein, "Minority Population Tops 100 Million," *U.S. Census Bureau News*, May 17, 2007, www.census.gov/Press-Release/www/releases/archives/population/010048.html (accessed October 4, 2008); Robert Bernstein and Tom Edwards, "An Older and More Diverse Nation By Midcentury," *U.S. Census Bureau News*, August 14, 2008, www.census.gov/Press-Release/www/releases/archives/population/012496.html (accessed October 4, 2008).

6 "Poll: 'Sharp Reversal' for Obama with Latino Voters," July 25, 2008, www.cnn.com/2008/POLITICS/07/24/pew.latino.poll/ (accessed October 4, 2008); www.gallup.com/poll/108040/Candidate-Support-Race.aspx (accessed October 12, 2008).

7 Ibid.

8 "Conventional Wisdom is Wrong Again: Latinos Overwhelmingly Favor Obama over McCain," *America's Voice*, www.americasvoiceonline.org/2008/pages/conventional_wisdom_is_wrong_again (accessed October 4, 2008).

9 Devin Dwyer, "Obama's Record-High Deportations Draw Hispanic Scorn," *ABC News Political Punch*, December 28, 2011, http://abcnews.go.com/blogs/politics/2011/12/obamas-record-high-deportations-draw-hispanic-scorn/ (accessed March 22, 2012).

10 Seth McLaughlin, "Romney on Illegal Immigration and the Dream Act," *Washington Times*, January 11, 2012, www.washingtontimes.com/news/2012/jan/11/romney-on-illegal-immigration-and-the-dream-act/ (accessed March 22, 2012).

11 Mark Memmott and Jill Lawrence, "Asian Americans Mostly Vote Democratic, Could Be Key in Some Early Primary States," *USA Today Blogs*, May 14, 2007, http://blogs.usatoday.com/onpolitics/2007/05/asianamericans_.html (accessed October 4, 2008).

12 See website at www.80-20initiative.net/news/press080118.asp (accessed October 4, 2008); Lisa Takeuchi Cullen, "Does Obama Have an Asian Problem?" *Time*, February 18, 2008, www.time.com/time/politics/article/0,8599,1714292,00.html (accessed October 4, 2008).

13 Bureau of Labor Statistics 2006; Bonacich has argued that this type of tension is common among middleman minority entrepreneurs, a label which tends to fit Korean immigrant entrepreneurs in these environs. However, Lee has argued that these interracial tensions are largely overstated. While this may be true, conflict has flared between Korean immigrant merchants and their predominantly black clientele, particularly in areas such as Los Angeles. One such example involves the murder of Latasha Harlin, a shopper who was shot in the back by a Korean storeowner who suspected Harlin of shoplifting. See Edna Bonacich, "A Theory of Middleman Minorities," *American Sociological Review* 38 (1973): 583–594; Jennifer Lee, "From Civil Relations to Racial Conflict: Merchant-Customer Interactions in Urban America," *American Sociological Review* 67 (2002): 77–98.

14 Lisa Takeuchi Cullen, "Does Obama Have an Asian Problem?" *Time*, February 18, 2008, www.time.com/time/politics/article/0,8599,1714292,00.html (accessed October 4, 2008); Jun Wang, "Asian Americans Outraged By CNN Election Report," *New America Media*, February 14, 2008, http://news.ncmonline.com/news/view_article.html?article_id=44cb40c466e5c8e91f4d0e557ef911bc (accessed October 4, 2008); see also Yen Le Espiritu, *Asian American Women and Men: Labor, Laws, and Love* (Thousand Oaks, CA: Sage, 1997); and Frank Wu, *Yellow* (New York: Basic Books, 2000) for more discussion of the "perpetual foreigner" stereotype.

15 Lisa Takeuchi Cullen, "Does Obama Have an Asian Problem?" *Time*, February 18, 2008, www.time.com/time/politics/article/0,8599,1714292,00.html (accessed October 4, 2008).

16 S. B. Woo, "Newest Poll: Asian Americans Support Obama/McCain by 3.4/1," September 22, 2008, http://80–20initiative.blogspot.com/2008/09/newest-poll-asamssupport-obamamccain.html (accessed October 4, 2008).

17 Dan Balz and Jon Cohen, "Blacks Shift to Obama, Poll Finds," *Washington Post*, February 28, 2007, www.washingtonpost.com/wp-dyn/content/article/2007/02/27/AR2007022701030.html (accessed October 5, 2008).

18 Jessie Daniels, "Pat Buchanan's Racial Analysis of 'Us' and 'Them'," *Racism Review*, May 16, 2008, www.racismreview.com/blog/2008/05/16/pat-buchanans-racial-analysis-of-us-and-them/ (accessed October 25, 2008).

19 On the role of emotions and voting, see Drew Westen, *The Political Brain: The Role of Emotion in Deciding the Fate of the Nation* (New York: Public Affairs Press, 2007).

20 See Yen Le Espiritu, *Asian American Women and Men*.

21 Frank Wu, *Yellow*.

22 Rosalind Chou and Joe R. Feagin, *The Myth of the Model Minority* (Boulder, CO: Paradigm, 2008); Yen Le Espiritu, *Asian American Women and Men*; Frank Wu, *Yellow*.

23 Adam Nagourney and Jennifer Steinhauer, "In Obama's Pursuit of Latinos, Race Plays Role," *New York Times*, January 15, 2008, www.nytimes.com/2008/01/15/us/politics/15hispanic.html?hp (accessed October 6, 2008).

24 Richard Rodriguez, "Hillary Clinton, the First Latina-in-Chief?" *Salon*, February 9, 2008, www.salon.com/opinion/feature/2008/02/09/latina_in_chief/ (accessed October 6, 2008); the quote is from Ryan Lizza, "Minority Reports: After New Hampshire, a Hint of Racial Politics," *New Yorker*, January 21, 2008, www.newyorker.com/reporting/2008/01/21/080121fa_fact_lizza?currentPage=all (accessed October 6, 2008).

25 Gregory Rodriguez, "Clinton's Latino Spin," *LA Times*, January 28, 2008, www.latimes.com/news/opinion/commentary/la-oerodriguez28jan28,0,1688217.column (accessed October 6, 2008).

26 Lisa Takeuchi Cullen, "Does Obama Have an Asian Problem?" *Time*, February 18, 2008, www.time.com/time/politics/article/0,8599,1714292,00.html (accessed October 4, 2008).

27 Rosalind Chou and Joe R. Feagin, *The Myth of the Model Minority*.

28 Sucheng Chan, *Hmong Means Free* (Philadelphia, PA: Temple University Press, 1994); Rosalind Chou and Joe R. Feagin, *The Myth of the Model Minority*; Stacey Lee, *Unraveling the Model Minority Stereotype* (New York: Teachers College Press, 1996); Frank Wu, *Yellow*.

29 C. W. Nevius, Marc Sandalow, and John Wildermuth, "McCain Criticized for Slur," *San Francisco Chronicle*, February 18, 2000, www.sfgate.com/cgi-bin/article.cgi?file=/chronicle/archive/2000/02/18/MN32194.DTL (accessed October 6, 2008).

30 Anthony Ramirez, "Word for Word/Asian Americans: McCain's Ethnic Slur: Gone, But Not Quite Forgotten," *New York Times*, March 5, 2000, http://query.nytimes.com/gst/fullpage.html?res=9A04E1DC1638F936A35750C0A966 9C8B63&scp=2&sq=gooks&st=nyt (accessed October 6, 2008).

31 Rosalind Chou and Joe R. Feagin, *The Myth of the Model Minority*.

32 See, for example, Irwin Tang, *Gook: John McCain's Racism and Why it Matters* (New York: Paul Revere Books, 2008), as well as Katie Hong's "John McCain's Racist

Remark Very Troubling," *Seattle Post-Intelligencer*, March 2, 2000, http://seattlepi. nwsource.com/opinion/hongop.shtml (accessed October 6, 2008).

33 Anthony Ramirez, "Word for Word/Asian Americans: McCain's Ethnic Slur: Gone, But Not Quite Forgotten," *New York Times*, March 5, 2000, http://query. nytimes.com/gst/fullpage.html?res=9A04E1DC1638F936A35750C0A9669C8B63 &scp=2&sq=goo ks&st=nyt (accessed October 6, 2008).

34 Jacob Weisberg, "What Will the Neighbors Think?" *Newsweek*, August 23, 2008, www.newsweek.com/id/155117/page/1 (accessed August 24, 2008); Ron Fournier and Trevor Tompson, "AP Poll: Racial Misgivings of Whites Loom Over Election," *Huffington Post*, September 20, 2008, www.huffingtonpost.com/2008/09/20/ap-poll-racial-misgivings_n_127996.html (accessed September 20, 2008).

7 November 4, 2008: A Dramatic Day in U.S. History

1 Alex Johnson, "Barack Obama Elected 44th President," Msnbc.com, November 5, 2008, www.msnbc.msn.com/id/27531033 (accessed December 12, 2008).

2 United States presidential election, http://en.wikipedia.org/wiki/ United_States_presidential_election,_2008 (accessed November 30, 2008).

3 "How They Voted: Search Exit Polls," *ABC News*, http://abcnews.go.com/Polling Unit/ExitPolls (accessed November 6, 2008).

4 These data are from various CNN and ABC exit polls. We are indebted to Shari Valentine for the Asian and Native American election counts here; see also Charles Franklin, "White Vote for Obama in the States," *Pollster*, November 12, 2008, www.pollster.com/blogs/white_vote_for_obama_in_the_st.php (accessed December 12, 2008).

5 Jody Herman and Lorraine Minnite, "The Demographics of Voters in America's 2008 General Election: A Preliminary Assessment," *Project Vote Research Memo*, November 18, 2008.

6 The best estimates exclude non-citizens and ineligible felons. Michael P. McDonald, "U.S. Elections Project," http://elections.gmu.edu/voter_turnout.htm (accessed December 17, 2008). His research shows variability in turnout across states, from a low of 50.6 percent in Obama's native state, Hawaii, and West Virginia to a high of 77.8 percent in Minnesota. Four in ten eligible voters did not turn out for this election.

7 Eliza Newlin Carney, "Where Are The New Voters?" *National Journal*, December 1, 2008, www.nationaljournal.com/njonline/rg_20081125_6075.php (accessed December 17, 2008); "Major New Report on Hispanic Electorate and the 2008 Elections: Hispanics Rising," *NDN*, May 30, 2008, www.ndn.org/hispanic/hispanics-rising-2.html (accessed December 18, 2008).

8 Andres Ramirez, "An Updated Analysis of the Hispanic Vote, 2008," *NDN Blog*, November 13, 2008, http://ndnblog.org/node/3249 (accessed December 17, 2008).

9 George Barna, as quoted at "How People of Faith Voted in the 2008 Presidential Race," *Barna Group*, November 11, 2008, www.barna.org/FlexPage.aspx?Page=Barna UpdateNarrow&BarnaUpdateID=321 (accessed December 19, 2008).

10 Scott Keeter, Juliana Horowitz, and Alec Tyson, "Young Voters in the 2008 Election," *Pew Research Center for the People & the Press*, November 12, 2008, http:// pewresearch.org/pubs/1031/young-voters-in-the-2008-election (accessed December 17, 2008); "How People of Faith Voted in the 2008 Presidential Race," *Barna Group*, November 11, 2008, www.barna.org/FlexPage.aspx?Page=BarnaUpdate Narrow&BarnaUpdateID=321 (accessed December 19, 2008).

11 "2008 Jewish Vote for Obama Exceeds All Expectations," *National Jewish Democratic Council*, November 5, 2008, www.njdc.org/site/page/jewish_vote_for_obama_exceeds_all_expectations (accessed December 18, 2008).

12 Joe R. Feagin and Clairece B. Feagin, *Racial and Ethnic Relations* (Upper Saddle River, NJ: Prentice Hall, 2008), pp. 114–132.

13 Scott Keeter, Juliana Horowitz, and Alec Tyson, "Young Voters in the 2008 Election," *Pew Research Center for the People & the Press*, November 12, 2008, http:// pewresearch.org/pubs/1031/young-voters-in-the-2008-election (accessed December 17, 2008).

14 CIRCLE Staff, "Young Voters in the 2008 Presidential Election," *CIRCLE Fact Sheet*, December 1, 2008, www.civicyouth.org/PopUps/FactSheets/FS_08_exit_polls. pdf (accessed December 17, 2008); Eliza Newlin Carney, "Where Are The New Voters?" *National Journal*, December 1, 2008, www.nationaljournal.com/njonline/ rg_20081125_6075.php (accessed December 17, 2008).

15 Lynn Vavreck, "Where Have All the Clinton Voters Gone and What Does Race Have to Do with It?" *Princeton Election Blog*, October 27, 2008, http://blogs. princeton.edu/ election2008/2008/10/where-have-all-the-clinton-voters-gone-and-what-does-race-have-to-do-with-it.html (accessed November 30, 2008). Most eventually seem to have voted Democratic.

16 Nate Silver, "For Obama, Will Familiarity Erode Contempt?" November 17, 2008, www.fivethirtyeight.com/2008/11/for-obama-will-familiarity-erode.html (accessed December 19, 2008).

17 Adam Nossiter, "For Some, Uncertainty Starts at Racial Identity," *New York Times*, October 14, 2008, www.nytimes.com/2008/10/15/us/politics/15biracial.html (accessed December 12, 2008).

18 Thomas B. Edsall, "Battle Royale: Center-Right Versus Center-Left in the Democratic Party," *Huffington Post*, November 29, 2008, www.huffingtonpost.com/2008/ 11/29/battle-royale-center-righ_n_147072.html (accessed January 6, 2009).

19 Jennifer Steinhauer, "Volunteers for Obama Face a Complex Issue,"*New York Times*, October 14, 2008, www.nytimes.com/2008/10/15/us/politics/15nevada.html (accessed December 12, 2008).

20 Jennifer Steinhauer, "Volunteers for Obama Face a Complex Issue," *New York Times*, October 14, 2008, www.nytimes.com/2008/10/15/us/politics/15nevada.html (accessed December 12, 2008).

21 The white volunteer responded with this comment to a summary post on our blog, www.racismreview.com.

22 These examples are reported in Jesse Washington, "Obama's True Colors: Black, White . . . or Neither?" *Associated Press*, December 13, 2008, http://news.yahoo.com/ s/ap/20081213/ap_on_re_us/obama_s_not_black (accessed December 22, 2008).

23 I. V. Blair, C. M. Judd, and K. M. Chapleu, "The Influence of Afrocentric Facial Features in Criminal Sentencing," *Psychological Science* 15 (2004): 674–679.

24 "How People of Faith Voted in the 2008 Presidential Race," *Barna Group*, November 11, 2008, www.barna.org/FlexPage.aspx?Page=BarnaUpdateNarrow&Barna UpdateID=321 (accessed December 19, 2008); "Inside Obama's Sweeping Victory," *Pew Research Center*, November 5, 2008, http://pewresearch.org/pubs/1023/exit-poll-analysis-2008 (accessed December 19, 2008).

25 Eliza Newlin Carney, "Where Are The New Voters?" *National Journal*, December 1, 2008, www.nationaljournal.com/njonline/rg_20081125_6075.php (accessed December 17, 2008).

26 The CNN exit poll data were posted at Slate's website, "2008 Presidential Candidates Share of White Vote by State," www.slate.com/id/2204464/sidebar/2204528 (accessed December 12, 2008).

27 Joe R. Feagin, "Racism among Obama Supporters," www.racismreview.com/blog/ 2008/10/18/racism-among-obama-supporters (December 15, 2008).

28 Charles Franklin, "White Vote for Obama in the States," *Pollster*, November 12, 2008, www.pollster.com/blogs/white_vote_for_obama_in_the_st.php (accessed December 12, 2008); "2008 Presidential Candidates Share of White Vote by State," www.slate.com/id/2204464/sidebar/2204528 (accessed December 12, 2008).

29 See the CNN exit poll data posted at Slate's website, "2008 Presidential Candidates Share of White Vote by State," www.slate.com/id/2204464/sidebar/2204528 (accessed December 12, 2008).

30 "How People of Faith Voted in the 2008 Presidential Race," *Barna Group*, November 11, 2008, www.barna.org/FlexPage.aspx?Page=BarnaUpdateNarrow& BarnaUpdateID=321 (accessed December 19, 2008).

31 Timothy Noah, "What We Didn't Overcome: Why You Can't Blame It All on the South," *Slate*, November 12, 2008, www.slate.com/id/2204464 (accessed December 12, 2008).

32 Adam Nossiter, "For Some, Uncertainty Starts at Racial Identity," *New York Times*, October 14, 2008, www.nytimes.com/2008/10/15/us/politics/15biracial.html (accessed December 12, 2008).

33 David Brady, Benjamin Sosnaud, and Steven M. Frenk, "The Shifting and Diverging White Working Class in U.S. Presidential Elections, 1972–2004," *Social Science Research* 38 (March 2009): 118–133.

34 Bill Bishop, "No, We Didn't: America Hasn't Changed as Much as Tuesday's Results Would Indicate," November 10, 2008, www.slate.com/blogs/blogs/bigsort/ default.aspx (accessed December 17, 2008); see also Paul Taylor and Richard Morin, "Americans Claim to Like Diverse Communities but Do They Really?" *Pew Research Center*, December 2, 2008, http://pewresearch.org/pubs/1045/americans-claim-to-like-diverse-communities-but-do-they-really (accessed December 17, 2008).

35 Bill Bishop, "No, We Didn't: America Hasn't Changed as Much as Tuesday's Results Would Indicate," November 10, 2008, www.slate.com/blogs/blogs/bigsort/ default.aspx (accessed December 17, 2008).

8 A "Post-Racial" America?

1 Katherine Rosman, "Before He Was President, Mistaken for a Waiter," *Wall Street Journal Blogs*, November 7, 2008, http://blogs.wsj.com/washwire/2008/11/07/before-he-was-president-mistaken-for-a-waiter-a-2003-obama-meeting (accessed December 30, 2008).

2 Alex Johnson, "Barack Obama Elected 44th President," *MSNBC*, November 5, 2008, www.msnbc.msn.com/id/27531033 (accessed December 12, 2008).

3 Alice Walker, "Letter to President Obama," *The Root*, November 5, 2008, www.theroot.com/id/48726 (accessed December 30, 2008).

4 Jackie Jones, "The Significance of Obama's Victory for African Americans," *Black America Web*, November 6, 2008, http://news.newamericamedia.org/news/view_article.html?article_id=be90e9bd27a4e1d4cc4afb9964217350 (accessed December 22, 2008).

5 "Woods Calls Obama's Election 'Absolutely Incredible'," *ESPN*, November 11, 2008, http://sports.espn.go.com/golf/news/story?id=3695226 (accessed December 29, 2008).

6 Kent Ninomiya, "Glove Gesture for Barack Obama," *Suite 101*, November 6, 2008, http://national-football-league-nfl.suite101.com/article.cfm/glove_gesture_for_barack_obama (accessed December 29, 2008).

7 Ibid.

8 "John McCain's Concession Speech," November 4, 2008, http://seoul.usembassy.gov/election08.html (accessed December 31, 2008).

9 Daily Mail Reporter, "Gordon Brown Joins World Leaders in Welcoming Obama's 'Inspirational' Election Victory," *Daily Mail*, November 5, 2008, www.dailymail.co.uk/news/worldnews/article-1083183/Gordon-Brown-joins-world-leaders-welcoming-Obamas-inspirational-election-victory.html (accessed December 31, 2008).

10 Tom Hundley, "Barack Obama: The First Jewish President?" *Chicago Tribune*, December 12, 2008, www.chicagotribune.com/news/nationworld/chi-obamajews-wrapdec12,0,1483597.story (accessed December 18, 2008).

11 Peter Hitchens, "The Night We Waved Goodbye to America, Our Last Best Hope on Earth," *Daily Mail*, November 10, 2008, www.dailymail.co.uk/news/article-1084111/PETER-HITCHENS-The-night-waved-goodbye-America-best-hope-Earth.html (accessed December 29, 2008).

12 Monica Davey, "Celebrating Obama in Grant Park," *New York Times Blog*, November 5, 2008, http://thecaucus.blogs.nytimes.com/2008/11/05/waiting-for-obama-in-grantpark/?pagemode=print (accessed December 30, 2008).

13 Matthew Bigg, "Black Americans Celebrate Obama's Victory," *Reuters*, November 5, 2008, http://thestar.com.my/news/story.asp?file=/2008/11/5/worldupdates/ 2008–11–05T141511Z_01_NOOTR_RTRMDNC_0_-363281–3&sec=Worldupdates (accessed December 31, 2008).

14 Monica Davey, "Celebrating Obama in Grant Park," *New York Times Blog*, November 5, 2008, http://thecaucus.blogs.nytimes.com/2008/11/05/waiting-for-obama-in-grant-park/?pagemode=print (accessed December 30, 2008).

15 Ibid.
16 Hardy L. Brown, "Celebrating Barack Obama as President-Elect of the United States," November 6, 2008, www.blackvoicenews.com/content/view/42793/18 (accessed December 30, 2008).
17 Bradley Brooks, "U.S. Election Inspires Hope for 'Obama Effect' in Brazil," *Associated Press*, December 8, 2008, www.sun-sentinel.com/news/nationworld/sflfla brazobama1208sbdec08,0,3321955.story (accessed December 30, 2008).
18 Ibid.
19 "World Welcomes President Obama," *Sky News*, November 5, 2008, http://news. sky.com/skynews/Home/World-News/President-Barack-Obama-World-Reaction-Leaders-Welcome-US-President-To-International-Community/Article/200811 115142585 (accessed December 31, 2008).
20 "In Poll, African Americans Say Election a 'Dream Come True'," *CNN*, November 11, 2008, www.cnn.com/2008/POLITICS/11/11/obama.poll/index.html (accessed December 28, 2008).
21 Nicholas Graham, "RNC Candidate Distributes 'Barack The Magic Negro' Song," *Huffington Post*, December 26, 2008, www.huffingtonpost.com/2008/12/26/rnc candidate-distributes_n_153585.html (accessed December 29, 2008).
22 "Fox News Airs 'Magic Negro' Message On New Year's Broadcast," *Think Progress*, January 2, 2009, www.huffingtonpost.com/2009/01/02/fox-news-airs-magic- negro_ n_154761.html (accessed January 5, 2009); on this contrivance in movies, see Hernan Vera and Andrew Gordon, *Screen Saviors: Hollywood Fictions of Whiteness* (Lanham, MD: Rowman & Littlefield, 2003).
23 Greg Mitchell, "Racial Incidents and Threats Against Obama Soar," *Huffington Post*, November 15, 2008, www.huffingtonpost.com/greg-mitchell/racial-incidents-andthre_b_144061.html (accessed December 29, 2008).
24 "Anti-Obama Racial Incidents Reported in Several Cities," *The Daily Voice*, http://thedailyvoice.com/voice/2008/11/antiobama-racial-incidents-rep-001342.php (accessed December 29, 2008).
25 Bill Bradley, "Why Is the National Press Ignoring Small-Town Racism?" *Vanity Fair*, November 12, 2008 www.vanityfair.com/online/politics/2008/11/why-is-the national-press-ignoring-smalltown-racism.html#entry-more (accessed December 26, 2008).
26 Sadiq Green, "Racist Incidents Follow Obama Victory," *Digital Journal*, November 14, 2008, www.digitaljournal.com/article/262339 (accessed December 29, 2008).
27 Duke is quoted in "David Duke Holds Memphis News Conference," http://white reference.blogspot.com/2008/11/dr-david-duke-holds-memphis-news.html (accessed December 26, 2008).
28 All are quoted in Sonia Scherr, "Hate Groups Claim Obama Win is Sparking Recruitment Surge," *Hatewatch*, November 6, 2008, www.splcenter.org/blog/ 2008/11/06/hate-groups-claim-obama-win-is-sparking-recruitment-surge (accessed December 26, 2008).
29 Quoted in David Holthouse, "Ideologues Call for Post-Election Militia Revival," *Hatewatch*, November 19, 2008, www.splcenter.org/blog/2008/11/19/ ideologues-call-for-post-election-militia-revival (accessed December 26, 2008).

30 Ibid.
31 Philip D. Carter, "Another of the 'New Souths'," *Washington Post*, October 10, 1971, p. 129.
32 Sandra Lopez-Rocha, "The Color of Culture: Post-Racial and Post-Ethnic Considerations in the United States," Fourth International Conference on New Directions in the Humanities Conference, 2006, http://h06.cgpublisher.com/ proposals/524/ index_html (accessed December 22, 2008).
33 Daniel Schorr, National Public Radio, January 28, 2008, www.npr.org/templates/ story/story.php?storyId=18489466 (accessed December 22, 2008).
34 "President-Elect Obama: The Voters Rebuke Republicans for Economic Failure," *Wall Street Journal*, November 5, 2008, http://online.wsj.com/article/ SB12258624 4657800863.html (accessed December 28, 2008).
35 Jesse Washington, "Obama's True Colors: Black, White . . . or Neither?" December 13, 2008, http://news.yahoo.com/s/ap/20081213/ap_on_re_us/obama_s_not_black (accessed December 15, 2008).
36 Ibid.
37 Ibid.
38 Joe R. Feagin, *Racist America* (New York: Routledge, 2000).
39 Chris Cillizza, "Impossibly High Expectations on Race Relations?" *Politics Blog, Washington Post*, http://voices.washingtonpost.com/thefix/2008/11/obamas_impossible_ high_expecta.html?hpid=topnews (accessed December 29, 2008).
40 For evidence, see Joe R. Feagin, *Racist America*; Thomas Shapiro, *The Hidden Costs of Being African American* (New York: Routledge, 2004); and Michael Brown, Martin Carnoy, Elliott Currie, Troy Duster, David B. Oppenheimer, Marjorie M. Shultz, and David Wellman, *Whitewashing Race* (Berkeley, CA: University of California Press, 2003).
41 For evidence, see Joe R. Feagin, *Racist America*; and Joe R. Feagin, *Systemic Racism: A Theory of Oppression* (New York: Routledge, 2006).
42 Editorial Board, "Will Obama Focus on Race Issues?" *Christian Science Monitor*, November 14, 2008, www.csmonitor.com/2008/1114/p08s01-comv.html (accessed December 29, 2008).
43 Ibid.
44 Ibid.
45 Uzodinma Iweala, "Race Still Matters," *Los Angeles Times*, January 23, 2008, http://articles.latimes.com/2008/jan/23/opinion/oe-iweala23 (accessed December 22, 2008).
46 Eduardo Bonilla-Silva, "The 2008 Elections and the Future of Anti-Racism in 21st Century America," Association for Humanist Society Meeting, Fall 2008, www. altrue.net/altruesite/files/humanist/2008bonillasilvaspeech.doc (accessed January 2, 2009).
47 Quoted in Joe R. Feagin, "Debating Obama's Actions," December 7, 2008, www. racismreview.com/blog/2008/12/07/debating-obama%E2%80%99sactions-right-left-or-centrist (accessed January 2, 2009); see also Newby's blogging at http:// sociologistsforobama.blogspot.com/2008/11/eduardo-bonilla-silva-problemwith. html (accessed January 2, 2009).

48   See Leslie Houts Picca and Joe R. Feagin, *Two Faced Racism: Whites in the Backstage and Frontstage* (New York: Routledge, 2007).

49   Helene Cooper, "Attorney General Chided for Language on Race," *New York Times*, March 7, 2009, www.nytimes.com/2009/03/08/us/politics/08race.html?_r=2 (accessed March 22, 2009).

50   "Hijacking of Conference on Racism Must be Avoided," *Irish Times*, March 26, 2009, www.irishtimes.com/newspaper/opinion/2009/0326/1224243442379.html (accessed March 28, 2009).

51   John Blake, "Could Obama Presidency Hurt Black Americans?" *CNN*, July 22, 2008, www.cnn.com/2008/POLITICS/07/22/obama.hurt.blacks/index.html (accessed January 11, 2009).

52   Rod Bush, "Black Solidarity & the Obama Election (Updated)," *Racism Review*, November 28, 2008, www.racismreview.com/blog/2008/11/28/black-solidarity-the-obama-election-updated (accessed January 7, 2009).

53   See Joe R. Feagin, *Racist America*; and Leslie H. Picca and Joe R. Feagin, *Two Faced Racism*.

54   Gwen Ifill, "The Candidate," *Essence*, October 2007, pp. 226, 230.

55   Dedrick Muhammad, *Forty Years Later: The Unrealized American Dream* (Washington, D.C.: Institute for Policy Studies, 2008), pp. 5–6.

56   Adam Nagourney and Megan Thee, "Poll Finds Obama Isn't Closing Divide on Race," *New York Times*, July 16, 2008, www.nytimes.com/2008/07/16/us/politics/16poll.html?pagewanted=print (accessed January 1, 2009).

57   Bill Bishop, "No, We Didn't: America Hasn't Changed as Much as Tuesday's Results Would Indicate," November 10, 2008, www.slate.com/blogs/blogs/bigsort/default.aspx (accessed December 17, 2008); see also Paul Taylor and Richard Morin, "Americans Claim to Like Diverse Communities but Do They Really?" *Pew Research Center*, December 2, 2008, http://pewresearch.org/pubs/1045/americans-claim-tolike-diverse-communities-but-do-they-really (accessed December 17, 2008).

58   Paul Taylor and Richard Morin, "Americans Claim to Like Diverse Communities but Do They Really?" *Pew Research Center*, December 2, 2008, http://pewresearch.org/pubs/1045/americans-claim-to-like-diverse-communities-but-do-they-really (accessed December 17, 2008).

9   President Obama's 2009–2013 Term and the 2011–2012 Primaries

1   See "Obama's Populism Circa 2007," *Smartypants Blog*, http://immasmartypants.blogspot.com/2012/01/obamas-populism-circa-2007.html (accessed February 14, 2012); and Andrew Sullivan, "How Obama's Long Game will Outsmart His Critics," *The Daily Beast*, January 15, 2012, www.thedailybeast.com/newsweek/2012/01/15/andrew-sullivan-how-obama-s-long-game-will-outsmart-his-critics.html (accessed February 14, 2012).

2   See James Fallows, "Obama Explained," *The Atlantic*, March 2012, www.theatlantic.com/magazine/archive/2012/03/obama-explained/8874/1/ (accessed February 12, 2012).

3   See "Obama's Populism Circa 2007," *Smartypants Blog*, http://immasmartypants.blogspot.com/2012/01/obamas-populism-circa-2007.html (accessed February 14,

2012); Andrew Sullivan, "How Obama's Long Game will Outsmart His Critics," *The Daily Beast*, January 15, 2012, www.thedailybeast.com/newsweek/2012/01/15/andrew-sullivan-how-obama-s-long-game-will-outsmart-his-critics.html (accessed February 14, 2012); and Andrew Buncombe and Issam Ahmed, "Protests Grow as Civilian Toll of Obama's Drone War on Terrorism is Laid Bare," *The Independent*, March 3, 2012, www.independent.co.uk/news/world/asia/protests-grow-as-civilian-toll-of-obamas-drone-war-on-terrorism-is-laid-bare-7494409.html (accessed March 27, 2012).

4   See Office of the Spokesman, Department of State, "Media Note," August 24, 2010, www.state.gov/r/pa/prs/ps/2010/08/146233.htm (accessed May 8, 2011); "When the Right Wing Gets the Story the Left Missed," *Smartypants Blog*, September 15, 2011, http://immasmartypants.blogspot.com/2011/09/when-right-wing-gets-story-left-missed.html (accessed February 9, 2012).

5   See "A Word on Greenwald's Worldview," *Booman Tribune*, August 16, 2011, www.boomantribune.com/story/2011/8/16/223210/466 (accessed August 19, 2011); and "With Billion-Dollar Settlement, Obama Administration Again Makes Good on Its Promises to Indians," *Daily Kos*, www.dailykos.com/story/2012/04/16/1083742/-Obama-administration-s-billion-dollar-settlement-with-tribes-again-makes-good-on-its-promises- (accessed April 16, 2012).

6   Jeffrey M. Jones, "Americans See U.S. as Exceptional; 37% Doubt Obama Does Majority Believe U.S. at Risk of Losing Status as Greatest Country in the World," *Gallup*, December 22, 2010, www.gallup.com/poll/145358/Americans-Exceptional-Doubt-Obama.aspx (accessed February 10, 2012).

7   Romney is quoted in John A. Gans, "American Exceptionalism and the Politics of Foreign Policy," *The Atlantic*, November 21, 2011, www.theatlantic.com/international/archive/2011/11/american-exceptionalism-and-the-politics-of-foreign-policy/248779/ (accessed February 10, 2012).

8   Ibid.

9   "Orange County GOP Official Refuses to Resign over Racist Email," *Los Angeles Wave*, Wire services, April 16, 2011, www.wavenewspapers.com/news/orange-county-racist-ape-chimp-email-gop-republican-obama-davenport-119993794.html (accessed February 10, 2012).

10 "Fox Nation's Gorilla Story Stirs Racist Frenzy," *News Corpse*, January 28, 2011, www.newscorpse.com/ncWP/?s=gorilla+&searchsubmit=Find (accessed February 10, 2012).

11 Claudio E. Cabrera, "Judge Admits Sending Racist Email About Obama," *The Root*, March 1, 2012, www.theroot. com/racist-obama-emails-judge-richard-cebull (accessed March 2, 2012).

12 Sabrina Tavernise, "4 Years Later, Race is Still an Issue for Some Voters," *New York Times*, May 3, 2012, www.nytimes.com/2012/05/04/us/politics/4-years-later-race-is-still-issue-for-some-voters.html?pagewanted=1&_r=2&emc=eta1 (accessed May 9, 2012).

13 B. Glenn Greenwald, "Obama v. Bush on Power Over Congress," *Salon*, August 18, 2011, www.salon.com/2011/08/18/obama_v_bush/(accessed February 9, 2012).

14 Ishmael Reed, "What Progressives Don't Understand About Obama," *New York Times*, December 11, 2010, www.nytimes.com/2010/12/12/opinion/12reed.html?_r=2&nl=todaysheadlines&emc=a212 (accessed February 9, 2012).

15 Ibid.

16 Melissa Harris-Perry, "Black President, Double Standard: Why White Liberals Are Abandoning Obama," *Nation*, September 21, 2011, www.thenation.com/article/163544/black-president-double-standard-why-white-liberals-are-abandoning-obama (accessed February 7, 2012).

17 Quoted in Chris Hedges, "The Obama Deception: Why Cornel West Went Ballistic," *Truth Dig*, May 16, 2011, www.truthdig.com/report/item/the_obama_deception_why_cornel_west_went_ballistic_20 (accessed May 18, 2011).

18 Melissa Harris-Perry, "Cornel West v. Barack Obama," *Nation*, May 17, 2011, www.thenation.com/blog/160725/cornel-west-v-barack-obama (accessed February 10, 2012).

19 Jamal Eric Watson, "Speaking Freely: Cornel West Takes Aim and Fires," *Diverse Issues in Higher Education*, February 9, 2012, http://diverseeducation.com/article/16821/ (accessed February 12, 2012).

20 Alexei Barrionuevo and Jackie Calmes, "President Underscores Similarities with Brazilians, but Sidesteps One," *New York Times*, March 20, 2011, www.nytimes.com/2011/03/21/world/americas/21brazil.html?pagewanted=1&_r=2&emc=eta1 (accessed February 10, 2012).

21 Desmond S. King and Rogers M. Smith, "On Race, the Silence Is Bipartisan," *New York Times*, September 2, 2011, www.nytimes.com/2011/09/03/opinion/on-race-the-silence-is-bipartisan.html?emc=eta1 (accessed February 10, 2012).

22 Gail Russell Chaddock, "Gay Marriage: Clooney Fundraiser a Hint of Coming Obama Money Boom," *Christian Science Monitor*, http://news.yahoo.com/gay-marriage—clooney-fundraiser-a-hint-of-coming-obama-money-boom.html (accessed May 11, 2012).

23 See early polls at www.surveyusa.com.

24 James Fallows, "Obama Explained," *The Atlantic*, March 2012, www.theatlantic.com/magazine/archive/2012/03/obama-explained/8874/1/ (accessed February 12, 2012).

25 Ibid.

26 Joe R. Feagin, *The White Racial Frame: Centuries of Racial Framing and Counterframing* (New York: Routledge, 2010); Joe R. Feagin, *White Party, White Government: Race, Class and U.S. Politics* (New York: Routledge, 2012).

27 See Joe R. Feagin, *White Party, White Government*.

28 See Joe R. Feagin, *White Party, White Government*. For a more pragmatic progressive analysis, see numerous blog posts of the head of a midwestern nonprofit organization at http://immasmartypants.blogspot.com (accessed October 26, 2012).

29 See Joe R. Feagin, *White Party, White Government*; and Thomas B. Edsall, "Battle Royale: Center-Right Versus Center-Left In the Democratic Party," *Huffington Post*, November 29, 2008, www.huffingtonpost.com/2008/11/29/battle-royale-center-righ_n_147072.html (accessed January 6, 2009).

30 See Kevin P. Phillips, *The Emerging Republican Majority* (New Rochelle, NY: Arlington House, 1969).

31 Quoted in D. Sunshine Hillygus and Todd G. Shields, *The Persuadable Voter* (Princeton, NJ: Princeton University Press, 2008), p. 138; see also Paul Krugman, "Bigger Than Bush," *New York Times*, January 1, 2009, www.nytimes.com/2009/01/02/opinion/02krugman.html?_r=1 (accessed January 2, 2009).

32 Here we draw on extensive arguments in Joe R. Feagin, *Systemic Racism: A Theory of Oppression* (New York: Routledge, 2006), especially Chapter 7.

33 Quoted in Kevin Sack, "South's Embrace Of G.O.P. Is Near A Turning Point," *New York Times*, March 16, 1998, p. A1.

34 "About Republicans for Obama," www.republicansforobama.org/?q=about (accessed January 7, 2009).

35 David A. Bositis, "Blacks and the 2004 Republican National Convention," Joint Center for Political and Economic Studies, Washington, D.C., 2004, pp. 1–10.

36 James Wright, "Black Republicans Ponder Their Future," *Afro Newspapers*, November 24, 2008, http://news.newamericamedia.org/news/view_article.html?article_id= (accessed December 18, 2008); Alexander Burns, "Steele: 'How do you like me now?'" *Politico*, January 30, 2009, http://dyn.politico.com/printstory.cfm?uuid=2A1BA222-18FE-70B2-A83323D0DB01F7E4 (accessed February 9, 2009); "Joint Center looks at Black Republicans post-RNC," www.amsterdamnews.com, September 6, 2012 (accessed September 6, 2012).

37 Elicia Dover, "New Gingrich Calls Romney 'Obama-Lite,'" *ABC News*, February 6, 2012, http://abcnews.go.com/blogs/politics/2012/02/newt-gingrich-calls-mitt-romney-obama-lite-little-food-stamp-and-rich-guy/ (accessed February 6, 2012).

38 Newt Gingrich, "In NYC Public Schools Unionized Workers Win, Pupils Lose; Schools Should Serve our Children—Not Interest Groups," *Human Events*, December 28, 2011, www.humanevents.com/article.php?id=48399 (accessed February 7, 2012).

39 Lucy Madison, "Santorum Targets Blacks in Entitlement Reform," *CBS News*, January 2, 2012, www.cbsnews.com/8301-503544_162-57350990-503544/santorum-targets-blacks-in-entitlement-reform/ (accessed February 7, 2012).

40 Mitt Romney, "What Kind of Society Does America Want?" *USA Today*, December 19, 2011, www.usatoday.com/news/opinion/forum/story/2011-12-19/romney-us-economy-entitlements/52076252/1 (accessed February 6, 2012).

41 Rachel Weiner, "Herman Cain and the 'Race Card'," *The Fix*, October 10, 2011, www.washingtonpost.com/blogs/the-fix/post/herman-cain-and-the-race-card/2011/10/10/gIQAVJsRaL_blog.html (accessed April 26, 2012).

42 Lee Siegel, "What's Race Got to Do With It?" *New York Times Blog*, January 14, 2012, http://campaignstops.blogs.nytimes.com/2012/01/14/whats-race-got-to-do-with-it/ (accessed February 7, 2012).

43 Sean Hannity and Dick Morris, "Obama's Radical Past Comes Back to Haunt Him Again," April 10, 2012, http://nation.foxnews.com/president-obama/2012/04/10/obamas-radical-past-comes-back-haunt-him-again (accessed April 17, 2012); Noah Rothman, "Fox & Friends Examines Rev. Wright 'Re-emergence,'

'Hate-Filled Easter Sermon'," April 10, 2012, www.mediaite.com (accessed April 17, 2012). See also "Rev. Wright Roars Back with Hate-Laced Easter Week Sermon," *Fox News*, April 9, 2012, http://nation.foxnews.com/rev-jeremiah-wright/2012/04/09/rev-wright-roars-back-hate-laced-easter-week-sermon (accessed April 17, 2012).

44 For detailed evidence, see Joe R. Feagin, *The White Racial Frame*, all chapters; and Joe R. Feagin, *Systemic Racism*, later chapters.

10 The 2012 National Election

1 Gallup.com. See "Obama Approval Sinks to New Lows Among Whites, Hispanics," September 7, 2011, Gallup, www.gallup.com/poll/149351/obama-job-approval-sinks-new-lows-among-whites-hispanics.aspx (accessed February 10, 2012).

2 Halimah Abdullah, "Could Obama's Struggles with White Voters Cost Him the Election?" CNN, www.cnn.com/2012/10/25/politics/obama-40-percent/index.html (accessed November 1, 2012).

3 Sonya Ross and Jennifer Agiesta, "AP Poll: Majority Harbor Prejudice Against Blacks," ap.com, http://hosted.ap.org/dynamic/stories/u/us_ap_poll_racial_attitudes ?site=ap&section=home&template=default (accessed Nov 1, 2012). We are indebted to analysts of the AP data for the figure for whites.

4 Joan Walsh, "What's the Matter with White People," salon.com, www.salon.com/2012/03/04/whats_the_matter_with_white_people/singleton/ (accessed May 11, 2012).

5 See Ruy Teixeira, "Why Obama's Re-Election is Going to Look a Lot Like 2008," www.tnr.com/article/politics/101258/president-obama-general-election-2012-chances-prospects (accessed March 2, 2012).

6 Ronald Brownstein, "Is Obama's Coalition Re-Emerging?" *National Journal*, February 6, 2012, http://decoded.nationaljournal.com/2012/02/is-obamas-coalition-reemerging.php (accessed February 9, 2012).

7 Alexander Keyssar, "The Strange Career of Voter Suppression," *New York Times*, February 12, 2012, http://campaignstops.blogs.nytimes.com/2012/02/12/the-strange-career-of-voter-suppression (accessed February 14, 2012).

8 Andrew Levison, "TDS Strategy Memo," February 2, 2012, www.thedemocratic strategist.org/strategist/2012/02/tds_strategy_memo_after_the_pr.php#more (accessed February 6, 2012).

9 See ibid.; and Jessie Daniels, *Cyber Racism* (Lanham, MD: Rowman and Littlefield, 2009), passim.

10 Richard Prince, "No Blacks, Latinos on Time Magazine Political Team," http://mije.org/richardprince/were-blacks-latinos-insulted-or-just-ignored#Time, *Journal-isms*, Maynard Institute, (accessed February 6, 2012); "Newsroom Diversity," 4th Estate, www.4thestate.net/bleached-lack-of-diversity-in-newsroom-front-page-election-coverage/ (accessed February 6, 2012).

11 Jeff Zeleny and Jim Rutenberg, "G.O.P. 'Super PAC' Weighs Hard-Line Attack on Obama," *New York Times*, May 17, 2012, www.nytimes.com/2012/05/17/us/politics/gop-super-pac-weighs-hard-line-attack-on-obama.html?_r=2&pagewanted

=1& www.nytimes.com/2012/05/17/us/politics/gop-super-pac-weighs-hard-line-attack-on-obama.html?_r=2&pagewanted=1&hp (accessed May 23, 2012).

12 Ashley Killough, "Romney Uses Welfare Attack in New Ad," CNNblog.com, October 31, 2012, http://politicalticker.blogs.cnn.com/2012/10/31/romney-uses-welfare-attack-in-new-ad/comment-page-1 (accessed November 5, 2012).

13 James Zogby, "Romney: Going Negative, Subtly," www.huffingtonpost.com/james-zogby/romney-going-negative-sub_b_1547611.html (accessed May 27, 2012).

14 Thomas B. Edsall, "Debt Splits the Left," February 5, 2012, http://campaignstops.blogs.nytimes.com/2012/02/05/debt-splits-the-left/?ref=opinion (accessed February 6, 2012).

15 Robert Creamer, "Romney's Bain Record: Playing By a Different Set of Rules Than Ordinary Americans," *Huffington Post*, May 18, 2012, www.huffingtonpost.com/robert-creamer/romneys-bain-record-playi_b_1527163.html (accessed May 23, 2012).

16 "Election Analysis," PBS Newshour, November 7, 2012, www.pbs.org/newshour/bb/politics/july-dec12/tactics_11-07.html (accessed November 7, 2012).

17 Steve Lohr, "The Obama Campaign's Technology Is a Force Multiplier," *New York Times* blog, November 8, 2012, http://bits.blogs.nytimes.com/2012/11/08/the-obama-campaigns-technology-the-force-multiplier/?nl=todaysheadlines&emc=edit_th_20121109 (accessed November 9, 2012).

18 Jodi Cantor, "For President, a Complex Calculus of Race and Politics," *New York Times*, October 20, 2012, www.nytimes.com/2012/10/21/us/politics/for-president-obama-a-complex-calculus-of-race-and-politics.html?pagewanted=1&_r=0&nl=todaysheadlines&emc=edit_th_20121021 (accessed November 8, 2012).

19 Halimah Abdullah, "Could Obama's struggles with white voters cost him the election?" CNN, October 26, 2012, www.cnn.com/2012/10/25/politics/obama-40-percent/index.html?hpt=hp_t2 (accessed November 8, 2012).

20 Associated Press Report, "Obama Wins the Way His Campaign Predicted, with Big Minority Turnout and Robust Ground Game," washingtonpost.com, November 8, 2012, www.washingtonpost.com/politics/obama-wins-the-way-his-campaign-predicted-with-big-minority-turnout-and-robust-ground-game/2012/11/08/15027660-2978-11e2-aaa5-ac786110c486_story.html (accessed November 12, 2012); Michael Scherer, "Inside the Secret World of the Data Crunchers Who Helped Obama Win," swampfeed.com, November 7, 2012, http://swampland.time.com/2012/11/07/inside-the-secret-world-of-quants-and-data-crunchers-who-helped-obama-win/2/ (accessed November 12, 2012).

21 See comments in Moni Basu, "Obama makes history, again," CNN, updated 5:36 a.m. EST, November 8, 2012, www.cnn.com/2012/11/07/politics/obama-identity/index.html (accessed November 9, 2012).

22 "President Exit Polls," *New York Times*, http://elections.nytimes.com/2012/results/president/exit-polls (accessed November 8, 2012); "President: Full Results (Exit Polls)," CNN, www.cnn.com/election/2012/results/race/president#exit-polls (accessed November 8, 2012). Exit data were collected by Edison Research for Associated Press and six major networks. Their summary: "National data are for 350 random

precincts and include phone interviews with absentee voters. The national exit poll survey includes 26,565 interviews with voters in all 50 states and the District of Columbia. The interviews were conducted at 350 polling locations on election day, along with 4,408 telephone interviews of absentee and early voters." "Edison Successfully Conducts the 2012 National Election Exit Polls," www.edisonresearch. com/home/archives/2012/11/edison-successfully-conducts-the-2012-national-election-exit-polls.php (accessed November 13, 2012).

23 Benjy Sarlin, "Poll: Latino Vote Devastated GOP Even Worse Than Exits," TalkingPointsMemo, November 7, 2012, http://2012.talkingpointsmemo.com/ 2012/11/poll-latino-vote-devastated-gop-even-worse-than-exits-showed.php? ref=fpa (accessed November 8, 2012); Hamed Aleaziz, "Jewish-American Voters Overwhelmingly Support President Obama," http://thinkprogress.org/security/ 2012/11/07/1159621/jewish-american-obama-poll-results/?mobile=North Carolina (accessed November 11, 2012).

24 Halimah Abdullah, "Could Obama's struggles with white voters cost him the election?" CNN, October 26, 2012, www.cnn.com/2012/10/25/politics/obama-40-percent/index.html?hpt=hp_t2 (accessed November 8, 2012).

25 "President Exit Polls," *New York Times*, http://elections.nytimes.com/2012/ results/president/exit-polls (accessed November 8, 2012); "President: Full Results (Exit Polls)," CNN, www.cnn.com/election/2012/results/race/president#exit-polls (accessed November 8, 2012). Political data were collected by Edison Research for National Election Pool, including Associated Press and major networks. National data are for 350 random precincts and include phone interviews with absentee voters. Native American estimates are from Shari Valentine.

26 Nate Cohn, "What Black Turnout for Obama in 2012 Means for the GOP in 2016," New Republic, November 13, 2012, www.tnr.com/blog/electionate/ 110068/the-overlooked-question-2016-the-future-black-turnout (accessed November 14, 2012); Jason Noble and Jennifer Jacobs, "Latinos Are Critical to a Victory, Obama Tells the Register," desmoinesregister.com, October 25 2012, www.des moinesregister.com/article/20121025/NEWS09/310250053/Latinos-critical-victory-Obama-tells-Register (accessed Nov 1, 2012); "First Thoughts: Romney's immigration challenge," msnbc.com, April 17, 2012, http://firstread.msnbc.msn. com/_news/2012/04/17/11245825-first-thoughts-romneys-immigration-challenge ?lite (accessed April 17, 2012).

27 Markos Moulitsas, "Mitt Romney's Latino Problem," in "Charts and Maps," March 20, 2012, www.dailykos.com/story/2012/03/20/1076099/-Romney-s-Latino-problem-in-charts-and-maps (accessed April 17, 2012).

28 Mark Hugo Lopez and Paul Taylor, "The 2010 Congressional Reapportionment and Latinos," Pew Hispanic Center, January 5, 2011, www.pewhispanic.org/2011/ 01/05/the-2010-congressional-reapportionment-and-latinos/ (accessed February 14, 2012).

29 Ibid; Arturo Vargas, "Simply Translating an Ad Isn't Enough," *New York Times*, www.nytimes.com/roomfordebate/2012/05/23/securing-the-hispanic-vote/simply-translating-an-ad-isnt-enough-to-win-the-latino-vote (accessed May 24, 2012).

30 Dante Chinni, "Election Exit Polls Provide Mountain of Data," PBS NewsHour, November 7, 2012, www.pbs.org/newshour/rundown/2012/11/patchwork-nation-from-election-exit-polls-a-mountain-of-data.html (accessed November 8, 2012); Rod Dreher, "Viewpoint: Republicans at a Crossroads," BBC News, www.bbc.co.uk/news/world-us-canada-20257611 (accessed November 11, 2012).

31 Ross Douthat, "The Obama Realignment," *New York Times*, November 7, 2012, http://campaignstops.blogs.nytimes.com/2012/11/07/douthat-the-obama-realignment/?hp (accessed November 8, 2012); Julia Preston, "Republicans Reconsider Positions on Immigration," *New York Times*, November 9, 2012, www.nytimes.com/2012/11/10/us/politics/republicans-reconsider-positions-on-immigration.html?hp (accessed November 11, 2012).

32 Ed Kilgore, "No 'Centrist Reforms' On Tap For Republicans," The Daily Strategist, November 8, 2012 www.thedemocraticstrategist.org/strategist/2012/11/lux_populist_message_fuels_dem.php (accessed November 8, 2012). Our italics.

33 Matthew Zook, Mark Graham, Ate Poorhuis, Monica Stephens and Taylor Shelton, "Mapping Racist Tweets in Response to President Obama's Reelection," *The Guardian*, www.guardian.co.uk/news/datablog/2012/nov/09/mapping-racist-tweets-president-obama-reelection (accessed November 11, 2012).

34 "Remarks by the President on Election Night," The White House, www.whitehouse.gov/the-press-office/2012/11/07/remarks-president-election-night (accessed November 9, 2012).

INDEX